Francis Penrose

Letters on Philosophical Subjects

particularly the creation, the deluge, vegetation

Francis Penrose

Letters on Philosophical Subjects
particularly the creation, the deluge, vegetation

ISBN/EAN: 9783337238148

Printed in Europe, USA, Canada, Australia, Japan

Cover: Foto ©Thomas Meinert / pixelio.de

More available books at **www.hansebooks.com**

ON PHILOSOPHICAL SUBJECTS;

PARTICULARLY

THE CREATION,

THE DELUGE, VEGETATION, &c.

THE POWERS PRODUCING THESE OPERATIONS ARE HERE SHEWN TO BE

HEAT, COLD, AIR AND WATER.

Since the Edition of these Letters printed at Plymouth, the late Experiments in the new Chymistry, have confirmed the above Theory. These Experiments prove, that Heat and Light, together with *Oxygen* or Cold, are the Powers which carry on both Animal and Vegetable Life: Light, Heat, Vital Air, and inflammable Gas, are thereby proved to be substances of the first class, and approach nearest to simplicity.

THE SECOND EDITION.

LONDON:

PRINTED FOR J. DEIGHTON, OPPOSITE GRAYS-INN, HOLBORN;

1794.

ADVERTISEMENT.

THE first Edition of these Letters were printed at Plymouth, under the Title of Letters Philosophical and Astronomical; but being informed, by some of my Friends, that the Title Page had prevented many Persons from reading them, supposing that none but Adepts in those Sciences could understand them, the contrary is the fact. The greater Part of these Letters may be fully comprehended by any Person of common understanding.

These Letters were reviewed by the Critical Reviewers in December 1788, who give the following Account of them: they say, " That the Mosaic Account of the Creation " is explained and defended, as well as the " Deluge; and Gravity accounted for by hot
" and

ADVERTISEMENT.

" and cold Ether; and that every ingenious
" man, and our Author's Ingenuity, we do
" not queſtion, when he ſteps out of the com-
" mon way, will neceſſarily expect atten-
" tion."

The Analytical Reviewers noticed them in April, 1789: they obſerve, " That the Au-
" thor (when diſſerting on vegetation) ex-
" hibits a conſiderable Degree of Ingenuity:"
And the very great improvements in the new Chymiſtry have proved the Author's ſentiments to be right.

F. PENROSE.

STONEHOUSE,
Plymouth, Jan. 1794.

SIRS,

THE following Letters contain many new Observations in Astronomy and Philosophy, which appear to be of sufficient Importance to be inquired into, in Order to ascertain whether they be Facts or not.—On that Persuasion, I have taken the Liberty to address them to you, and hope they will meet with an impartial Examination; and that they will not be discarded because they contain some Things which differ from Opinions generally received and taught.—Was this *always* to be the Case, there would be

DEDICATION.

be an End to Improvements in the Sciences; for every Thing *new must differ* from what was before known.

It would have given me great Satisfaction, could I have obtained the Honour for some of the most important Matters in them, to be read at a Meeting of your Society; I should then have been properly informed whether they were of sufficient Importance to trouble the Publick with or not; but, as I had not Interest enough to get that done, I take this Method to crave your liberal Decision on them.

I am,

With great Deference and Respect,

Your most obedient, humble Servant,

F. PENROSE.

STONEHOUSE,
Plymouth, June 30, 1788.

EXPLANATION

Of the SOLAR DIAGRAM

Month, *according to the Julian Calendar, when the Sun and Moon are in Conjunction.*

O.—Full Moons; *pointing out the Day of the Month when she is in Opposition to the Sun, in her Passage through the Ecliptick.*

S.—Sunday, *or every Seventh or Sabbath-Day throughout the Year.*

●.—The Earth, *in the Meridian of the twelve Signs, in her Orbit, or Path through the Ecliptick, viz. when she has the Sun and these Stars in Conjunction, in her annual Orbit. Astronomers tell us that the Ecliptick is* equally divided *into twelve Signs of* 30 *Degrees each. But it is not so.—It is the Equinoctial which is* divided equally *by these twelve Signs.—Some of these Signs are of such a Length, as to require the Earth to make more than* 31 *Rotations while she is passing through them, while others require little more than* 29; *and the six Northern Signs are so much longer than the six Southern, that*

B *th*

EXPLANATION

Of the SOLAR DIAGRAM.

the Earth takes more than a Week longer in traverfing them, than fhe does in traverfing the others.—See Introduction, P. 16, 19.

E E—The Equinoctial, *divided into twelve equal Parts, by the twelve fixed Stars, which are called* Signs, *each Sign into* 30 *Degrees; the whole Equinoctial containing* 360 *Degrees, anfwering to the fame Number of Degrees on the Equator.*

D D. — The Anticipation of Time. — This is not in Nature, *but occafioned from the Julian Year not anfwering exactly in Length of Time, to the Length of Motion the Earth takes to perform her annual Orbit round the Sun, viz. the Julian Year contains* 365¼ *Days, whereas the Earth compleats her Revolution round the Sun, in* 365 *Days,* 5 *Hours,* 49 *Minutes.—Hence, as we calculate according to the Julian Reckoning, the Earth will finifh her annual Orbit eleven Minutes of Time before the Julian Reckoning ends.* Introduct. P. 3, 97, 105.

Thus

EXPLANATION

Of the SOLAR DIAGRAM.

Thus the Motion of the Earth anticipates Time, according to the Julian Calendar, eleven Minutes every Year, and throws it back.—See P. 98.—*Let us postulate that Motion and Time, began, according to the Julian Period, at the autumnal Equinox, 706, (which is the Time the best Interpreters of Moses's History, say he placed it) from that Year to this, 1786, (which is the 6499th, according to that Period,) the Earth will have made 5793 annual Revolutions; by which Means, Motion will have anticipated Time 44 Days, 6 Hours, 3 Minutes, according to O. S. viz. from Oct. 25, to Sept. 11, or according to the N. S. from Oct. 25, to Sept. 22.*

F. F.—*The Precession of the Equinoxes. According to the last Article, the solar or true Time, has fallen short of the Time, (as reckoned according to the Julian Calendar,) 11 Minutes every Year.—Hence, the Sun will appear eleven Minutes more forward in the Ecliptick, every Year, than she ought to do.—Thus, in 5793 Revolutions,*

EXPLANATION

Of the SOLAR DIAGRAM.

Revolutions, she will not appear to be in the Beginning of Aries, *as she was observed to be* A. I. P. 706, *but in the third Degree of* Taurus, *(if we reckon by the N. S.) and in the* 14*th according to O. S. See Introduction,* P. 98.

Hence *it may be observed, that the fixed Stars and Equinoxes, are just in the same Places in the Heavens, they were* 5793 *Years ago, and that the Anticipation of Time, and Precession of the Equinoxes, are not in Nature, but occasioned by an erroneous Calculation of the exact Length of the solar Year and the lunar Cycle. See* P. 97, 105.— *This may be observed by* G. G.— *The Difference between* O. S. *and* N. S. *made A. D.* 1752.

EXPLANATION

An Explanation of the LUNAR DIAGRAM, for A. D. 1786, (anſwering to the Year of the World, 5793, and to the Year of the Julian Period, 6499,) ſhewing the Place of the Sun, Earth, and Moon, every Day in the Year, according to the Julian Calendar.

―――

A.—*The* Sun *in the Centre of the Syſtem.*

B. B.—*The* Equinoctial Circle, *divided by the twelve Stars or Signs, into twelve equal Parts, of* 30 *Degrees each.*—*The Whole into* 360 *Degrees.*

(E) (E) *The* Earth, *in her Place in the Ecliptick, when the Moon is at Full, or in Oppoſition.*

C. C.—*The annual Path of the Earth round the Sun, which is divided into Days, Weeks, and Months, according to the Julian Calendar. It is an Ellipſe, within the Equinoctial, and forms an Angle of* 23 *Days,* 28 *Minutes, with it;—and is divided into* 365¼ *of Parts or Degrees*

EXPLANATION

Of the LUNAR DIAGRAM.

grees, answering to the Number of Rotations the Earth makes during her Revolution round the Sun.—Was the Earth, throughout her annual Revolution, to keep at the same Distance from the Sun, which she is at the Equinoxes, she would then go round that Luminary in a Circle, and perform and measure it in 360 Days or Rotations.—But now, as it is performed by Nature, she goes so far beyond the Periphery of the Circle, at the Summer Solstice, as to require $5\frac{1}{4}$ more Rotations to do it.

m. m.—*Meridians, which pass from the Sun in the Centre, to the first Point of each Sign, in the Equinoctial.*—As the Circle of the Equinoctial and the Elliptical Path of the Earth, answer each other geometrically, so these Meridians cut the Julian Calendar at the true Day, and Month, when the Sun will be found to enter them; and thereby shew the Places of the Sun and Moon every Day throughout the Year.

D. D.—*The* Moon's Orbit *round the Earth,*
E. *going*

EXPLANATION

Of the LUNAR DIAGRAM.

E *going forward through the Ecliptick.—This View is as it may be seen from a Planet or Star, without that Orbit, and perpendicular to the Plane of the Ecliptick.—By this Side View may be observed the* Loops *the Moon makes, in her Orbit round the Earth, in her Passage through the Ecliptick, (in the same Manner as other Satellites do round their Planets,) being sometimes a Semi-diameter of her Orbit before the Earth, and sometimes the same Distance behind her, always keeping about* 240,000 *of Miles from her, and going round the Ecliptick with her.— She is kept in her Orbit by two Forces, viz. the* Light *proceeding from the Sun, and the* Light *reflecting from the Earth.—— This is the Power,* (Light) *which expands and projects her towards the Extremities;—the other is the* Ether *proceeding from the Extremities, which Sir Isaac Newton calls* Spirit.—*He often makes use of* Attraction, *to express the first, and* Gravitation *the last, without enquiring into the Causes of these Phenomena; therefore, to be short, clear, and better understood, I shall do the same.—See Let.* IV. P. 165, XIV. P. 283.

EXPLANATION

Of the LUNAR DIAGRAM.

In her Orbit round the Earth, (which is about 240,000 Miles, from her,) these two Powers or Forces ballance each other.—Thus, here all is still, calm, and neither prevails.—Here also the projectile Force, which carries the Earth from *West* to *East*, through the Ecliptick, meets the gravitating Power, which carries the Moon from *North* to *South*, round the Earth. See Let. XVII.—As these two Powers act perpendicularly to each other neither prevails; but they act jointly, and they force the Moon round the Earth in a Diagonal *between* them.—Thus, at her Change, she goes N. W. till she comes to 1, (her first Quarter,) at which Place she is Half the Diameter of her Orbit behind the Earth.—Here, instead of going on N. W. she changes her Course, and goes nearly E. N. E. till she comes to her Opposition or Full, when she is due North of the Earth.—She continues still to go Eastward, but changes from E. N. E. to N. N. E. till she arrives at 3, (the End of her third Quarter,) where she is at the East Point of her Orbit, and a Semi-diameter

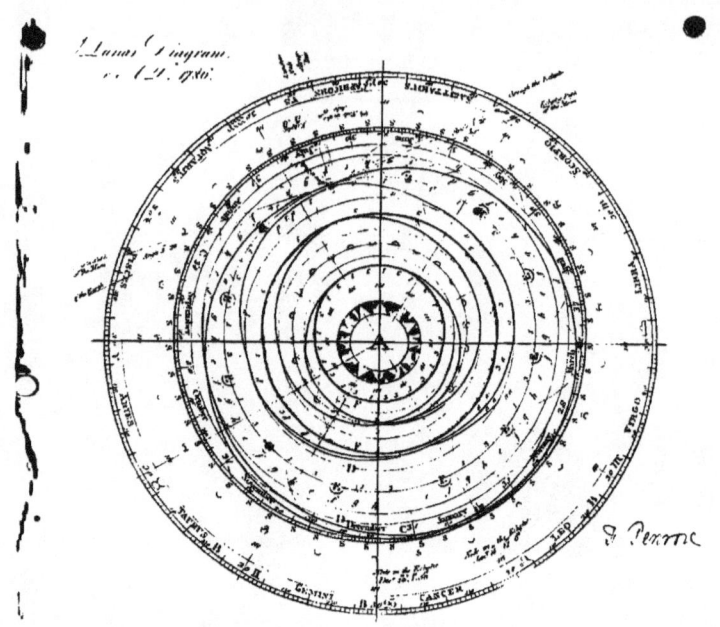

EXPLANATION
Of the LUNAR DIAGRAM.

of her Orbit before the Earth.—From hence she goes *Westward* at S. W. till she comes to her Change, where she is due South of the Earth. See Let. XXII.

Besides the above described Forces, there is another which goes from *West* to *East*,—the ethereal Current of the Eclipses.—This Current goes from *West* to *East*, and round the Ecliptick, in a progressive Circle, but so slow as to require 18 *Julian Years*, 10 Days, 19 Hours, 46 Minutes, 0 Seconds, 15 Thirds, to compleat it, and to meet the Moon again, exactly in the same Point of the Ecliptick from which they parted, when the Cycle began.—Hence, as Observations prove, at the End of this Cycle, there is a Return of all the Eclipses which touch the Earth.—Let. XXII.

Thus the Moon performs her Orbit, round the Earth, in 29 Days, 12 Hours, 44 Minutes, 1 Second, 45 Thirds, (which is called a Lunation,) in which Time the ethereal Current of Eclipses has moved forward and *Eastward*,
C 1 Day,

EXPLANATION

Of the LUNAR DIAGRAM.

1 *Day*, 14 *Hours*, 6 *Minutes*, 11 *Seconds*, 19 *Thirds*.—By which Means the Moon croffes that Current, before fhe comes to the Star.—This occafioned Aftronomers to imagine that the Nodes moved backward to the Weftward.—The Point where the Moon croffes the Current of Eclipfes is called her Node.—At the End of every fixth Node, or 172 *Days*, 12 *Hours*, 59 *Minutes*, this Path of the Nodes croffes the ecliptick Path of the Earth, and if that Point is then within 17 Degrees of the Sun, it caufes an Eclipfe, but if farther from it, the Shadow of the Earth or Moon will not reach each other.

F F.—The Moon's Path, *as obferved from the Earth*.—At the End of the firft Quarter, fhe is Half illuminated.—At the End of her Second, fhe is wholly fo.—At the End of her Third fhe is again Half illuminated; and at her laft Quarter or Change, fhe appears quite dark.

S S.—The Sabbath, or Seventh Day throughout the Calendar.

The following is a Defcription of the Eclipfes

EXPLANATION

Of the LUNAR DIAGRAM.

Eclipses for the Year 1786.—*January* 14, *at Noon, the astronomical Day ends, and January* 15 *begins; at this Point the Moon's Node was in the Ecliptick; and* 44 *Minutes after the Moon was opposite the Sun, and caused an Eclipse of the Moon.*—To *January* 15, *add six Nodes, or* 172 *Days,* 12 *Hours,* 59 *Minutes, and it will make* 187 *Days,* 12 *Hours,* 59 *Minutes; from this substract the* 181 *Days from the Calends of January, and it will leave July* 6th *Day,* 15th *Hour,* 59th *Minute, the exact Place of the Node.*—*Six Nodes are short of six Lunations,* 4 *Days,* 15 *Hours,* 25 *Minutes;*— *this Node therefore will be in the Ecliptick so much before the Sun; and as the Nodes are diametrically opposite to each other, so the other will want just as much, and therefore meet the Moon in the Ecliptick, July* 11th *Day,* 4th *Hour,* 24th *Minute.*—*If we add six Lunations, or* 177 *Days,* 4 *Hours,* 24 *Minutes, to Jan.* 15th *Day,* 0 *Hour,* 44th *Minute, it will give July* 11, 5, 8, *for the Moon's Opposition, which is* 44 *Minutes only from the Node, and will cause a total Eclipse of the Moon, but, as*

it

EXPLANATION
of the LUNAR DIAGRAM.

it happens about five o'Clock in the Afternoon, must be invisible to us.—In 14 Days, 9 Hours, 4 Minutes, (Half the Length of a Node,) the other Node will get round the Earth into the Ecliptick, which added to July 11th Day, 4th Hour, 24th Minute, brings it to July 25th Day, 13th Hour, 28th Minute.—In Order to find when the Moon will be in Conjunction, add Half a Lunation, 14 Days, 18 Hours, 22 Minutes to July 11th Day, 5th Hour, 8th Minute, (the Time when the Moon was in Opposition,) it will cause an Eclipse, but not visible to us.

In Order to find when the Node will again cross the Ecliptick, add 345 Days, 1 Hour, 58 Minutes, (the Quantity of twelve Nodes,) to Jan. 15.—It will bring it to Dec. 26th Day, 1st Hour, 58th Minute, when the Node will again be in the Ecliptick; but as neither Node will then be within 20 Degrees of the Sun, no Eclipse can happen.

a, a, a.—The Path of the ascending Node.
d, d, d.—The Path of the descending Node.

EXPLANATION

Of the SOLAR DIAGRAM.

liquity of the Ecliptick, *and since the Ecliptick and Equinoctial are both great Circles, they must bisect each other; as it is found they do, in the Beginning of* Aries *and* Libra; *so that six of these Signs lye on the North Side of the Equinoctial, and are called the* Northern Signs; *and the other Six, on the South Side of it, and are called the* Southern Signs.—*This Ecliptick is divided into* 365¼ *Parts, answering to the Number of Meridian Altitudes of the Sun, during the Revolution of the Earth thro' it, corresponding to the Number of solar Days or Rotations the Earth makes during that Time. As the elliptical Figure of the Ecliptick makes it five Degrees, and almost a Quarter longer than the Equinoctial, which is a Circle; so we find the Earth requires so much longer Time to traverse it, than she would require, did she go round the Sun in a Circle,* at the same Distance from the Sun, *she is at the Equinoxes; as the Earth makes equal Areas in equal Times.* See Introduction, P. 16.

☽.—New Moons; *shewing the Day of the Month,*

An Explanation of the SOLAR DIAGRAM, for the Year of our Lord, 1786, (answering to the Year of the World, 5792, and to the Year of the Julian Period, 6499) shewing the Place of the Sun, Moon, and Earth, every Day in the Year, according to the Julian Calendar.

———

S.—*The* Sun *in the Centre of the System.*— a, a— Meridians, *going from the* Equator, *through the Ecliptick, to the twelve Signs, or fixed Stars in the* Equinoctial; *shewing the Day of the Julian Month, when the Sun comes into these Meridians, or enters these twelve Signs.*

B. B.—*The* Equatorial Circle *divided into 360 Degrees.*—*If the* Plane *of the Equator be produced to the Heavens, it will there mark out a Circle, called the Equinoctial,* marked E. E· *which will divide the Earth and Heavens into two Halves or Hemispheres.*

C. C.—*The* Ecliptick, *an* Ellipse, *which is found to be inclined to the Equinoctial, at an Angle of* 23° 28ʹ, *which Angle is called the* Obliquity

CONTENTS.

INTRODUCTION.

SOME Notions in these Letters contrary to general received Opinions. Page 2.

Equinoctial equally divided by the twelve Signs, but the annual Orbit of the Earth unequally, and measured by the Number of Rotations the Earth makes during that Time. 3

Retrocession of Time, how occasioned; shewing the Cause of the Difference between Calendar Measure and true Time:—Chronology of Time when began: 4, 98—Style altered. 5

Time when it began; that Point described by Moses. 6

Certain Points from which Astronomers begin their Computations, as described by Dr. Keil. 7

Creation when it happened. 6, 8

Observations of some eminent Astronomers on the Diagrams, with their Remarks thereon. 10, 342

CONTENTS.

INTRODUCTION.

	Page
Remarks on the Aſtronomers Remarks.	13

The Reaſon why the Seaſons of the Year have not been pointed out, exactly, by any Nation beſides the Iſraelites and Jews   14

Olympiads deſcribed.   15

The Revolution of the Equator, the only true Meaſure of Time.   16

Annual Orbit of the Earth round the Sun, an Ellipſe, and divided unequally.   16

Time and Motion anſwering exactly to each other; both meaſured by the Rotations of the Equator, and anſwering each other preciſely, ſo that they may be turned into each other reciprocally.   17

The Quantity of Time the Earth goes forward in the Ecliptick, during one Rotation of the Earth, or a natural Day.   42

All

CONTENTS.

INTRODUCTION.

                           Page

All Nature measured by the Rotations of the Equator.   18

The Division of the Ecliptick examined, and the Length of the Solar Year.   19, 20

Observation thereon, only one Year apart, precarious.   21

Dr. Keil's *Method of ascertaining the Length of the solar tropical Year.*   22

The Length of it examined and proved, by Mr. Kennedy, *according to* Dr. Keil's *Method, from Observations made 168 Years Distance from each other.*   23

Solar Period, or Cycle of the Sun described.   24

Dr. Bradley's *Observation, A.D. 1753, ascertained the first Meridian.*   25

Calendar of the Israelites described, and the Method

CONTENTS.

INTRODUCTION.

            Page

Method they used to measure and record Times, viz. by Days and Years.   26

Though the Israelites appear to measure Times and Seasons mechanically, yet they do it at the same Time, astronomically, according to the Operations of Nature.   30

The Method of calculating Times and Seasons by the Israelites.   31

The Year of the Quadriennium at the Creation.   34

The Method of adjusting the lunar with the solar Year, by the Epact, and both measured by integral Days.   36

The solar Months of the Israelites, agreeing with the twelve Signs, beginning and ending on the same Point with them.   38

The Use the Israelites made of their solar Months, and the Courses of their Priests described.   39

CONTENTS.

INTRODUCTION.

The Beginning of the Year, the Month, and the Week altered by the Command of God, as a Memorial of their Deliverance from the Egyptian Bondage. Page 41

The Jews, in celebrating their Feast, for their Deliverance from the Egyptian Bondage, celebrate the Birth of Christ also. 41

The true Time of the Birth of the Messiah examined, and found to be at the Feast of Ingathering and Tabernacles. 42

How it happened that Christians kept the Birth of Christ at the Winter Solstice, instead of the autumnal Equinox. 45

The Julian Year, when it began.—The Cause why Julius Cæsar altered it, and the Method of that Alteration. 50

The Names and Animals, denominating the twelve Signs, ideal, and descriptive of the Seasons,—whence derived. 53

CONTENTS.

INTRODUCTION.

Agency of Nature believed by the ancient Philosophers, to be in Heat and Cold. Page 60

The Death of the Messiah *foretold by Daniel; this Prophesy examined.* 65

The issuing of the Decree for the Return of the Jews to Jerusalem, and the End of the Prophesy compleated, by the cutting off the Messiah. 67

When the Paschal Lamb was to be slain. 70

The old seventh Day Sabbath restored;— the Birth of Christ, how kept. 71

The aforesaid Observations proved by the Calculations of Equinoxes, new and full Moons, and Eclipses.—Deists and Skepticks *called on to point an Equinox, new or full Moon, or an Eclipse, which contradict it.* 74

The Point where these Calculations were began. 74

Why

CONTENTS.

INTRODUCTION.

Why the Introduction was dated Sept. 22, 1787. Page 76

The Age of the World, and Day of the Week, proved mathematically and astronomically, by the Number of Days, Years, and Lunations. 78

A Calculation of the Eclipse which happened during Herod's last Illness. 79

Calculation of the Birth of Christ. 82

Prophesy of Christ's Death foretold and calculated. 85

A Calculation of the Eclipse, A. D. 1787, also of the next Full Moon after it. 92

Explanation of the aforesaid Calculations;— their Method described, with Instructions how they were performed. 97

Difference between Calendar Measure and true Time, explained by Dr. Keil. 98

Lunar

CONTENTS.

L nar ANTICIPATIONS *explained and proved to have no Foundation in Nature.* P.104

The 19 Years Cycle of the Moon proved to be longer than the 19 Years Cycle of the Sun, which is contrary to the general received Opinion of Astronomers. 105

Issue joined with the Skeptick, to try whether what is asserted, (viz. that Moses gives us the Place of the Sun and Moon at the Creation) be true or not.

What gave Occasion to the following Letters. 118

LETTER I.

On the DELUGE.

An Answer to some Queries proposed by Mr. Heaviside;—whether Ore, Metal, or Coal were ever found under Chalk?—Observations where Ore and Metals are found, with Remarks on the Formation of this terraqueous Globe.—How Metals, Salts, &c. were dissolved, and reformed

at

CONTENTS.

at the Deluge; together with the Method by which the different Strata *were formed.—The Flood described.* Page 119

LETTER II.

On the DELUGE.

Mr. Heaviside's Answer to the former Letter, with his Remarks thereon; together with his Theory of the Deluge.—That he cannot think that the Earth underwent a general Dissolution at that Time.—That he believed the central Nucleus was Fire;—with Objections to the Dissolution of the Earth at the Deluge. 130

LETTER III.

On the DELUGE.

Facts which prove that in all Parts of Europe, Asia, Africa, *and* America, *the Exuviæ of Animals and Vegetables, particularly Sea Shells, are found in different* Strata *of Stone, both on the Tops of the highest Mountains in the World, and also at the greatest Depths that have been*

CONTENTS.

been dug below the Surface of the Earth.— Some farther Account of the Deluge. Page 137

LETTER IV.

On the CREATION.

Original Names, ideal.—The Reason why it has been asserted and generally believed, that the Scriptures do not speak strictly true, with Regard to Philosophy, on the Motion of the Sun, Earth, &c. but is accommodated to vulgar Apprehensions.—The Mosaic Account of the Creation and Formation of this System;—describing the Agents which carry on the mechanical Operations of Nature; together with some Extracts from Sir Isaac Newton, *to shew that he supposed the Agents of Nature to be the same as those revealed in the Scriptures.* 145

LETTER V.

On VEGETATION.

Vegetation, when it first began.—The Agents which carry it on described; together with the Method

CONTENTS.

Method Nature makes use of for that Purpose. The Vegetation of a Seed and Bud.—Experiments from Dr. Hales, *to ascertain the Effects of* Heat *and* Cold *on that Operation of Nature.*
Page 167

LETTER VI.

On VEGETATION.

Experiments from Dr. Hales, *which prove that Vegetables inspire and expire according to the Dryness and Moisture, and the Heat and Coldness of the Air.—The Method Nature makes use of to perform Vegetation.—Trees and Vegetables grow in the Form of a Pyramid, unless prevented.—The Cause assigned why Plants in a Green-house, or other Room, point towards the Window.—The Juices of Vegetables always in Motion, but do not circulate like the Blood in Animals.— Some more Experiments from* Dr. Hales, *to explain the Method Nature makes use of in the bleeding Season, (in the Spring of the Year) to force out the Buds and Leaves.* 184

LETTER

CONTENTS.

LETTER VII.

On VEGETATION.

A Recapitulation of the Method Nature makes use of to carry on Vegetation.—The natural Agents hot *and* cold Ether.—*Fire and Motion synonimous.—The Phenomenon of Vegetation a proper One to explain the* Agency of Nature. *The Cause why Trees shed their Leaves in Autumn, and the Means made use of to push forth their Buds and Leaves in the Spring.—The Scripture Account of Vegetation perfectly agreeable with Nature.*—Cold *and* hot Ether, *the* Agents *which support and carry on Animal as well as Vegetable Life.*   Page 203

LETTER VIII.

On the DELUGE.

Mr. Heaviside professes a great Inclination for the Study of Natural Philosophy, though he had been prevented from attending to it so much as he wished.—He then puts the following Query. In that general Dissolution of Substances, which you

CONTENTS.

you suppose at the Deluge, why were not Shells, Bones, Shrubs, &c. dissolved, as well as Rocks, Stones, &c.? Page 216

LETTER IX.

On the DELUGE.

Prejudices of Education hard to be overcome, therefore many Things in Mr. Penrose's Theory may appear doubtful at first, as they differ from some which are generally taught.—There may be Arcana *in Nature, which human Reason may not be able to explain.—Answer to Mr. Heaviside's last Query.—A Constitution and Custom observed by the Royal Society, concerning Disquisitions.—The Waters outside of this terraqueous Globe, not sufficient for the Flood.—Centre of Gravity altered at the Flood.—Causes assigned why* Bones, Shells, &c. *were not dissolved.* 220

LETTER X.

On CHRONOLOGY and ASTRONOMY.

As the first material Agents cannot come within the Knowledge of our Senses, so different Philosophers

CONTENTS.

Philosophers have formed different Opinions; but Astronomy may be proved by mathematical Demonstration.—History is no more than a Romance without Chronology, which is not certain unless proved by Astronomy.—Where to begin our astronomical Epoch.—Moses's Account of the Place of the Sun and Moon at the Creation, proved by mathematical Demonstration.—First Meridian proved by an Observation of Dr. Bradley's.—As Mr. Penrose is not fearful of being convicted of Error, Leave is given to Mr. Heaviside to shew this Letter to any Proficient in Astronomy, and to get his Criticisms on it.

Page 231

LETTER XI.

On CHRONOLOGY and ASTRONOMY.

Mr. Heaviside having shewn Mr. Penrose's Letter to some eminent Astronomers, Members of the Royal Society, they " all agree that his " Calculations were perfectly right, *and* proved " what he intended they should; *and that they* " would have desired Leave to have read the " Paper at the Meeting of the Royal Society,
but

CONTENTS.

" *but that it was deemed to be connected with*
" *religious Subjects, which they never meddle*
" *with there.*"—Queries *to Mr. Penrose, occasioned by the aforesaid Letter.* Page 241

LETTER XII.

On CHRONOLOGY and ASTRONOMY.

Moses's History of the Creation ought to be examined by Chronology and Astronomy, which is the true *Test of History.—The Cycle of Years explained.—Answer to Mr. Heaviside's last Queries.—*Ether *the Cause of Gravitation.—Gravity and Levity relative Terms.—The* Agency of the Ethers *explained;—they are the Cause of* Winds, Hurricanes, Earthquakes, &c.—*They alter or destroy* Attraction, Gravitation, Cohesion, &c.—*Is the Cause of the different Motions of the Earth, and its spheroidical Shape.—The Cause of Tides, &c.* 247

LETTER XIII.

On NATURAL PHILOSOPHY.

Doubts proposed concerning some Parts of
Mr.

CONTENTS.

Mr. Penrose's Philosophy, in Order that Truth may be ascertained.— Queries concerning cold Ether, *and the Pressure of that cold Ether into the hot, or where it is more rare.—What is the Cause of the Motion of the Earth? What is the Cause that the Earth does not fall into the Sun? Do you impute it to a Current of Ether? Answer to the last Queries conclusive, if it be allowed that Moses was so far ignorant of Astronomy, as to be incapable of calculating the Eclipses which preceded his Time.—He is said to be learned in all the Learning of the Egyptians. State of the Sciences in Chaldea and Egypt.*
Page 263

LETTER XIV.

On NATURAL PHILOSOPHY.

*Mr. Heaviside's Query answered.—Calculations of the Motions of the heavenly Bodies demonstrably true; but the Principles of natural Philosophy cannot be demonstrated with that Clearness and Precision, as those in Astronomy. Three Principles of Matter ;—Gravity explained.—*Cold *and* hot Ether *described according to*
Sir

CONTENTS.

Sir Isaac Newton.—Centre *of* Gravity *supposed formerly to be placed in the Centre of the Earth, but late Experiments prove that* Gravity *does not tend to the Centre of the Earth, but to the Superficies, and to the Place where there is the greatest expansive Heat.*—Gravity *proved to be increased or lessened in Proportion as* Heat *and* Cold *prevail.*—The Pressure *of the* cold Ether *or* Gravity *acts exactly in the same Proportion on the Poles and the Equator, as the spheroidical Shape of the terraqueous Globe shews it does.*—The Centre *of* Gravity *to be near the Surface of the Earth, where every Thing tends.*
Page 271

LETTER XV.

On NATURAL PHILOSOPHY.

State of the Sciences about two thousand Years ago. — *The former Query repeated,* " If the
" Earth, &c. were first put in Motion by the
" Heat of the Sun, rarefying the Atmosphere
" between these Bodies, why did not the Earth
" immediately gravitate into the Sun? Must not
" a trajectile Force have been first necessary to
" cause its annual Orbit?"
293

CONTENTS.

LETTER XVI.

On NATURAL PHILOSOPHY.

Heat and Cold first Agents, according to Sir Isaac Newton, Boerhaave, &c. — *Internal Make of this terraqueous Globe described.—The Thickness of the Shell of the Earth.—The confused Appearances on this terraqueous Globe, prove that it has underwent tremendous Convulsions from within, and that the earthy Shell has been burst into Millions of Pieces.—Earthquakes examined, and their Effects described.— These Effects occasioned by Fire.—The Causes of Earthquakes explained; which prove that there is an immense Quantity of Fire within the Earth.— The above Account agreeable with what is given in the Scriptures.* Page 299

LETTER XVII.

On NATURAL PHILOSOPHY.

Mr. Heaviside's *Question, " Why does not the Earth gravitate into the Sun, &c." answered. All Space filled with* ETHERS, *which reach from the Sun to the Extremities of this System, and*

CONTENTS.

and are in continual Conflict, and cause a vibrating Motion, by their Endeavour to get the better of each other.—These Ethers the Cause of Projection and Gravity.—The Earth and Planets of different specifick Gravities, according to their Distances from the Sun.—The diurnal and annual Motion of the Earth accounted for.—The Phenomena of Nature, and the Scriptures, confirm the Testimony of each other.
Page 321

LETTER XVIII.
On ASTRONOMY.

With a DIAGRAM. 337

LETTER XIX.
On ASTRONOMY.

Observations of Mr. Heaviside's astronomical Friend, on Mr. Penrose's Diagram, not conclusive. 339

LETTER XX.
On ASTRONOMY.

Mr. Penrose's Design to get the Opinion of some

CONTENTS.

some of the Geometricians and Astronomers, concerning his Diagram.   Page 343

LETTER XXI.

On ASTRONOMY.

The Difficulty in getting a decided Opinion on the Diagrams.   347

LETTER XXII.

ASTRONOMY.

On the MOON and LUNAR MOTIONS.

The Moon not a Planet, but a Satellite attending the Earth.—The recorded Observations of Astronomers, concerning her, collected.—Her Make and Motion described.—The Chaldean Cycle, with the Methods they made use of for calculating their Eclipses.—The physical Causes of these Motions explained, and confirmed by the Observations of Mr. Herschel, and the French Astronomers.   349

LETTER XXIII.

CONTENTS.

LETTER XXIII.

On ASTRONOMY.

To confirm what Mr. Penrose has observed in his last and former Letters.—He has sent Mr. Heaviside a Calculation of the Eclipse which is to happen July the 25th.—It is calculated by the Method made use of by the Ancients, *to measure and record Time:—But to shew how certain their Method was, it is also calculated according to the* present, *by Equations and Anomalies.—It may be remarked, that both these Methods differ from each other only* 8 M. 11 S. *That the Patriarchs and Chaldeans had more Knowledge in Astronomy than is generally allowed them.—This is proved by the* 18 *Years Cycle of Eclipses, and also the* 19 *Years Cycle of the Moon, both which, it is certain, we received from them, and without these Cycles, Astronomers would be at a great Loss.—Data on which the Calculations are made, and Conclusions infered from them,* Page 380

Introduction.

The INTRODUCTION.

THE following Letters are real Copies of genuine ones, which passed between me and an intimate Friend, for our own Amusement, according to their Dates; but not with the most distant View that they should ever appear before the Public.—The Gentleman,* who was the first Beginner of this Correspondence, died about the Middle of last February.— Some Days before his Death, he desired his Son to write me, that
" He

---

* JOHN HEAVISIDE, Esq. of Princes's-Street, Cavendish-Square; a Gentleman whose Loss is already experienced by many of his Acquaintance, who were very numerous; his whole Attention, for many Years past, having been employed to serve his Friends and Neighbours, particularly those in Distress; this was his greatest Pleasure! and he had Inclination, Fortune, and Abilities to do it.—Therefore, as a Person of his unbounded Benevolence is so rarely to be met with, his Loss will be the more severely felt.

The INTRODUCTION.

" He was paſt all Hopes of Recovery, and
" begged to know what I would have done
" with thoſe very valuable Papers which he
" had of mine, his Health having made him
" unable to attend to them as he wiſhed."
About ten Days after this, the Son wrote me
a ſecond Letter, " to let me know that his
" Father was dead, and that he had found
" the Letters of mine which his Father or-
" dered ſhould be ſent me."

Some Time after this, I mentioned his Death to ſome of our Friends, with the Circumſtance of his Son's ſending me ſome Letters which had paſſed between us.—They deſired to read them; after which they returned them to me again, with a Requeſt that they might be printed; I conſented thereto, and hope they will receive the Approbation of the Public.

As ſome of the Notions in theſe Letters are contrary to *general received Opinions*, I truſt they will not be diſcarded on that Account, without being firſt examined, and the Evidence

Evidence I produce tried, if sufficient to support these Notions or not; which are, principally,

First, That the Equinoctial, or great Circle of the Heavens, is equally divided by the twelve Signs, of 30 Degrees each, making in the Whole 360°.

Secondly, That the annual Orbit of the Earth must be measured by the Earth's rotary Motion, which is absolutely, and without any Exception, the true Measure of Time.

Thirdly, That the Anticipation of Time, and the Precession of the Equinoxes, have not any Foundation in Nature, but are occasioned by the Calendar Computation, not answering exactly to the Length of the annual Orbit.— According to our Calendar Measure, the solar Year contains $365\frac{1}{4}$ Days, or Six Hours; but the solar tropical Year, or the Time she is performing her annual Orbit, is only 365 Days, 5 Hours, 49 Minutes,

which

which is 11 Minutes short of her Quadrant, or six Hours. Therefore the Earth precedes, beyond the Meridian, where it began, 11 Minutes in equatereal Time, or 2ⁿ· 45' in Measure. Hence, as the Earth goes, every Year, 11 Minutes beyond the Place where it began ; so it had occasioned, (in the Year 1753) the Equinoxes to have preceded forward 44 Days, and the Calendar Computation to fall back the same Number; and thereby to anticipate Time so much. For the Autumnal Equinox, in the Year 706, of the Julian Period (which was the Year of the Creation, according to the Mosaic Chronology) fell on October 25th; but in A. D. 1753, which was the 6466th of the Julian Period, it was observed to enter Libra, Sept. 11, O. S. so that in 5760 Years, the Calendar Measure had *anticipated* the true 44 Days.

At the Council of Nice, which was held A. D. 325, the Sun was observed to enter Libra, Sept. 22; therefore in order to bring the Calendar Measure back to that Time, and so to commemorate the Festival of Easter,

at

at a more exact Season; an Act of Parliament was passed, A. D. 1752, to throw 11 Days out of the Calendar Computation for that Year; so that this Year contained only 354 Days, instead of 365. By this Means the Equinox was brought back from the 14th of *Taurus* to which it was got, (from the first of Aries,) to the third of the same Sign, and the Sun entered Libra that Year, Sept. 22, N. S. instead of Sept. 11, O. S. which was the Time it entered it the Year before. (a)

Fourthly; The general Opinion is, that Moses, in his History of the Creation, does not point out, or give us any Instruction, in what Place of the Heavens the Sun and Moon were at the Creation.

First.—In answer to this I observe, that he has told us, 1st, That they were placed there on the fourth Day of the Creation Week.
2dly

(a) See Letter XII. XIV. and Diagram.

2dly.—That the Moon could not give her Light till the going down of the Sun: As the Sun was in the Meridian of the Place where it began to shine; so the Earth must have made one Quadrant of her Rotation, before the Moon could enlighten Her.— As soon as that was performed, the Sun sat in the West, and the Moon rose directly after in the East, when they both together enlightened the whole Earth from Pole to Pole. Hence, it may be remarked, that the Rotation of the Earth measured one Quadrant of solar Time, before she began to measure the lunar; therefore as the Sun and Moon were, jointly, to point out the Seasons, the Days, and the Years; so the Chronology of Time must begin at this Period, as Moses tells us it did.

(b) 3dly.— In Regard to the Place of the Sun and Moon in the Heavens, Moses informs us, that the Feast of Ingathering at the End or Revolution of the Year, was to commemorate the Creation, which happened at

---

(b) Levit. XXIII, 32.

at that Seafon.—That the Feaft was to be kept at the autumnal Equinox.—That the Moon muft begin to fhine in the Evening, at the going down of the Sun, being fifteen Days old, and juft paffed her Oppofition or Full.—Here then we have a Point to begin our Calculations from, viz. the firft Degree or Point of Libra; the Epact 15, (the Moon then being fifteen Days old) the fourth Day of the Week; and, as one Quadrant of folar Time was to be added to the Beginning of the Year, viz. from twelve o'Clock Midday, to Six in the Evening; fo it muft be the fecond Year of the folar Quadriennium.—Had we not had thefe *Data*, we muft be in the Dark for a Point where to begin our Calculations from; for, as Dr *Keil* obferves, Lect. XXVIII. " As there are certain Points from " which Aftronomers begin their Computa- " tions of the Planets Motions, fo alfo there " muft be certain Points, as Inftants of Time, " from which, as from Roots, all Calcula- " tions muft begin."

Now, I have poftulated that my Interpretation

8   The INTRODUCTION.

pretation of the Mosaic History is true; and I find by Calculation, that all the Equinoxes, Solstices, new Moons, full Moons, and Eclipses, will be pointed out by these Calculations, according to the observed Times. Here then we have two Points to measure from, 1st. the postulated Point of the full Moon, at the autumnal Equinox 706, according to the Julian Period; and 2dly. the observed Time, when the Sun entered Libra, A. D. 1786, which Year we know answers to the Year 6499 of that Period; during that Time the Earth has made 5793 annual Revolutions through the Ecliptic, and 2115849 Rotations round her Axis. Therefore, it must be allowed, that if the Number of the Earth's Rotations (or natural Days) and the Number of Years, or annual Revolutions, measure the exact Length between these two Points, it must be mathematically true.—Now, I prove by Calculations (c) that they do.—These Calculations have

(c) See Letter, No. XVII.

The INTRODUCTION.

have also this farther Evidence, *viz.* That you may begin them, either at the autumnal Equinox, 706, A. I. P. or when, (by Observation,) the Sun was seen to enter Libra, A. D. 1786, and the Calculations will come out the same to a Minute, which no astronomical Tables, yet extant, will do.—During this Time, the Moon will have made 71647 Lunations or Revolutions round the Earth, and Half another, when She intersected the Earth's Orbit, through the Ecliptic, and caused an Eclipse of the Sun, A. D. 1786, July 25 D. 8 H. 43 M. P. M.

If, after this, any one should dispute the Point, whether Moses has given proper Instructions concerning the Place of the Sun and Moon, the Day of the Week, &c. at the Creation.—He must allow that we have been very lucky in getting Information for doing it. (d)

These Notions being different from those
B adopted

(d) See Letter, No. XVII.

adopted by Writers on the Subject, I remained diffident of my own Opinions, notwithstanding my Calculations of the Motions of the Heavenly Bodies, confirmed me they were true, till I defired Mr. Heavifide, who had fome Friends among the Royal Society, eminent in Aftronomy and Philofophy, to fhew them thefe Letters, with my Diagram, and to get their Opinions and Remarks on them.

The Gentlemen returned him for anfwer, that I had proved, to Demonftration, that the Sun and Moon were in the fame Places in the Heavens, in the Year 706 of the Julian Period, (as they muft have been in the Year in which the Creation happened, according to the Mofaic Chronology,) and that the Earth had made juft the fame Number of Rotations, which I had poftulated it had. But with Regard to thofe Points in the Diagram, wherein I differed from the general received Opinions, they did not determine.(e)

That

(e) See Letter **VII.**

That they liked my Letters fo well, that they would have read them before the Royal Society, had they not been joined with Religion, which was contrary to one of their Rules to enter on.

Not receiving the Satisfaction from thofe Gentlemen I hoped for, concerning the Points wherein I differed from general received Opinions, I got another Friend, who was intimately acquainted with an eminent Aftronomer, to requeft his Remarks thereon; to whom I alfo fent one of my Diagrams.—After fome Time, he fent his Remarks in the following Words, " I have examined " fome Parts of it, and find it to be fufficient-" ly exact; I muft however obferve, that the " Method of reprefenting the Sun's Place, " and alfo the new and full Moons, for a " given Year, by a Diagram, is by no Means " new; fince not only that has been done, " but, by certain moveable Circles, the Lu-" nations and Seafons of the Eclipfes have " been fhewn for a given Number of Years. " There are, however, feveral Affertions in
" the

"　the Explanation which accompanies the
" Diagram, which, I believe, will not be
" readily granted.—The Conſtructor of the
" Diagram, ſays— *Aſtronomers, tell us, that*
" *the Ecliptic is equally divided into* 12 *Signs,*
" *of* 30 *Degrees each; but it is not ſo.* —Now
" the Truth is, that the Ecliptic is equally
" divided by the twelve Signs, and when
" theſe twelve Signs are *referred* to the Equa-
" tor, they neceſſarily occupy unequal Por-
" tions of that Circle, from the Inclination
" of the *two Circles*. (f) Beſides, the Ecliptic
" *cannot with any Propriety*, be called an
" Elipſe.—It is *only* the Line deſcribed ap-
" parently by the Centre of the Sun, viewed
" from the Earth, during the annual Revo-
" lution of that Planet round that great Lu-
" minary.—That I am not at all diſpoſed to
" enter into any Diſcuſſion concerning the
" Accuracy either of the ancient Iſraelites, or
" the modern Jews, in calculating the Times
" of their Feaſts.—I muſt however obſerve,
" that the Length of the tropical Year is not
" exactly

(f) The Equator is a Circle——The Ecliptic an Elipſe.

"exactly 365 D. 5 H. 49 M. but is at pre-
"sent a few Seconds shorter, and has been
"continually diminishing, somewhat unequal-
"ly, for several Centuries past; and will, in
"all Probability, continue to diminish for
"many Ages to come."—On this I beg
Leave to remark, that there, certainly, have
been formed very exact Diagrams, representing the Sun's Place, &c. for a given Year—
But then these have been made by the Assistance of Equations and Anomilies, to make
the 365 Rotations of the Earth, to tally with
the 360 Degrees of the Equator.—Thus, as
he has very justly observed, when the 365
Rotations of the Earth, through the Ecliptic,
is referred to the Equator, they necessarily
occupy unequal Portions of that Circle, so
unequal as 365 is to 360. From which it is
agreed, that a Diagram has been formed to
shew the Sun's Place, &c. in a given Year,
by the *artificial* Means of *Equations* and *Anomilies*; but mine, on the contrary, is formed
according to Nature; that is, by the Rotations of the Equator *only, the sole Measure of
Time,* without Equations or Anomilies.—I
will

will now beg leave to remark, that Moſes in his Hiſtory tells us, that the Sun and Moon were *both* placed in the Heavens, to meaſure and point out the Seaſons, the Days, and Years: (g) Hence the Reaſon why thoſe Nations who have made Uſe of one of them *only*, have never yet been able to keep the appointed Seaſons of the Year they were deſigned or inſtituted for.

The only ancient People, whoſe Hiſtory can be confirmed by true Chronology, and proved by Aſtronomy, were the Iſraelites, whoſe Years were formed by the Sun and Moon, jointly.—That is, the Moon, by interſecting the Earth's Orbit, prevented the Beginning of the ſolar Year going from the appointed Seaſon; their Year always ended at the firſt full Moon which happened either upon, or, the firſt which ſucceeded, after the

(g) Gen. I. 14. Moſes ſays, that the Sun and Moon were jointly appointed to meaſure, mark, or point out the Times and Seaſons; for God ſaid, let them (in the Plural) be for Signs, and for Seaſons, and for Days, and Years.—The Scriptures farther inform us, Pſalm LXXXIX. 37, and CIV. 19. That the Moon is eſtabliſhed in Heaven as a faithful Witneſs, to point out the Seaſons.

the autumnal Equinox.—In Imitation of this, were formed the Olympiads of the Greeks, who followed the Posterity of Abraham in this Particular, *viz.* by governing the Seasons of the solar Year, by the Moon's Intersections of the annual Orbit of the Earth; indeed they differed from them in ending their solar Year at the Summer Solstice; whereas the Israelites finished theirs at the autumnal Equinox.—Thus the Chronology of Years was truly recorded by the Olympiad Games, which were celebrated every four Years, on the first full Moon which happened upon or after the Summer Solstice.—By this Means they kept the Beginning of their Years at the true Seasons; and this no other Nation has been able to do, notwithstanding the great Improvements which have been made in Opticks and other Sciences; neither will it be done *now*, by the *Gregorian* Calendar, which will vary more than an Hour in one Hundred Years.

With Regard to the Measure of the Earth's annual Orbit, through the Ecliptic, whether

or

or not it is equally divided by the twelve Signs, of 30 Degrees each; let it be remembered, that the rotary Motion of the Earth is the *only* Measure of Time, and that every Rotation of the Equator is 360 Degrees, *in Measure*, and 24 Hours *in Time*.— Now when the Sun is in Conjunction with any one of the Signs, suppose *Libra*.—The annual Orbit is measured by the Number of Rotations the Earth makes during her Passage through the Ecliptic, or till the Sun is in Conjunction with the same Star, *Libra*, again.

Had the annual Orbit of the Earth been a Circle, instead of an Elipse, (as the Earth performs equal Areas in equal Times,) these twelve Signs would have equally divided the annual Orbit, as well as the great Circle of the Heavens, and all concentrick Circles; but as it is not a Circle, but an Elipse, and that Part of the eliptic Orbit which the Earth traverses in Summer, being much larger and farther from the Sun, than the other Half which it traverses in Winter, must, of Consequence,

sequence, make a greater Number of Rotations in going through that Half than the other; indeed by Observation we find it to be more than seven.

The Earth measures the Orbits of all the Heavenly Bodies, as well as her own annual Orbit, by the Number of Rotations she makes during those Orbits, and adding the Overplus of Degrees beyond the last Rotation.— For this Purpose, the whole Equator, or Circumference of the Earth, is, as has been observed, divided into 360 Degrees in Measure, whilst she makes one Rotation round her Axis, from Sun to Sun, and is called a solar or natural Day; which 360 Degrees in Measure, are divided into 24 Hours, by a well regulated Clock.—Hence it may be observed, that, as every Rotation of the Equator contains exactly 360 Degrees, whilst a well regulated Clock points out 24 Hours in Time, *precisely*; so Time may be turned into Measure, and Measure into Time, reciprocally.—This has been evinced to Demonstration by the Trials of Mr. *Harrison*'s Time Piece.

Piece.—While the Earth is performing this Rotation or natural Day, She is carried forward, four Minutes of Time, in her annual Orbit viz. That Space of Time which She takes in going from the Star She fat off from the Day before, (which was then in Conjunction with the Sun) till She comes in Conjunction with the Sun again, is juft four Minutes.—But this is a different and diftinct Motion of the Earth's, *forward*, in its annual Orbit, which has no other Connection with the diurnal Rotation, than that it is meafured by a ftated Part of that Rotation.— In this Manner the Earth meafures the Length of her annual Orbit, or folar tropical Year; the Period of a Lunation, or the Time while the Moon is going from one Oppofition or Conjunction of the Sun, to her next Oppofition or Conjunction.—The Length of a Lunar Year, or twelve Lunations.—The Length of the Orbits of the Planets, Comets, &c.— And alfo the Times when the Eclipfes are to happen, or that particular Time, when the Moon croffes the Earth's annual Orbit, either in Conjunction with

with the Sun, and in a direct Line between the Earth and the Sun; or in Oppofition, when the Earth is in a direct Line between the Sun and Moon.—The Moon does not meafure her own Orbit, but, points out the Seafons, by Her Interfections of the annual Orbit of the Earth.

Let us now examine whether the annual Path of the Earth is equally divided, by the twelve Signs, or not.—She goes from *Libra* to *Aries*, or the fix Winter Signs, or Winter Half, in 178 D. 17 H. 58 M. But the Summer Half, or fix Signs, viz. from the Vernal to the autumnal Equinox, require 186 D. 11 H. 51 M. to compleat it; which fhews us She is more than a Week longer in traverfing the Summer fix Signs, than She is in traverfing the Winter fix Signs.—From whence it may be obferved, that She increafes her Diftance from the Sun, greatly, after She has paffed the vernal Equinox, and that She muft be many thoufands of Miles farther from the Sun, at the Summer Solftice, than She is at the Winter Solftice.—She is alfo
31 D.

31 D. 5 H. 0 M. in going through the Sign *Virgo*, and but 29 D. 4 H. 35 M. going through the Sign *Capricorn*; which shews, that, notwithstanding the twelve Signs or Stars, divide the great Circle of the Heavens into twelve *equal* Parts, yet the Path of the Earth's Orbit, (which is an Elipse within that great Circle,) is so much enlarged when She is passing through the Sign *Virgo*, that it requires more than two Rotations of the Equator, to measure it, than it does to measure the Sign *Capricorn*.—Thus, it is evident, that She traverses more than 720 Degrees, or more than forty-nine thousand Miles, in going through the *Sign Virgo*, than She does in going through the *Sign Capricorn*.—Hence also it is evident, that the Earth's Path or Orbit through the Ecliptic, is certainly an Elipse; which, I believe, few will dispute. *

We will now endeavour to try whether the following Assertion of his is true or not, viz. " That the tropical Year is not exactly 365 D. " 5 H.

---

* " The Orbits of all the Planets are Elipses, very little different from " Circles; but the Orbits of the Comets are very long Elipses; and the " lower Horns of them all are in the Sun."—See Ferguson's Astronomy, §. 155.

"5 H. 49 M. but *at present* a few Seconds shorter, and has been continually decreasing, somewhat unequally, for some Years past, and in all Probability will continue to diminish for some Ages to come."— This appears to be an Assertion without Evidence to support it.—It is true, that different Astronomers, by their Observations, have made the annual Orbit of different Lengths, hardly any two agreeing about what is the Length of it, except those who have made it 365 D. 5 H. 49 M.—The Length of it, according to Sir *Isaac Newton*, is 365 D. 5 H. 48 M. 57 S.—Hence is *partly* the Reason why the ancient Eclipses, of more than two thousand Years standing, cannot be calculated by the present Tables, which come short of them.—This Error, has been attributed, to the Moon's being nearer the Earth now than She was then; but, in Fact, the Cause does not arise from this, but from the erroneous tabular Measure.

The measuring the annual Orbit of the Earth, by two Observations, only *one* Year between

between is so precarious, that almost every Astronomer will make a different Observation this Year from that he does the next; hence it may be observed, that different Astronomers will not only vary from one another, but also the same Astronomer will differ from Himself.—Dr. Keil tells us, [h] that " by
" Observations that are made at the Distance
" of one Year, we *cannot safely* rely upon the
" Quantity of the Year collected from them;
" for a small Error of one Minute, being
" constantly increased, and multiplied by
" the Number of Years, in Process of Time,
" would amount to a prodigious Mistake in
" the Place of the Sun, therefore the Astron-
" omers more accurately determine the Quan-
" tity of the Year, by taking the Observati-
" ons of two Equinoxes, at *many* Years Dis-
" tance from one another; and dividing the
" Time, by the Number of Revolutions the
" Sun has made, the Quantity will shew the
" Time of one Revolution, or *nearly* the
" Period of the Earth in her Orbit.—For,
" by

[h] Lect. 22. P. 271.

"by this Means, if there be any Miſtake
"made in the Obſervation, it will be divid-
"ed into ſo many Parts, according to the
"Number of Years, that it will be inſenſible
"for the Space of one Year."

Dr. Keil, as above, having remarked the great Difficulty there is, in obſerving when the Sun is in the Plane of the Meridian; of the Place of Obſervation; and alſo the Uncertainty of it was ſuch, that he calls the Error of a *Minute* a *ſmall Error*; and, therefore, in order to come *near* the Truth, we are to take the Obſervations of two Equinoxes, at many Years Diſtance from one another, and dividing the Time by the Number of Revolutions the Sun has made, the Quantity will ſhew the Time of one Revolution *nearly*.

Now in Order to find the Length of the tropical Year, Mr. Kennedy took Dr. Keil's Direction, and tried it by the Obſervations of two remarkable great and exact Aſtronomers, which were made 168 Years Diſtance from each other,—The firſt Obſervation was made by by *Tycho Brake*, at *Uraniberg*, A. D. 1585, and the laſt by Dr. *Bradley*, at *Greenwich*, 1753. By this he found the Length of the ſolar tropical Year to be exactly 365 D. 5 H. 49 M. (i) From which may be deduced, that 365 D. 5 H. 49 M. is the exact Length of the ſolar tropical Year, and alſo, that it is no ſhorter now than it was 168 Years ago. (k)

A natural Day, or one Rotation of the Equator, contains 24 Hours in Time, or 1440 Minutes; theſe may be called equatoreal Minutes, as there are Terminations, in Meaſure, on the Equator, which anſwer to every one of them.—The Equator precedes forward 11 of theſe Minutes, every ſolar Year; and in 1440 Years, it paſſes through all its meridional Variations, and at the End of that Period, it returns again to the original Point of the Day, in the ſame Place or Meridian, where it began, but not on the ſame Day of the Week.—As this is an exact Cycle

---

(i) Kennedy, P. 159.—— (k) Introduction, Page 23.

cle of the Sun, fo all the Multiples of this Number will be fo too, as 2880, 3420, 5760, &c. will compleat folar Cycles; therefore if you know the Time when the Sun enters *Libra*, or any other Point in the Heavens, on any one of the Years of any Cycle; by that you will alfo know the Time when the Sun enters *Libra*, the fame Year, in all other Cycles. (1)

The fourth Cycle ended A. D. 1783.—Here we have 5760 Revolutions to try the exact Length of the folar tropical Year by; and throughout all this Period of Time, the Sun will be found to enter *Libra* at the Times calculated, according to the Length of the folar Year being exactly 365 D. 5 H. 49 M. Thus let the autumnal Equinox 706, of the Julian Period, be one Point, and the autumnal Equinox, 6466 of the fame Period, be the other Point.—Between thefe two Points, the Earth has made 5760 Revolutions; and by an accurate Obfervation that Dr. Bradley made that Year, A. D. 1753, at Greenwich,

D. which

(1) See Letter, No. 8, 10.

which was the Year in Connection with 6466, of the Julian Period, the Sun was observed to enter Libra at the Day, Hour, and Minute it did 5760 Years before, and Calculations, according to this Length of the Year, will be found to agree with the Observations made every Year throughout this Period, and also all succeeding ones. (m) Is not this Demonstration, that this Length of the Year is perfectly right?

In Order to understand some Parts of these Letters the better, I shall give a Description of the patriarchal or israelitish Year, according to the Calendar of it, as it is found in the Scriptures, or as it was observed by the ancient Israelites.

It appears clear, that the Seasons in which Moses ordered the Feasts to be kept, and the Directions which he gave to the Israelites for keeping them, were pointed out by a well known and simple Calendar; which, at that Time,

(m) See Letter, No. 6.

Time, may be supposed to be understood by all; therefore, there was no Occasion to describe it.—This Calendar seems to be formed in a most simple, clear, and exact Manner. They calculated their Months *astronomically*, by the Number of Rotations made by the Earth, (in Appearance) as mechanically as a Clock points out the Hours of the Day.—They did not seem to have any Regard to the Motions of the heavenly Bodies, any more than if they had no Motion at all.—Thus, we may remark, that the Patriarchs, instead of being left to find out, by Observations on the Heavenly Bodies, the Length of the Years, whereby their Festivals and Seasons were to be calculated and observed, they were instructed by a Calendar of *integral Days*, and Quadrants, to calculate astronomically the Times appointed for keeping of them, and thereby to record the Ages of the Patriarchs, and therewith the Age of the World; this they were to do by the solar tropical Year, but to record Events by Days and Months of the lunar.—Indeed had not Moses, at the Time he ordered them to keep these Festivals

at

at their particular Seasons, given them Directions how to know when these Seasons came, it would be very absurd to expect it from them.—But he instructed 'them to measure both the solar and lunar Year, by a certain Number of the Rotations of the Earth, or natural Days.—In this Manner the Patriarchs and the Israelites always expressed their Ages, viz. by *Days of Years*, to shew that their Years were measured by Days.—Thus when *Pharoah* asked *Jacob* how old he was. (n) In the English Text it is, " *And Pharoah said unto Jacob, how old art thou.*"—In the Margin, you have a literal Translation of the Hebrew.—" *How many are the Days of the Years of thy Life;*" Jacob answered him in the same Stile—" *The Days of my Years, &c.*

Thus it may be infered, that their annual Calendars contained a certain Number of Days, and that their Years were measured by those Days.

They began to count the Beginning of their

(n) Gen. XLVII. 8, 9.

their Days, at Six o'Clock in the Evening, (o) at the going down of the Sun, (which it always did in the Latitude where Paradife is fuppofed to be placed, and, nearly fo, in Egypt and the Wildernefs.)—Thus, as foon as the Sun was out of Sight, they added that Day to the former Number; and the next Day immediately began.—Six Days of the Week they were to work, which fixth Day ended at the going down of the Sun that fame Evening, when the feventh or Sabbath began; and at the going down of the Sun, the Evening of the Sabbath, their Week, or Cycle of feven Days ended, and the firft Day of the next Week began; and, in Order to keep and to commemorate their Sabbath, they had a holy Convocation thereon, which was their firft and principal Feftival.

Their Day was divided into four Quadrants or Quarters, and had four cardinal Points; the firft began at Six o'Clock in the Evening, and ended at Mid-night; the fecond ended at Six in the Morning; the third at Mid-day, and

(o) Levit. XXIII. 32.

and the fourth at Six in the Evening; when the next Day began.—This is the Method which Moses ordered Time to be measured and recorded by, and the Method that the Sun and Moon do it, viz. by the Number of the Earth's Rotations.

Thus, notwithstanding in Appearance they measured mechanically by Calendar Numbers only, yet at certain Times, these Numbers met the Motions of the Heavenly Bodies, and their Calculations turned out astronomically true.—They made Use of two Years to measure and record Times and Seasons by; the one by the apparent Motions of the Sun, (or more properly the Motions of the Earth,) and the other by Lunations or the Revolutions of the Moon; which two Years, being measured by Days *only*, prevented the Times appointed, at particular Seasons of the Year, from ever altering; and to prevent their forgetting or mistaking the appointed Seasons, when these Transactions began and ended; Moses ordered Festivals and holy Convocations to be kept at these appointed Times, to commemorate them.

Their lunar Year confisted of 354¼ Days; and was divided into twelve Months; the first Month of the Year began at the new Moon before the Feast of Tabernacles. The first Day of the Feast of Tabernacles, or the Ingathering of the Fruits of the Earth, was appointed to commemorate the Place of the Sun and Moon at the Creation, and was always to be celebrated on the 15th Day of this Month, or (as expressed in the Hebrew) the Moon; which was at its first Appearance, on the going down of the Sun, after the full, in Commemoration that that was the Place of the Moon, on the fourth Evening of the Creation; as the autumnal Equinox was the Point where the Sun was first placed, at that Time.* As has been already observed, they began

---

* As this was the first Day that the Chronology of the World commenced, the Israelites, (which is still continued amongst the Jews to this Day,) "on their Return from the Synagogue, salute each other with saying, "to a good Year shall you be writ, for according to Tradition, this is the "Day that God created the World, so it is that on which God judges it; "and therefore (says David Levi) (p) in our Prayers, on this Festival; we "pray to God, to renew unto us a good Year."—As Trumpets were always made use of on the first Day of this Feast, so it was called the Feast of Trumpets, a Memorial of blowing of Trumpets. (q) David Levi tells us, (r) "that their Trumpets are always made of a Ram's Horn, in Re-

(p) P. 75.—(q) Levit. XXIII. 24.—(r) P. 70.

began their Days at Six o'Clock in the Evening; their lunar Year began at the same Point, and consisted of 354¼ Days; so the first lunar Year began, at the same cardinal Point with the Day, and it ended at the cardinal Point of the next Quadrant, viz. at Mid-night; the second ended at Six in the Morning; the third at Noon, and the fourth at Six in the Evening; at which Point of the Day, the lunar Year was compleated and ended; and was then added to the End of the fourth Year, which contained 355 Days, whereas, the first three of this Cycle of four Years, contained only 354.

This lunar Year was divided into twelve Months, and was calculated by the Patriarchs, and ancient Israelites, by Calendar Numbers only, and continued to be so till after the Captivity

---

" membrance of Abraham offering his Son Isaac, when the Angel of the
" Lord called to him out of Heaven, and said, lay not thine Hand upon
" the Lad—and Abraham seeing a Ram, caught by the Horns, in a
" Thicket, he went and offered Him up for a Burnt Offering, instead of
" his Son; our Traditions inform us, that happened on this Day, (s) we
" therefore make Use of a Trumpet, made of Ram's Horn, as a Memorial
" of it."

(s) Gen. XXII. 8, 9.

Captivity of the Jews, when they learned and introduced a different Method of pointing out, and of calculating this lunar Months. It is fuppofed they learned their Method during their Captivity amongft the Babylonians and Greeks; from that Time, to this Day, they calculate their Months by the Appearance of the Moon, next after the Change, and by 29 and 30 Days, according as it appeared; but they never made their Months to contain more than thirty Days. But, according to the Calendar Numbers of the Ifraelites, their firft eleven Months contained 30 Days each, and their twelfth 24 Days only; and at the End of their Cycle of four Years, 25 Days.—At this Point, their Calendar Numbers met the Lunations aftronomically.

The firft Day of every lunar Month was called the Month or Moon-day; on this Day they had a Feftival, and holy Convocation, as a Memorial that the laft Month was ended, and another began.—By thefe lunar Months

Months, all Events and Transactions were recorded.

The solar Year, (by which the Ages of the Patriarchs were recorded, whose Ages were always made to begin and end at the autumnal Equinox, and thereby to run parallel with the Years of the World,) contained 365¼ Days; but then this Quadrant at the End of the Year, like the Lunar, did not come into the Reckoning till at the End of the Quadriennium, or Cycle of four Years, was compleated; so that the first three Years of the Quadriennium consisted of 365 Days each, and the fourth of 366.—The solar Day began at Noon, as it did on the fourth Day of the Creation, therefore it anticipates the lunar one Quadrant of a Day, as that did not begin till Six in the Evening.—Thus, as this Quadrant reached from Noon to Sunsetting, so it shews us that the first Year of the World must be reckoned as the second of the Quadriennium; therefore, when we would know the Quadriennium of the World's Age,

Age, we muſt add 1 to A. M. and then divide by 4—this will always give you the Quadriennium ſought.—The ſolar Day was divided into Quadrants, as the lunar, at the four cardinal Points.

Hence, it may be obſerved, that the lunar Year conſiſted of 354¼ Days, and the ſolar 365¼.—If we ſubſtract the lunar from the ſolar, it leaves 11 Days, (the Difference in Length between the two Years;) which is called the *Epact*, and is a great Means to diſtinguiſh one Year from another.

As the two Years were carried on together, and both meaſured by integral Days; ſo they regulated each other in the following Manner; the firſt ſolar Year was one Quadrant and eleven Days longer than the lunar; this odd Quadrant was occaſioned by the ſolar Time beginning ſo long before the lunar.— The two firſt ſolar Years contained 730¾ Days, while the two lunar contained only 708½, ſo that the *Epact*, at the End of this Year,

Year, was 22¼ Days, the lunar Year being so far short of the solar.—The first Day of the Month, of the lunar Year, was on the first Appearance of the Moon, after the Conjunction, which was nearest to the autumnal Equinox, and came before it: Now, as the Moon was 15 Days old, or passed its Full, on the first Year of the Creation, so if we substract 15 from 22, it will leave 7 for the Epact; and so much the new Moon Year will precede the Solar.—The next lunar Year, added to these two, will make 1096 Days, while the three lunar contain 1062¾ Days only, which are 33¼ short of the solar.— Now as the twelfth lunar Month contained no more than 24 Days, so it over-ran the full Moon 9 Days; therefore as the first Day of the Feast of Ingathering was to be on the full Moon which happened either upon the autumnal Equinox, or the next which followed, they added a Month of 30 Days, and the next new Moon, lunar Year, began 6 Days after the solar Year ended. The Number of Days contained in the solar Quadriennium,

The INTRODUCTION.

driennium, are 1461, while the lunar have but 1417; to which add the Month of 30 Days, and it makes 1447; which fubſtract from 1461; the Days of the folar, leave 14, and fo many Days the full Moon, lunar Year, precede the next folar.

Hence it may be obferved, that both Years are meafured by integral Days, and that the annexed Quadrant was not reckoned till the Day was compleated, which it always was at the End of every four Years.—At firſt View, this annexed Quadrant, at the End of each Year, has the Appearance as if it would caufe a Confufion between them; but the contrary is found to be the Fact; for it may be obſerved, that the Quadrant, annexed to both Years, rectify each other in fo exact a Manner, that it appears to be appointed by God himfelf, as the Medium or Bond of Connection between them.

From what has been faid, it may be remarked, that take any four Years of the World,

World, the lunar Computation is not only included in the folar, but is equal to it.

For firft, every four folar Years in Succeffion, include firft four lunar Years, three of which confift of 354, and one of 355 Days, whofe Sum is 1417. Secondly. They include four lunar Epacts, three of which confift of 11 Days, and one of 10 Days, whofe Sum is 43 Days, which being added to 1417, make 1460. Thirdly. They include four Quadrants, which make one Day; to 1460 add that one Day, and the whole Amount of lunar Days will be 1461, the fame as the Solar.

The folar Year, like the Lunar, was divided into twelve Calendar Months;—the firft eleven contained the fame Number of Days that the Lunar did, viz. of 30 Days each; but the twelfth had 35 Days.—Thefe twelve folar Months began and ended at the fame Point of Time with the twelve Signs—they began when the Sun entered Libra, till

after

after the Exodus of the Israelites out of Egypt, when they altered the Beginning of the Year by God's express Command, from the autumnal Equinox, to the Vernal; their first Month was altered to the seventh, and their seventh to the first; (t) their Sabbath was altered from the seventh Day to the sixth. — The Israelites counted these Months by Calendar Numbers, in the same Manner they did their lunar Months, but at the End of every Quadriennium they met the Sun *Astronomically*, at the same Point of the Day, in the same Sign.

The Use which the Israelites made of the Months of the solar tropical Year, was for the coming in and going out of the twelve Courses of Military Officers, and of the 24 Courses of Priests, (u) who waited in the Temple; these Priests went in and came out every Sabbath Day; so that it came to the Turn of each Priest (v) to wait two Courses in the Year, besides the three Festivals; when all

---

(t) Exod. XII. 1.

(u) 1 Chron. XXIV. 7.— XXVII. 1.— (v) 2. Kings, XI. 5, 7.

all the Courses waited. (w) They began their Year at the Feast of the Passover, which lasted till the Morrow after the Sabbath, when the wave Sheaf was offered, after which they began to count the seven Weeks, between that and Pentecost, or the Feast of Weeks; the third Feast was the Feast of Tabernacles, or Ingathering, which lasted eight Days. These Feasts made four Weeks, when all the Courses waited; and the 24 Courses twice over, made 48 Weeks; which, with the four Weeks of the Festivals, make in the Whole 52 Weeks, with one Day for all the Courses to go out and come in, will compleat the solar tropical Year, which contains 52 Weeks and one Day.

After the Exodus of the Israelites, from their Bondage out of Egypt, they kept their Feast of Tabernacles and Ingathering, according to Moses's Directions, as do the Jews to this Day, (x) *on the fifteenth Day of the seventh Month,* (from the vernal Equinox) when

---

(w) 2 Chron, V. 11.—— (x) Levit. XXIII. 29.

when ye have gathered in the Fruit of the Land, ye shall keep a Feast unto the Lord, seven Days. On the first Day shall be a Sabbath, and on the eighth Day shall be a Sabbath.—And ye shall take you on the first Day, the Boughs of goodly Trees, and ye shall rejoice before the Lord your God; ye shall dwell in Booths seven Days.

It is worthy of Observation, (says Mr. Kennedy) (y) that when the Jews celebrate the Feast of Tabernacles, as above directed, in Remembrance of the Creation of the World, which they never fail to do at the appointed Season; they celebrate at the same Time, not only the Birth-day of the World, but of the promised Messiah too, who was born on the first Day of the Feast of Tabernacles, and circumcised on the eighth, or great Day of the same.—But as this is a Season of the Year, contrary to the general received Opinion, when Christ was born; I shall endeavour to find the real and true Season when that happened.

(y) Kennedy's Introductory Discourse, P. 19.

pened.—In order to do this, let us examine the Scriptures, and try what Affiftance may be received from them, for when they are examined carefully, and with a good Intention, we often find that they contain more than we expected to find in them.—It is generally agreed, that the Ceremonies and Works of the Law were typical of thofe Things which were fulfilled in the Gofpel; both Teftaments being a Counter-part to each other, as our Saviour told the Jews; *fearch the Scriptures, for in them ye think ye have eternal Life; they are which teftify of me. If ye had believed Mofes, ye would have believed me: for he wrote of me.* (z) That the Temple typified the Body of Chrift we are certain, for our Saviour himfelf told us fo. (aa) The Feaft of Dedication of Solomon's Temple, was kept on the Feaft of Tabernacles, (bb) in the feventh Month,—and on the eighth Day they made a folemn Affembly for its Dedication. If this was a Type of Chrift, there

(z) John V. 39. 46,—(aa) John II. 19. 21.— (bb) II. Chron. V. 3. 7. 8.

there is no Doubt but that it was fulfilled by its Antitype.

St. Luke tells us, (cc) *That in the Days of Herod the King, of Judea, that a certain Priest named Zacharias, of the Course of Abia. And it came to pass, that as soon as the Days of his Ministration were accomplished, that he departed to his own House; and that after those Days, his Wife Elizabeth, conceived and hid herself five Months — And in the sixth Month, the Angel Gabriel was sent from God, to a Virgin, and said unto her — behold thy Cousin Elizabeth, she has also conceived a Son in her old Age, and this is the sixth Month with her.*

In order to know the Season of the Year when this happened, St. Luke tells us, that it was directly after *Zacharias's* Days of Ministration were accomplished — And that *Zacharias* was of the Course of *Abia*. — And in Chronicles (dd) we are informed that *Abia* belonged

---

(cc) Luke I. 1. 23, &c. — (dd) I. Chron. XXIV. 15.

longed to the eighth Courſe. — Now the Prieſts began theſe Courſes of Miniſtration after the Sabbath (which followed the Paſſover) was over.—During the Feaſt of the Paſſover, or Feaſt of Unleavened Bread, (which was ſeven Days,) all the Courſes of the Prieſts miniſtered together.— That the Beginning of the fifty Days, between the Feaſt of the Paſſover, and the Feaſt of Weeks, was to commence on the Morrow after the Sabbath, when the wave Sheaf was offered (ee) ſo that the firſt Courſe were to begin their Miniſtration on the ſecond Sabbath after the Paſſover, which was (ff) *Jehajorib*; the ſecond *Jedaiah*; the third *Horim*; the fourth *Searim*; the fifth *Milchijah*; the ſixth *Mijamin*; the ſeventh *Hahhez*—the next Week came the Feaſt of Weeks or Pentecoſt.— Hence the Courſe of *Abiah*, (which was the *eighth*) did not come in till the Week after Pentecoſt.— Now if we count the Weeks they will be, the Paſſover two Weeks, between that Feaſt and Pentecoſt ſeven Weeks,

Pentecoſt

(ee) Levit. XXIII. 15.—(ff) I. Chron. XXIV. 7 to 10.

The INTRODUCTION. 45

Pentecoſt one Week, and *Abias*, the Week after, one Week; in all eleven Weeks.—So that the Week after his Miniſtration muſt be the twelfth after the Paſſover Day.—Subſtract 12 from 52, the Number of Weeks in a ſolar tropical Year; and there will remain 40 Weeks, the exact Time of Geſtation, to which add one Day for the Day of the Birth, and that will bring it to the Paſſover Day, when John Baptiſt was born.—Add to this ſix Months, (the Difference between the Conception of Elizabeth, and when the Angel Gabriel was ſent to the Virgin) and it will bring it to the 15th of the ſeventh Month, when Chriſt was born.

Now multiply the 40 Weeks by 7, and the Product will be 280; add 1 for the Day of the Birth, and it will make 281 Days, (as theſe are lunar Months) ſubſtract 266 Days for the nine Months of Geſtation, and the Remainder 15 will expreſs the true aſtronomical Day when the Baptiſt and Meſſiah were born.—John the Baptiſt was born on the

the 15th of the first Month, or Passover Day, and the Messiah on the 15th of the seventh Month, when the Feast of Tabernacles commenced.

The vulgar Era of Christ's Birth was not settled till A. D 527, when it was done by Dionisius, a Roman Abbot, since which it has been generally received and followed by Christians.—Had this Era began in the Time of the Apostles, there is no Doubt but it had been right, but as it did not become an Era till the sixth Century, it is not at all to be wondered at, if it should be found to be not exactly right, as it certainly is not.—As there is no Certainty in Chronology, without it is confirmed by Astronomy, I shall endeavour to settle it according thereto.

We are told in the Gospel (gg) that Christ was born while Herod was King of Judea; who sought to kill Him, as soon as he heard of his Birth; but *Joseph*, being warned of God,

(gg) Matthew II. 16.

God, fled into Egypt with him, where he remained till he heard of Herod's Death, which happened in the Year 4711 of the Julian Period; but the vulgar Era, settled by Dionifius, makes his Birth to have happened in the Year 4713 of that Era.

Jofephus informs us (hh) that Herod died in the 26th Year of Auguftus Cæfar, and a little before the Paffover, and that there was an Eclipfe of the Moon during his laft Illnefs.— Now, if we calculate that Eclipfe of the Moon, it muft fettle aftronomically the Year when Herod died.

This Eclipfe is not to be found amongft the Catalogue of Eclipfes, but Mr. Fergufon (ii) fays, " It appears by our Aftronomical " Tables to have been in the Year of the Ju- " lian Period, 4710, March 13th, at 3 " Hours paft Mid-night, at Jerufalem."—

At the End of this Introduction (kk) I fhall add

(hh) Jofephus lib. XVII. Cap. 8 and 11.— (ii) Fergufon, P. 385, S. 395.
(kk) Page

add a Calculation of this Eclipse, by which it will appear, that Mr. Ferguson has made a Mistake of one Year in his Calculation, for you may observe, from my Calculation, that this Eclipse must have happened A I P 4711, and not 4710, and that it happened according to Mr. Ferguson's Time, March 13, N. S. 3 H. 40 M. 33 S. It could not be on the 13th of March, 4710, because the Full Moon, in that Year, happened on the 23d Day of March, instead of the 13th, when the Moon's Node was too far Distant, at that Time, from the Sun, to cause an Eclipse.

As it may be observed from these Calculations, that our Saviour was born on the first Day of the Feast of Tabernacles, in the 26th of Augustus Cæsar, on a Sunday, the seventh Day of the Week from the Creation, in the Year of the World, (according to the Mosaic Chronology) 4005, about five Months before Herod died, which *Josephus* tells us was a little before the Passover Day, or the 14th of Nisan, which happened that Year on April 11,

11, of the Julian Calendar.—This corrects the vulgar Era, two Years and 89 Days: It was then propofed to bring the Beginning of the Year, from the autumnal Equinox, (nearly the Place it had got by irregular Intercalations,) back to the Calends of January.

Soon after the Feaft of Tabernacles, when Chrift was born, and Herod fought his Death by ordering all the young Children in Bethlehem, of two Years old and under, to be flain; Jofeph carried him into Egypt, where he remained till after Herod's Death, which happened about five Months after.

As the Reader may be defirous to know the Reafon why Chriftians kept the Feftival of Chrift's Birth, at the Winter Solftice, inftead of the Autumnal Equinox, which appears to be the true Seafon; and, as Hiftory is filent hereon, I fhall give the moft probable Account I can concerning it.—In order to do this, it appears proper to examine the Method of recording Events at that Time.

In the first Place, it must be observed, that the Romans were Masters of the then known World, and that they obliged all the conquered People to obey their Laws.

Forty-six Years before the vulgar Era, Julius Cæsar, finding great Inconveniencies to proceed from the Irregularity of the Roman Calendar then in Use, which was of a lunar Year, and required an Intercalation every Year to make it agree with the Solar; and that by the bad Management of the *Pontifices*, who had the ordering of it, the Calends of January were got from the Winter Solstice, (to which they had been placed by Numa, about 560 Years before,) nearly to the autumnal Equinox; he therefore, to make a more perfect Calendar of the Year, called to his Assistance an Astronomer from Alexandria; who, in order to put the Seasons into their right Places, very carefully observed the Sun's Place in the Ecliptic; and by reckoning the greater Part of October, November, and December, twice over, he effected it.—Thus, when by the old Calendar,

dar, the Year was got to the Calends of January, he brought it back and began it again nearly to the autumnal Equinox; by this Means, the Winter Solstice of the new Calendar, (as *Ovid* informs us,)* was made the Point where the old Year ended, and where the new one began.

Other Roman Writers also inform us the same; but *Pliny* and *Columella* tell us, that the Calends of January, with the other Equinox, and the Solstices, were placed in the 8th Degree of each Sign, and were much perplexed to account for it; but the Fact appears to be, that the Alexandrian Astronomer, finding that the Equinoxes had preceded the Calendar Measure, he ordered the Beginning of the political Year to be placed in the 8th Degree of *Capricorn*, instead of the first, thinking thereby to place the Calendar Computation where it might agree with the Solar.

About ten Years before our Saviour was born,

* *Bruma novi prima est veterisque Novissimus Anni, Principium capiunt Phœbus et Annus idem.*   Ovid.

born, they found that an Error had been committed, by adding the Day of the Leap Year to every third Year, instead of every fourth, whereby three supernumerary Days had got into the Calendar; but by *August Cæsar's* ordering that no Leap Year should be again put into the Calendar for the twelve Years next ensuing, brought it right again; and then imagined that the Calendar would never more want any farther Correction.—This was believed so late as the Council of Nice, which was held, according to vulgar Era, A. D. 325. For by their paschal Canons, they erroneously fixed the 21st of March for the Sun's Entry into the Equinoctial Point, and took it for granted, that it would be immoveably fixed to that Day of the Julian Calendar.—For it does not appear that Astronomers were capable of observing the exact Time of the Sun's entering the Equinoctial Points, till *Tycho Brahe*, by his Improvements in Astronomy, did it.—After this Reformation by Julius and Augustus Cæsar, to prevent Confusion by different Calendars, *Strauchas* informs us, [11] that severe Laws were made to punish any

---

[11] Book XV. Chap. 42, (Salt's Translation.)

any People who did not conform thereto, or who made Use of any other.

Now the above was the State of Calendar Computation at the Coming of Christ.—All the Roman Empire knowing what Pains Julius Cæsar had taken to set all the Seasons in their true Places, and to make a true Calendar of the Year, it would have been strange, and have the Appearance of great Obstinacy, for any one to have acted in Contradiction to it; and therefore, the Christians, no doubt, did conform to it, and made Use of it; for, it was one of the Principles of Christianity, taught by St. Peter himself, (mm) " to submit " themselves to every Ordinance of Man for " the Lord's Sake, whether it be to the " King as Supreme, or unto his Governors."

Thus it may be observed in what a State of Confusion the Calendar Computation had been in, about the Birth of Christ; and what Pains had been taken, by the Roman Emperors, to set it upon a right Foundation.—
He

(mm) I. Peter, II. 13.

He was born amongst the Jews, who, with the Patriarchs and Israelites, from the very Beginning to this Time, have always believed, that the Creation happened at the Full Moon nearest after the Autumnal Equinox, and that the Feast of Ingathering was appointed by God, and ordered by Moses to be kept in Commemoration of it.—The Feast of Tabernacles was ordered to be kept at the same Time; but as that was to be a Memorial of their Deliverance from the Egyptian Bondage, when they dwelled in Tabernacles, so they were ordered to dress their Habitations with green Boughs, to commemorate it; (nn) Christ being born amongst the Jews, on *the first Day of this Feast*, the Christians dressed their Houses also with green Boughs, for a Memorial that Christ was born on that Day.

Now as Christ was born on *New Year's Day*, and as St. Paul tells us (oo) that in his Time, " there were many unruly and vain " Talkers and Deceivers, especially they of
" the

(nn) See P. 41.—(oo) Titus, I. 10.

"the Circumcifion," (foon after which the Circumcifion and Uncircumcifion feparated themfelves from each other); it would have been aftonifhing had the Chriftians obferved their Seafons by any other Calendar than that which Julius Cæfar and Auguftus had taken fo much Pains to make compleat: But though they kept the Feftival in Commemoration of the Birth of Chrift, on *New Year's Day*, according to the Julian Computation, yet ftill they continued their Cuftom of drefling their Habitations with green Boughs, to fhow that it was on the Feaft of Tabernacles that He was born.—It may be obferved, that they alfo fettled every other Feaft and Feftival according to the Julian Calendar.—The Names of the twelve Signs begin in the Latin Language, it appears probable they were given to them at this Time.—For though they are the fame with the folar Months of the Ifraelites, yet the Knowledge and Ufe of them were almoft loft.—It does not appear that any People befides the Jews and Greeks made Ufe of the folar Year, all others had the lunar, with Intercalations; this was *Numa*'s Year.   For

For the Reasons before-mentioned, Julius Cæsar, with the Assistance of an Alexandrian Astronomer, altered it to the solar; and they then believed they had settled the Calendar in so exact a Manner, that the Seasons would always thereafter be kept to their true Places. The Israelites distinguished their solar Months, as well as their lunar, by Numerals; but, it seems, (as Julius Cæsar was not willing to make so great an Alteration in all the civil Months, as to make them to tally exactly with the Signs in the Heavens,) that the Astronomer gave Names to the Signs, expressive of the Season of the Year which they pointed out.

Thus *Aries*, the *Ram*, the Point when the Sun enters the Vernal Equinox, was represented by a Ram, the Horns of Animals being always made Use of to shew the Strength of the Sun; so the Ram, the Head of the Flock, was a proper Emblem to exhibit to us, by his *Horns*, the increasing Strength of the Sun's Heat.

The 2d was *Taurus*, the Bull, the strongest of all domestic Animals! who, together with *his Horns*, gave us a proper Idea of the great Strength of the Sun, whilst it passed through this Sign, which it entered about the 13th of April.

The 3d was *Gemini* or *Twins*, informing us, that at the End of this Sign, the *Heat* of the Sun, and his twin Brother, the *cold* Ether, then bore an equal Share in the Government of Nature. The Sun ended this Sign about June 21, when

The 4th began, which was represented by *Cancer*, a Crab, to inform us, that as the Crab went backwards, whilst other Animals walked forward, so this Animal exhibited to us the retreating Power of the Sun at this Season.

The 5th is *Leo*, the Lion, the most powerful Beast of the Forest! and is very expressive of the violent Heat of the Sun, whilst it passes through this Sign, which it enters about

bout July 21.—Notwithſtanding the Aſtronomer did not alter the civil Months, to begin and end according to the Signs in the Heavens, yet he named one of theſe Months, which anſwered nearly to this Sign, *Julius*, in Honour to his Patron *Julius Cæſar*, letting us know, that as the Heat of the Sun was then at the greateſt, ſo it commemorated the greateſt Emperor of the World.

The 6th Sign was *Virgo*, repreſented by a young Woman, into which the Sun enters about the 22d of Auguſt: a young Woman grown to Puberty, is the Inſtrument by which the Increaſe of the Human Species is brought forth! during this Sign, the Trees and Vegetables produce their Fruit and Seed.—Hence, the Aſtronomer thought it proper to exhibit the Reign of Auguſtus Cæſar; in whoſe Time Peace and Plenty reigned, and Arts and Sciences flouriſhed.

The 7th is *Libra*, into which the Sun enters about Sept. 22d, where one Year ends, and another begins! Here alſo the Twin-Brothers,

Brothers, *Heat* and *Cold*, ballance each other; what can more properly represent these than a Pair of Scales?

The 8th Sign is *Scorpio*, a Scorpion; a destructive Animal! who does its Mischief by his hinder Part or Tail; representing to us the Injury done by the *cold Ether following* the departing Heat.—The Sun enters this Sign about Oct. 22, and on Nov. 21 comes

The 9th, *Sagittarius*, the Shooter, to exhibit to us the great Power of the *cold Ether*, during this Sign; which greatly hurts, kills, or destroys a large Part of the Productions of Nature; whose Arrows are so subtile and piercing as to enter the Pores of all Matter.

The 10th Sign is *Capricornus*, a horned Goat; an Animal who gets his living by climbing Hills and Precipices! A very proper Emblem to represent the rising Strength of of the Sun! which it begins to do about the 21ſt of December, when the Sun enters this Sign.

The 11th is *Aquarius*, repreſented by flowing Water, to denote this watery Seaſon.

The 12th and laſt is *Piſces*, Fiſhes; the moſt prolific of all Animals! repreſenting to us the approaching Fertility of the Seaſon; when Seeds and Plants are made to vegetate by the growing Power of the Sun.

From the above Account of the Signs, it may be remarked, that *Heat* and *Cold* were then believed to be the Agents which governed the *Mechaniſm* of Nature.—In this they agreed with the ancient Philoſophers; for *Plato* tells us, " that they maintained " that *Fire* and *Heat* govern all other Things," and " that *Fire expands* all Bodies outward, " and that *Air compreſſes* them together in-" ward, and counteracts the *internal Fire:* By " the *Miniſtry of theſe Cauſes* a perpetual Cir-" culation is kept up." Theſe, (ſays he),
" are

"are *secondary and co-operating* Causes, which
"*God* makes use of as his Ministers." And
Cicero, in describing the Tenets of the ancient *Platonists*, does it in the following
Words.—" *De Naturâ* autem ita dicebant,
" ut eam dividerent in *Res duas:* ut altera
" esset efficiens, altera autem, quasi *huic se*
" *prebens.*—Neque enim Materiam ipsam
" cohærere potuisse, si nulla vi contineretur:
" neque vim sine aliquâ Materiâ.—Illa Initia
" Elementa dicuntur, e quibus *Aer & Ignis*
" movendi vim habent & efficiendi, reliquæ
" Portes *accipiendi* & quasi *patiendi, Aquam*
" dico & *Terram.*" *Acad* Quæst. lib. 1, or
in English thus.—" That they divided Nature into two Parts, one of which was
" *active*, and the other *passive*.—They held
" it impossible for Bodies to *cohere*, unless
" they were kept together by some Force;
" and that it was necessary this Force should
" be exerted *by some Matter*.—In distinguishing the several Uses of the Elements, they
" attributed to *Air* and *Fire*, the Power of
" giving Motion, and *causing* Effects; to
" *Earth*

" *Earth* and *Water* a *Paſſiveneſs*, or Diſpoſi-
" tion to receive their Impreſſions."

Hence we are taught the Doctrine of ancient Philoſophers; which they received, by Tradition, from their Anceſtors, and from their Obſervations on the *Phænomena* of Nature.—Perhaps if we diveſt ourſelves of the Prejudices imbibed by our Education, we ſhall find it to be true.—It is probable, that theſe Philoſophers received their Traditions from Noah and the Patriarchs, as it appears to be the ſame taught by Moſes, who informs us, (pp) that God created the Heavens and the Earth; " that the *Heavens* and *Skies*
" were in continual *Conflict*, *Motion*, and
" *Expanſion*; to which he gave the Name of
" the *Placers*, the *Diſpoſers*, or *Governors*,
" *under God*, of all Nature."—We are told in Samuel, (qq) that the Vegetable is *puſhed out of the Earth by a ſhining Light and by Rain*; and in the 19th Pſalm we are informed, *that the Mechanical Circulations of the Heavens repreſent the Glory of God; and the Firmament*

(pp) Gen. I. Chap. 1.— (qq) II. Samuel, XXIII. 4.

The INTRODUCTION. 63

Firmament (Expansion) his handy Work; and that their Fulness and Influence reach unto the End of the World.—That in them he has placed the Tabernacle of the Sun's Light, which coming out like a strong Man, prevails to the Extremities of them, and nothing is hid from the Heat thereof. To return from this Digression,

In regard to the Death of Christ, it is agreed, that he died on a Friday, the Full Moon Day, on the 14th of Nisan.—Hence it is no difficult Matter, to calculate the Year when this happened; as, two Passover Days could not happen on *a Friday* for many Years following.

The Time of this Passover, or the Death of the Messiah, was foretold by the Prophet Daniel, 562 Years before. (rr) In the first Year of the Reign of *Darius* I. Daniel prophesied, (ss) " That seventy Weeks (of Years)
" are determined upon thy People, and upon
" thy holy City, to finish Transgressions,
" and to make an End of Sin, and to make
       " Reconciliation

(rr) Daniel, IX. 1.——(ss) Daniel, IX. 24, 25, 26, 27.

"Reconciliation for Iniquity, and to bring in everlasting Righteousness, and to seal up the Vision and Prophecy.— Know therefore that from the going forth of the Commandment, to restore and build Jerusalem, unto Messiah the Prince, shall be seven Weeks; and three-score and two Weeks the Street shall be built again.—And after three-score and two Weeks, shall Messiah be cut off, but not for Himself.—And the People of the Prince that shall come, shall destroy the City and the Sanctuary, and he shall confirm the Covenant with many for one Week; and in the *midst* of the Week he shall cause the Sacrifice and the Obligation to cease, and *(as in the Margin)* upon the Battlements shall be the Idols of the Desolator."

Josephus, who was a Jew, and lived to see these Things accomplished, could not help giving the Prophet Daniel, the following Character, (u) "That Daniel did not only foretell *Things to come*, which was common
"to

(u) Joseph, lib. X. C. 12.

"to him with other Prophets, but alfo *fet a Time* for their coming to pafs."—He did not only foretell the Calamity that befell our Nation, from *Antiochus*, before it happened; but he alfo wrote of "the *Dominion of the Romans*, and of the *great Defolation* they fhould hereafter bring upon the People." And St. Matthew tells us, (uu) "That the Difciples came unto Jefus privately, faying, when fhall thefe Things be," Jefus anfwered, "When ye therefore fee the Abomination of Defolation fpoken of by Daniel, the Prophet, *ftand in the Holy Place*, (whofo readeth, let him underftand.) Let them which be in Judea, flee into the Mountains.—For then fhall be great Tribulation, fuch as was not fince the Beginning of the World to this Time.—And they fhall fall by the Edge of the Sword, (ww) *(in Number* 1,100,000, *fays Jofephus)* and they fhall be led Captive, *(in Number fays Jofephus,* 97,000) into all Nations, and Jerufalem fhall be trodden *(or inhabited by Gentiles)* until the Time of the Gen-
"tiles

(uu) Matthew **XXIV**, 3, 15, and 21.—(ww) Luke XXI, 24.

"tiles be fulfilled."—Ver. 32, " Verily I say unto you, *this Generation* shall not pass until all be fulfilled," *which it was in the 70th Year of the vulgar Era.* For

Josephus, who was an Eye Witness of the miserable Desolation by the Romans, tells us, (xx) of the Accomplishment of all these Predictions; when *Titus* laid Siege to the City; when Jerusalem was encompassed with the *(Roman)* Armies; when they cast a Trench about it, and enclosed it in on every Side; and when they caused the daily Sacrifices and Oblations to cease; and when *Titus*'s Soldiers, in Spite of all his Endeavours to prevent it, set the Temple on Fire; and whilst it was in Flames, they set up the Standards of the Legions, on the Eastern Porch, and there they sacrificed before them after their idolatrous Manner. He also records the Month and Day of the Month when Jerusalem was taken and plundered, and the Temple destroyed; and remarks, that the second Temple was burnt by the Romans

the

(xx) Lib. XI. Chap. 47.

the same Month, and Day of the Month, on which the first Temple was burnt by the Babylonians. Lib. VII. Chap. 9, 10.

Sixty-three Years after Daniel had made the above Prophecy of the Commandment, for the Return of the Jews, and for the restoring the Polity of Jerusalem, both civil and ecclesiastical, *Artaxerxes Longimanus* gave forth, (in the seventh Year of his Reign, A. M. 3550, which answers to A.I.P. 4256) his Decree and Command to *Ezra*, the Priest, (yy) " to go up to Jerusalem, and with
" him all the Priests and Levites, and all the
" People of Israel, which are minded of their
" own free Will, to go with him, and to
" carry in his Hand the Silver and Gold,
" which the King and his Counsellors had
" offered unto the God of Israel, and all the
" Silver and Gold, the free will offering of
" the People and the Priests, and whatsoever
" more shall be needful for the House of thy
" God, which thou shalt have occasion to
" bestow."

Now

(yy) Ezra VII. 11 to 27.

The INTRODUCTION.

Now let it be observed that the seventh Year of the Reign of Artaxerxes, begins and ends astronomically at the Vernal Equinox, as all Kings Reigns recorded in Scripture, after the Exodus of the Israelites out of Egypt, do.—Here begins the first Point of the Period of 70 Weeks, or 490 Solar Years, containing 365 D. 5 H. 49 M. each—and we are informed by Moses, (zz) that they numbered by Sabbaths of Years.

Now these 490 Years begin in the solar tropical Year of the World, 3550, when the sixth Year of the Reign of Artaxerxes Longimanus, King of Persia, ends, and the seventh Year of his Reign begins.—Now if to A.M. 3550 the 490 Years are added, it will make 4040, the Passover when the Messiah was cut off, as is proved by the Calculation at the End of this Introduction.—(1) Also, as the Mosaic Chronology places the Creation in the 706th Year of the Julian Period; so, if we add that Number to it, it will shew us that it was the 4746th Year of that Period when Christ suffered.

Ezra

(zz) Levit. XXV. 8.—(1) Page .

Ezra informs us, (a) it was in the Month of Niſan, in the Beginning of the ſeventh Year of Artaxerxes, in the ſolar tropical Year of the World, 3550, when he ſet off from Babylon to reſtore the eccleſiaſtical and political State of Jeruſalem.—And as may be obſerved by the Calculations at the End of this Introduction, it was on the 14th of Niſan, A. M. 4040, juſt 490 Years after Ezra received this Commandment, that the Meſſiah was cut off A. I. P. 4746, on the 3d of April, on a Friday, in the 19th Year of the Reign of Tiberius Cæſar, when Pontius Pilate was Procurator of Judea; when Daniel's Prophecy of ſeventy Weeks was completed, by the Death of Chriſt, who died on the Croſs, on the Day, Hour, and Minute that the paſchal Lamb was ordered to be Slain; for God directs it to be killed on the *fourteenth Day of the Month, between the two Evenings*. (a)

That the exact Time may be known when the paſchal Lamb was ordered by Moſes to be ſlain, I will give you the Time according to

---

(2) Ezra VII.— (a) Exod. XII. 6.

to *David Levi*, who cannot be supposed to give a partial Account of it in Favour of Christ.—He tells us (4) the Manner of solemnizing the Passover while the first Temple stood.—" It must be observed, (says he) that " the Lamb was to be without Blemish, a " Male, of the first Year, from the Sheep or " the Goats, and brought to the Temple, " and there to be killed on this fourteenth Day " of Nisan, between the two Evenings, that " is, according to the common and very an- " cient Tradition, betwixt the Time of the " Sun's declining from his Meridian Alti- " tude, till three o'Clock in the Afternoon, " and from Three till Six: after which, the " Sun going below the *Horizon*, the fifteenth " Day commences."—St. Matthew (5) and St. Mark (6) both tell us, that Christ gave up the Ghost the ninth Hour, which was at Three o'Clock in the Afternoon, or between the two Evenings, the Time precisely when the paschal Lamb was to be slain.—Thus, Christ died on a Friday, lay in the Grave all Saturday, or the Jewish Sabbath, and was raised

(4) Page 45.—(5) Matthew XXVII. 50.—(6) Mark XV. 34.

raised again on Sunday, the Morrow after the Sabbath, when the original seventh Day was again restored, and kept as such by Christians ever since, which was the Day appointed to wave the Sheaf before the Lord, explaining and fore-shewing the Resurrection, which both our Saviour (7) and St. Paul tell us was typical, and gave us an Idea of it; for as the Grain was the first Fruits of the Earth, so was the Resurrection of Christ the first Fruits of the Spirit.

The first Christians were Jews; therefore, in order to keep a Memorial of the Birth of Christ, which happened as has been observed, at the Feast of Tabernacles; they took the *Boughs of green Trees*, to dress up their Houses and Churches, or Places of Worship, in the same Manner as the Israelites and Jews were commanded and used to do, and to dwell therein, and to rejoice therein, till the eighth Day, or Christ's Circumcision, or of the great Feast,—(8) This Custom, this Memorial of the Birth of Christ, has been kept by Chris‑
tians,

(7) John XII. 24, and Corint. XV. 26, 23, 36.—(8) Levit. XXIII. 39.

tians, without Interruption, from the Birth of our Saviour to this Time; and though now almost left off, except in our Churches, and amongst the common People, who do not think it Superstition to commemorate the Birth of Christ; but our fashionable Gentry are now so wise in their own Conceit, (9) that they think it Foolishness to believe any Mysteries at all; and Superstition to make use of Memorials or Ceremonies,—They are also so charitable to give the Name of Enthusiasts to all those who do; believing nothing but what they can explain, according to their own Reason or Imagination.—But this is contrary to the Instruction which St. Paul gives us, (10) that without Controversy, (says he) great is the Mystery of Godliness: God was manifest in the Flesh—that by Grace we are saved through Faith—(11) that Faith is the Substance of Things hoped for; the Evidence of Things not seen, (12) for we are saved by Hope; but Hope that is seen, is not Hope. (13)

Now,

---

(9) Proverbs XXVI, 12.—(10) I. Tim. III. 16.—(11) Ephesians II. 6. (12) Hebrews XI. 1.—(13) Romans VIII. 24.

Now, as I am going to conclude this Introduction, and begin my Calculations, with some critical Remarks on the Holy Scriptures, let the Reader join with me in Prayer to our God Jehovah, that he will open our Eyes, that we may behold wondrous Things out of thy Law, (14) and that his Holy Spirit may assist us with Grace, whereby we may serve God acceptably with Reverence and Godly Fear. (15)

F. Penrose.

Stonehouse, Plymouth, Sept. 22.

In the Year of our Lord, 1787, (according to the Vulgar Era)
In the Year of the World, 5794.
In the Year of the Julian Period, 6500.

N.B. To prevent any spurious Editions being imposed on the Public, I shall sign my Name at the Bottom of the Diagrams, and at the Conclusion of the Introduction in each Book. *F. Penrose*   CALCULATIONS.

(14) Psalm CXIX, 18.—(15) Hebrews XII. 28.

Having now concluded my Introduction, I shall add some Calculations of Equinoxes, new, full Moons, and Eclipses, to confirm what has been observed therein.— All of these begin at the Point wherein Moses places the Sun and Moon at the Creation, and they come out at the observed Time when they happened. Now,

If the unbelieving Deist, or the doubting Sceptic is not satisfied herewith, I call on either one of them, in the friendly Words of *Horace*, to find out one Equinox, full, new Moon, or Eclipse, which do not confirm it; if he cannot, let him shew Cause why he withholds his Assent to it; as the Sun and Moon bear Witness that it is as true as that they are in Heaven.

Si quid novisti rectius istis,
Candidus imperti ; si non, his utere Mecum.
                            HORACE,

The Point I begin the following Calculations from, is the Autumnal Equinox, in the

the Year 706, of the Julian Period. The Sun, the Earth, Moon and her Node being then all in the firſt Point of Libra, when an Eclipſe of the Moon muſt have happened, had they been in Being.—This is an exact Point to begin my Calculations, and from that Point, to the preſent Time, I calculate with a Mathematical Exactneſs.—I ſay, that Moſes, (in his Account of the Creation, together with his Directions for keeping the Feſtivals, in Commemoration of that great Event,) has informed us, where the Sun and Moon were placed at that particular Inſtant of Time.—If my Calculations are true, you muſt admit that I received my Inſtructions either from Moſes, or that I obtained them ſome other Way.—Now, it does not appear, that this can be obtained otherwiſe than either by Calculation, Obſervation, or Revelation.—As to the firſt it is impoſſible to be done; and, it could not be obtained by the ſecond, as there was no Human Being to obſerve it; but Moſes ſays, it was revealed by God, and to confirm his Hiſtory and Chronology, he tells us the Places of the
Sun

Sun and Moon at that Time, which was 2370 Years before he was born; and this alſo at a Period of Time, when, (as the generality of People think) that all Sciences were in their Infancy.—But the following Calculations prove that his Relation is true. Is not this ſufficient Evidence to prove any other Hiſtory to be true; if ſo, why ſhould Moſes's Hiſtory be excluded?

I have dated this Introduction, Sept. 22, A. D. 1787, which agrees with the 6500th Year of the Julian Period.—This is the real Day I have finiſhed it; but, had it not been ſo, it would have been a very proper Day to have dated it from; as this Day, at 46 Minutes paſt Five in this Afternoon, (16) the Earth will have made and finiſhed 5794 Revolutions through the Ecliptic, in the firſt Meridian; and in the Meridian of Greenwich Obſervatory, at ten Minutes paſt Four To-morrow Morning.—This is the preciſe Point of Time when A. M. 5794 ends, and 5795 begins, according to the Moſaic Chronology

(16) See Page 88.

nology of the World.—But as Moses directed the Israelites to measure Time by the Sun and Moon jointly, (whose Motions were to be a Check on each other, and by that Means to prevent any Mistake in keeping the Seasons) so it was measured by the Sun; and the Seasons were pointed out by the Moon. (17) Thus, as the Moon was fifteen Days old at the Creation, or a little past its Opposition or Full, so this Feast of Ingathering, (which was ordered to be observed in Commemoration of it,) was not to be kept, till the 15th Day of the Moon, next after the Sun had entered Libra.—— Now, as has been observed, the Sun will enter Libra this Day, but the Moon will not be Full, or in Opposition to the Sun, at Greenwich, till Thursday the 27th Instant, at 22 Minutes past One in the Morning; and the Jews will begin their Feast of Tabernacles at Six o'Clock in the Evening. And with it they must celebrate the Birth of Christ, who was born on the first Day of that Feast, and circumcised on the eighth or the great Day; at which Time

(17) Psalm CIV. 19.

Time the Moon will have made 71662 Lunations or Revolutions round the Earth.—The Length between these two Points has been measured by 2116214 Rotations of the Equator round its Axis, which being divided by 7, make 30216 Weeks, and leave in Remainder two Days, to which add the four Days of the Creation Week, (before the Sun and Moon were placed in Heaven to measure and point out the Seasons, the Days, and the Years,) and it will bring it to the Sixth Day of the Week, or Saturday, regularly from the Creation.—This proves, besides thousands of others, that Sunday was the original Seventh or Sabbath-Day.—The Saturdays Sabbath can claim no higher than the Exodus of the Israelites out of Egypt.

If this is not mathematical Demonstration that the Sun and Moon, in the Year 706, A. I. P. where in the Places which Moses informs us; I shall be glad to know in what it falls short of it.

CALCULATION

CALCULATION

Of the Eclipse which happened in the Year 4711, of the Julian Period; which was the 26th of Augustus Cæsar, during Herod's last Illness.

The Mosaic Chronology places the Year of the Creation in the 706th of the Julian Period; therefore if we substract 706 from 4711, it will give 4005. The Year of the World answering to the 26th of Augustus Cæsar.

Substract One to find where A. M. 4004 ends, and 4005 begins.

SOLAR.

CALCULATIONS.

SOLAR.

A. M. 4004 Julian Years
Minutes ✕ 11 Julian Excess

4004
4004

Minute } ÷ 1440) 44044 (30 Days
in a Day   4320

844
Hours in a Day ✕ 24

3376
1688

÷ 1440) 20256 (14 Hours
1440

5856
5760

96
Minutes in an Hour ✕ 60

÷ 1440) 5760 (4 Minutes
5760

(0)

SOLAR.

CALCULATIONS. 81

SOLAR.

```
              4004
           × 1461  Quadrants in a Year
           ─────
              4004
             24024
             16016
              4004
           ─────────        Days      H.  M.
Quadrants ⎫ ÷4)5849844( 1462461    0   0  Julian Years
in a Year ⎭        (0)        30  14   4  Julian Excefs
                          ─────────────
                           1462430    9  56  Sun in Libra, 1ſt
                                              Meridian
     Add to bring Merid. of Jerufalem 13   4
                           ─────────────
                           1462430   23   00 Sun in Libra, Je-
                                              rufalem.
           Add, to Oct. 25.       298
                           ─────────────
                           1462728   23   00
  Julian Biſſext. 4004     1462461
                           ─────────────
                              267   23   00
                Aug. 31       243
                           ─────────────
            Sept. O. S.        24   23   00 at Jerufalem, P.M
                                             that is Sept. 25  11  0 O.S.
                           ─────────────
                           1462728   23   00
add to bring to Aries         178   17   58
                           ─────────────
                           1462907   16   58
  Julian Biſſext. 4005     1462826    6
                           ─────────────
                               81   10   58
                Feb. 28        59
            March 22 O.S.      22   10   58 Sun in Aries, Je-
                                             rufalem.
```

L

CALCULATIONS.

LUNAR CALCULATION, A. M. 4005.

$$\text{Years in a Cycle} \div 19 \overline{\smash{\big)}4004}\,(\,210 \text{ Cycles} \quad \text{A. M.}$$
$$\underline{38}$$
$$20$$
$$\underline{19}$$

$$14$$
$$\text{Lunations in a Year} \times 12$$
$$\overline{28}$$
$$14$$
$$\overline{168}$$
$$\text{Intercalary Lunations} \quad 5$$
$$\overline{173}$$

$$210 \text{ Cycles}$$
$$235 \text{ Lunations in a Cycle}$$
$$\overline{}$$
$$1050$$
$$630$$
$$420$$
$$\overline{}$$
$$49350$$
$$\text{Lunations} \quad 173$$
$$\overline{}$$
$$49523 \text{ Lunations}$$

CALCULATIONS. 83

LUNAR CALCULATION, A. M. 4005.

	Days	H.	M.	S.
In 40,000 Lunations are—	1181223	00	46	40
9,000 Ditto	265775	4	22	30
500 Ditto	14765	6	54	35
20 Ditto	590	14	40	35
3 Ditto	88	14	12	5
	1462442	16	56	25
Substract 1 Day for 49680 Lunations	1			
Moon full 1st Meridian, Libra	1462441	16	56	25
add to bring to Merid. of Jerusalem		13	4	
Moon full Jerusalem	1462442	6	00	25
To bring to Oct. 24.	297			
	1462739	6	00	25
Julian Bissextile 4004	1462461			
	278	6	00	25
Sept. 30	273			
Oct.	5	6	00	25
and one Day for Apparition	7	Feast of Tabernacles when Christ was born		

84   CALCULATIONS.

LUNAR CALCULATION, A. M. 4005.

	Days	H.	M.	S.
Moon full in Libra	1462442	6	00	25
add 5 Lunations to bring to Pisces	147	15	40	8
Moon full in Pisces	1462589	21	40	33
To bring to Oct. 24.	297			
	1462886	21	40	33
Julian Bissextile 4005	1462826	6		
	60	15	40	33
Feb.	59			
March O. S.	1	15	40	33
To N. S.	11			
	12	15	40	33 F.M.

Eclipse of the Moon in Herod's last Illness, March 12 D. 15 H. 40 M. 33 S. that is March 13 D. 3 H. 40 M. Morn.

	D.	H.	M.
add Half Lunation	14	18	22
March N. S.	27	10	2 New
			Moon
Apparition	1	12	1 of Nisan
	28	22	2
Add	14		of Nisan
	42	22	2
March	31		
April	11		Passover Even.

CALCULATIONS. 85

CALCULATION SOLAR, A. M. 4040.

Of CHRIST's Death on the Cross.*

```
Minutes        ) 4039  ( Julian Years
               ) ✕ 11  ( Julian Excefs
                 ─────
                  4039
                  4039
                 ─────
         1440 ) 44429 ( 30 Days
                4320
               ──────
                 1229
Hours            ✕ 24
                ─────
                 4916
                 2458
               ──────
         1440 ) 29496 ( 20 Hours
               ) 2880 (
               ──────
                  696
Minutes         ✕ 60
                ─────
         1440 ) 41760 ( 29 Minutes
               ) 2880 (
               ──────
                12960
                12960
                ─────
                  (0)
```

* In the first Year of Darius the first, which answers to A. M. 3488, Daniel prophefied, (18) that a future Decree should be made for the Reftoration of the Jews, (who were then in Captivity,) again to Jerufalem; and from the going forth of that Commandment, to the cutting off of the Meffiah, should be 70 Weeks, or 490 Years.—63 Years after; and, after

two

(18) Daniel IX. 24, 25, 26, 27.

86 CALCULATIONS.

CALCULATION SOLAR, A. M. 4040.

Of CHRIST's Death on the Cross.

```
      4039
      1461
      ────
      4039
     24234
     16156
      4039
                          D.    H.  M.
  ÷4 )5900979 (1475244   18    0  Julian Reduction
       (3)              30   20  29 Julian Excess
Solar Reduction         1475213  21  31  Sun in Libra, 1st
                                          Meridian
add to bring to Jerusalem         13   4
                        ─────────────────
                        1475214  10  35  Sun in Libra, Je-
                                          rusalem
add to bring to Aries        178  17  58
                        ─────────────────
                        1475393   4  33  Sun in Aries, Je-
                                          rusalem
add to bring to Oct. 25      298
                        ─────────────────
                        1475691   4  33
Julian Reduction 4040   1475610
                        ─────────────────
                             81   4  33
             Feb.            59
                        ─────────────────
          March O. S.        22   4  33  Sun in Aries, Je-
                                          rusalem
```

two future Kings Reign, this Commandment was issued by Artaxerxes Longimanus, at the End of the Sixth and Beginning of the Seventh Year of his Reign, A. M. 3550, to Ezra, (19) to restore the ecclesiastical and political State of Jerusalem.——Now if we subtract 3550 from 4040, it will leave the 490 Years exactly, between issuing that Decree, to the cutting off of Christ. See Page 21.

(19) Ezra, Chap. VII.

CALCULATIONS.

CALCULATION, LUNAR, A. M. 4040.

$$\text{Years in a Cycle} \div 19 \overline{)4039}^{A.\,M.} (212 \text{ Cycles}$$

$$\underline{38}$$
$$23$$
$$\underline{19}$$
$$49$$
$$\underline{38}$$
$$11$$
$$\text{Lunations} \quad \times 12$$
$$\overline{132}$$
$$\text{Intercatory Lunations} \quad 4$$
$$\overline{136}$$

$$212 \text{ Cycles}$$
$$235$$
$$\overline{1060}$$
$$636$$
$$424$$
$$\overline{49820}$$
$$\text{Lunations} \quad 136$$
$$\overline{49956} \text{ Lunations}$$

1st of Nisan   1475391
before the Sun, extra. D.   4
$$7\overline{)1475395}(210770 \text{ Friday}$$
$$(5)$$

to 14th of Nisan   14
$$7\overline{)1475409}(210772 \text{ Friday}$$
$$(5)$$

CALCULATIONS.

CALCULATION, LUNAR, A. M. 4040.

	Days	H.	M.	S.
In 40,000 Lunations are	1181223	00	46	40
9,000 Ditto	265775	4	22	30
900 Ditto	26577	12	26	15
50 Ditto	1476	12	41	27
5 Ditto	147	15	40	8
½ Ditto	14	18	22	

                         1475214 16 19 0 Moon New, 1
                                                           Merid. Libra

Subſ. 1 for 49680 Lunations   1

                         1475213 16 19 0
add to bring to Meridian }   13   4
  of Jeruſalem   }

                        1475214 5 23 Moon New, Jeru-
add to bring to Aries   177   4 24   ſalem, Libra

                       1475391 9 47 New Moon 1 Niſan
add to bring to Oct. 24   297

                       1475688 9 47
Julian Reduction 4040   1475610

                          78 9 47
       Feb.   59

    March O.'S.   19 9 47   1 Niſan
                             12

                          14 21 47

                          33 21 47
       March   31

     April P. M.   2 21   4   14 Niſan, Paſſover
                                              when Chriſt died

Days from the Creation, to the 14th of Niſan, when Chriſt died.
                         1475405
4 Days before the Sun   4
                       _____   Weeks.
                  7)1475409 (2107722
                     (5)   5th Day, Friday

CALCULATIONS. 89

I shall add one Calculation more in order to confirm what I have observed; which will also be an Explanation to some of the following Letters.

In A. D. 1715 there was a remarkable and total Eclipse of the Sun, which was seen in London, about Ten o'Clock in the Morning. According to Mr. *Whyston*'s Calculations, the Middle of it was April 22 D. 9 H. 51 M.—Therefore as this Eclipse was so well observed and recorded, there can be no Mistake about it; and as it is so certain a Point, I shall calculate that Eclipse from the original Point at the Creation, when the Moon was Full and in her Node, and the Sun in the first Degree of *Libra*.—I shall then calculate from that Eclipse, to the Full Moon next Thursday Sept. 27, 1787.—This, if it comes out right, will be Demonstration, that the Point we calculate from, according to Moses's Chronology, is true, and that the Length of the Solar Year is exactly 365 D. 5 H. 49 M. and the Length of a Lunation 29 D. 12 H. 44 M. 1 S. 45 T. as we have assigned it.

M   The

CALCULATIONS.

The vulgar Era of Chrift is placed in A. M. 4007, to which add A. D. 1715, and it will make A. M. 5722, to which add 706, the Number of Years the Julian Period begins before that Time; and it will bring it to the 6428th of that Period.

Subftract 1 from A. M. 5722, to make the Calculations at the End of that Year.

SOLAR CALCULATION.

A. M. 5721 Julian Years
11 Julian Excefs

$$5721$$
$$5721$$

Minutes in a Day 1440) 62931 (43 D.
5760

5331
4320

1011
Hours × 24

4044
2022

1440) 24264 (16 H.
1440

9864
8640

1224
Minutes × 60

1440) 73440 (51 M.
7200

1440
1440

(0)

CALCULATIONS. 91

SOLAR CALCULATION.

$$5721 \text{ Julian Years}$$
$$\times 1461 \text{ Quadrants in a Julian Year}$$

```
     5721
    34326
    22884
    5721
```

Quadrants in a Day ÷ 4) 8358381 (2089595 Days 6 H. 0 Julian Reduction
                   (1)   43 16 51 Julian Exc.

Sun in Libra, 1ft Meridian	2089551	13	9
add to bring to Aries	178	17	58
Sun in Aries, 1ft Meridian	2089730	7	7
add Meridian of Greenwich		10	24
	2089730	17	31
add for Oct. 25	298		
	2090028	17	31
Julian Reduction, 5722	2089960		
	68	17	31
To Feb. 28	59		
March O. S.	9	17	31 P. M. that

is March 10, 31 M. paft 5 Morning.

CALCULATIONS.

CALCULATION SOLAR, A. I. P. 6500. A. D. 1787.
A. M. 5794.

$$
\begin{array}{r}
5794 \\
\times\ 11 \\
\hline
5794 \\
5794 \\
\hline
\end{array}
$$

1440) 63734 (44 D
      5760

$$
\begin{array}{r}
6134 \\
5760 \\
\hline
374 \\
\times 24 \\
\hline
1496 \\
748 \\
\hline
\end{array}
$$

1440) 8976 (6 H.
      8640

$$
\begin{array}{r}
336 \\
\times 60 \\
\hline
\end{array}
$$

1440) 20160 (14 M
      1440

$$
\begin{array}{r}
5760 \\
5760 \\
\hline
(00)
\end{array}
$$

CALCULATIONS. 93

A. D. 1787.
CALCULATION SOLAR, A. I. P. 6500.

```
    5794
 ×1461  Quadrants
 ───────
    5791
   34764
   23176
    5794
```

```
                    Days      H.
∴ 4)8465034    2116258  12   0  Julian Reduction
      (2)(         44    6  14  Julian Excess
               ─────────────────
               2116214   5  46  Sun in Libra, 1 Merid.
add Meridian }           10  24  P. M. 5 H. 46 M. Af-
of Greenwich }                   ternoon
               ─────────────────
               2116214  16  10  P. M. 4 10 Morning
to Oct. 25        298
               ─────────────────
               2116512  16  10
Julian Reduction 2116218
               ─────────────────
                        10  10
To the End of August    243
               ─────────────────
   Sept.  S.         11  16  10
    N. S.            11
               ─────────────────
Sept. N. S.          22  16  10  P. M. that is Sept. 23,
                                 10 M. past 4 Morning
```

```
         Days since the Creation.
              2116215
                    4
              ───────
         7)2116219(302317 Weeks since the Creation
              0
              7 Sunday
```

```
         1794
            1
         ─────
      4)1795(448  Year of Quadrienium
         3
```

LUNAR CALCULATION.

```
                           A. M.
Years in a Cycle ÷ 19  ) 5721 ( 301
                         57
                         ─────
                           21
                           19
                         ─────
                            2
Lunations                  12
                         ─────
                           24
Intercalary                 6
                         ─────
                          (25)


                    301 Cycles
                  × 235 Lunations in a Cycle
                  ─────
                   1505
                    903
                    602
                  ─────
                   70735
                      25
                  ─────
                   70760  Moon Full in Libra
to bring to Aries    6½
Lunations in  ⎫        ⎛ 70766½ ⎛ Moon New in Aries
  a Year      ⎭ ÷ 12 ⎝   60    ⎝ 5897 Lunar Years
                       ─────
                        107
                         96
                       ─────
                        116
                        108
                       ─────
                         86
                         84
                       ─────
                         (2) ½ Lunations
```

CALCULATIONS. 95

LUNAR CALCULATION.

```
Years in a Period ÷ 30)5897(196
                      30
                      ———
                      289
                      270
                      ———
                      197
                      180
                      ———
                     (17) Years
```

```
                 2089774
Extra. Days            4
                 ————————
              7)2089778 (298539 Weeks
                    (5)( Friday
```

	Days	H.	M.	S.
In 138 Periods are	1467078	(24)	9	00
50 Ditto———	531550	8	45	00
8 Ditto———	85048	1	24	00
17 Years are	6024	5	41	57
2 Lunations	59	1	28	3
½ Ditto	14	18	22	
New Moon, 1st Merid. Aries	2089774	11	50	0
add for Meridian Greenwich		10	24	
	2089774	22	14	
add for Oct. 24.	297			
	2090071	22	14	
Julian Reduction, 5722	2089960			
	111	22	14	
To March 31	90			
April O. S.	21	22	14	P. M. that is

April 22 D. 10 H. 14 M. in the Morning

LUNAR CALCULATION.

From the Eclipse A. D. 1715, New Moon Aries, and add 895½ Lunations. to bring to Full Moon in Libra, 1787.

		Days	H.	M.	S.
To 70766¼ Lunations		2089774	22	14	0
add	800 Ditto	23624	11	3	20
	90 Ditto	2657	18	2	37
	5 Ditto	147	15	40	8
	¼ Ditto	14	18	22	
		2116219	13	22	5
add to bring to Oct. 24		297			
		2116516	13	22	5
Subſtract Julian Reduction, 5794	2116258				
		258	13	22	5
Calends of Jan. to the End of Aug.	243				
Sept. O. S.		15	13	22	5 Moon
					Full in Libra
add N. S.		11			
N. S.		26	13	22	5 P. M.

that is Sept. 27 D. 11 H. 22 M. 5 S. in the Morning

A. M.
5794
1
———
4)5795(1448
    3(of Quadriennium

2116219
Extra Days   4
———
7)2116223 (302317 Weeks
      (4) Thurſday.

By our Calculations, both from the original Point of the Full Moon at the Creation, and alſo from the Eclipſe which happened at London, 1715, there have been 71662 Lunations ſince the Moon was Full at the Creation, and that the laſt will end with a Full Moon next Thurſday Morning, Sept. 27, at 22 M. paſt One.

The

EXPLANATION

Of the Method made Use of in the foregoing Calculations.

The above Calculations of Equinoxes and Solstices are made in a different Manner from the Method generally used; which is, first to find the Places of the Sun and Moon in the Ecliptic, and then, by Equations and Anomilies, to make the 360 Degrees of the Equator to agree with the $365\frac{1}{2}$ Rotations of the Earth, through the Ecliptic.

These Calculations are not made in that Manner, but from the Method observed by Nature, viz. by the Number of Rotations the Earth makes between each of them; in the same Manner as Moses taught the Israelites to calculate their Seasons; and that in the most simple, easy, and (I will add) exact Manner, and requires no farther Knowledge in the Sciences, than the first four Rules of Arithmetic—and this Method I shall explain in as clear and concise a Manner as I can.

The Julian Period is a certain Measure of Time, for that Reason I calculate by that Period.

Of the Method made Use of in the foregoing Calculations.

Period.—But, as the Julian Year contains 11 Minutes more than the Solar Tropical, so we must subtract that Sum from every Julian Year, to make it agree with it.—Dr. Keil, in his XXVIIIth Lecture, has explained this in so clear a Manner, that I shall give it in his own Words.—" It must be acknowledged,
" says he, that the Time appointed by Julius
" Cæsar, for the Solar Year, is too much;
" for the Sun finishes his Course in the Eclip-
" tic, in 365 Days, 5 Hours, and 49 Mi-
" nutes; and therefore he begins again his
" Round 11 Minutes before the Solar Year
" is ended: so that if the Sun in any Year
" has entered the Equinox upon the 20th of
" March, at Noon Day; after four Years
" he will arrive at the Equinox 44 Minutes
" before Noon; and so every Year, 11
" Minutes sooner than by this Reckoning;
" so that in 131 Years, he will *anticipate*, or
" enter the Equinox a whole Day before the
" 20th of March; and therefore the *Celestial*
                                        " *Equinox*

EXPLANATION

Of the Method made Use of in the foregoing Calculations.

" *Equinox* will not always fall upon the same
" Day of the Month, but by Degrees it will
" move towards the Beginning of the Year."(a)

Hence, you may obferve, in our firft Calculation on the Birth of Chrift, that we multiply A. M. 4004, by 11 Minutes.—The Product of which is the Number of Minutes that 4004 Julian Years contain more than 4004 Tropical Solar.—Then, in Order to bring thefe Minutes to Days, we divide that Sum by 1440, the Number of Minutes in a natural Day, or whilft the Equator compleats one Rotation from Sun to Sun.—The Remainder we multiply by 24, to bring it to Hours, and that Remainder by 60, to bring it to Minutes.

In Order to find the Number of Days, we multiply 4004 by 1461, the Number of Quadrants, or Quarters of a Day in a Julian Year.—We then divide the Product by 4, which

(a) See Diagram and Calculations.

Of the Method made Use of in the foregoing Calculations.

which brings them to Days.—If there is any Remainder, it is Quadrants.—Hence we have the Number of Days and Quadrants in 4004 Julian Years; from this Sum we Subſtract the Days, Hours, and Minutes of the Retroceſſion, and the Remainder gives the exact Quantity of Days, Hours, and Minutes, in the fame Number of tropical folar Years; and this, by Obfervation, will be always found exactly true, from the Creation to this Time.— Hence we can calculate the Day when the Sun will enter *Libra*, in any Meridian, but not the Hour and Minute.—This appeared the greateſt Difficulty to get over, but by a lucky and accurate Obfervation of Dr. *Bradley*, A. D. 1753, it has anſwered our Purpoſe ſo far, as that all our Calculations made by it come out true.

1440 is the Number of Minutes in a Day, which has the fame Number of Points or Terminations, on the Equator, anſwering to every one of them; ſo that in 1440 Years, the

EXPLANATION 101

Of the Method made Use of in the foregoing Calculations.

the tropical folar Year will have began on every one of them, and at the End of that Period, the Sun will again begin a new Cycle, in the fame Meridian, and on the fame Point of the Day it did 1440 Years before, but not on the fame Day of the Week, which is the Characteriftick of each Cycle.

A. D. 1753 is in Connection with A. M. 5760, and A. I. P. 6466, when the fourth Cycle of the Sun was finifhed; and the Sun entered Libra on the fame Point of the Day, the fame Hour and Minute it began it 1440 Years before. (b)

Dr. Bradley obferved it to enter Libra that Year, at Greenwich, Sept. 22d Day, 10th Hour, 24th Minute.—Now, as the Sun was placed in Libra, at the Creation, at Noon, in the firft Meridian; but, at the Time when he made his Obfervation, it was paffed on 10 Hours, 24 Minutes to the Weftward; by turning Time into Meafure, the firft Meridian

(b) See Page 24.

EXPLANATION

Of the Method made Use of in the foregoing Calculations.

dian will be found to be 156 Degrees to the Westward of Greenwich Observatory.—We have accordingly made this the Root, and postulated it as true, and have found all our Calculations to turn out right on that *Postulatum*.—As Jerusalem is 35° 20 M. of Longitude, East of Greenwich; so if we turn this Measure into Time, it will produce 2 Hours, 40 Minutes, which added to 10 Hours, 24 Minutes, (the Meridian of Greenwich) it will make 13 Hours, 4 Minutes.— On this Principle the above Calculation was made; and by it the Sun was found to enter Libra that Year at Jerusalem, Sept. 24th D. 23d H. 0 M. P. M. that is Sept. 25th Day, 11th Hour, 00 Minutes, Morning.— To which we add 178 Days, 17 Hours, 58 Minutes, the Distance between the first Point of Libra, and the first Point of Aries; by which the Sun was found to enter Aries at Jerusalem, March 22d Day, 5th Hour, 58th Minute, P. M. or Afternoon.—As the Sun was placed in Libra, Oct. 25th, A. I. P. 706,

EXPLANATION 103

Of the Method made Use of in the foregoing Calculations.

706, according to the Julian Calendar, so, in all our Calculations, we add 298 Days to the Sum, (the Number of Days from the Calends of January, to Oct. 25, when Time began) and then subſtract the Julian Reduction from it.—The Remainder will give the Day of the Julian Month ſought.—Hence, as the firſt of the Month was not to be counted from the *Synod*, but from the Apparition, we poſtulate that the Moon, if ſhe had been in Being, would be in one of her Nodes, and exactly oppoſite to the Sun, on the third Day of the Week, juſt 24 Hours, or one whole Day, before the Sun entered Libra.—This is a moſt exact Point, and from it we begin all our Calculations, and they always come out according to the obſerved Times; this we call the original Radix or Root, and from this Root we calculate by Years and Lunations, and thoſe Years and Lunations, are meaſured by Days.—In all theſe Calculations we make the tropical ſolar Year to contain 365 Days, 5 Hours, 49 Minutes

Of the Method made Use of in the foregoing Calculations.

nutes precisely, and a Lunation 29 Days, 12 Hours, 44 Minutes, 1 S. 45 T.

It may be observed by these Calculations, that in every 49680 Lunations, we throw off one Day.—This Day is thrown off for much the same Reason that 11 Minutes were thrown off every Year from the solar Computation.—For in a Period of 30 Years, the Reckoning over-runs the compleat Days, 10 Minutes and 30 Seconds.—In this determinate Proportion, the Moon makes a slow, gradual, and uniform Progression quite round the Ecliptic, and in 49680 Lunations, gets a Day, in the same Manner as the Sun gets one Day in 131 Years, according to the Julian Reckoning; therefore it must be discharged, otherwise we shall count one Day more than is performed by Nature.

Before the late Regulation, it had been observed, that the lunar Reckoning had *anticipated* the Astronomical four Days, and so much

EXPLANATION

Of the Method made Use of in the foregoing Calculations.

much Difference there were between the Ecclefiaftical and Aftronomical Full Moons.—This Anticipation was attributed to the Moon being now nearer the Earth than fhe was fome Years ago, and that fhe performed her Lunations in lefs Time now than fhe did formerly; and what appears the more extraordinary is, that Aftronomers fhould afcribe thefe lunar Anticipations to the Moon's coming to the End of the lunar Cycle of 19 Years, one Hour and Half before the Sun; whereas, it may be obferved, by comparing the 19 Years Cycle of the Sun and Moon together, that inftead of the Moon coming to the End of that Cycle an Hour and Half before the Sun, the contrary is the Fact; for the Sun comes to the End of the Cycle 1 H. 55 M. 51 S. 15 T. before the Moon.——

Here it follows.

	Days	H.	M.	S.	T.
A Lunar Cycle containing 235 Lunations	6939	16	26	51	15
A Solar Cycle of 19 Tropical Solar Years	6939	14	31	00	00
Excefs of Lunar Computation above the Solar		1	55	51	15

EXPLANATION

Of the Method made Use of in the foregoing Calculations.

From the above it may be remarked, that the Contrary to what Astronomers maintain is true, viz. that the Moon comes to the End of the Cycle before the Sun; she indeed departs from the Sun at the End of every Cycle, but then it is by a Progression Eastward, and not by a Retrocession Westward; for the New Moons and Full Moons in that Space of Time fall out almost two Hours later, and not an Hour and Half sooner.

On comparing 19 Julian Years with 19 Lunisolar, we shall find that the Julian Reckoning over-runs the Lunar 1 H. 33 M. 8 S. 45 T. just in the same Manner as it was observed the Julian Year over-runs the Tropical Solar; and must be expunged for the same Reason.—Here follows the Comparison.

	Days.	H.	M.	S.	T.
19 Julian Years contain	6939	18	00	00	0
19 Lunisolar Years contain	6939	16	26	51	15
Excess of the Julian above the Lunar—		1	33	8	45

Hence

EXPLANATION 107
Of the Method made Use of in the foregoing Calculations.

Hence appears the Reason why Astronomers maintain, that in 19 Lunisolar Years, the mean New Moons and Full Moons happen an Hour and Half sooner, than they did at the Beginning of the Cycle.—Instead of which, it is found, on comparing 19 Solar with 19 Lunar, that the Sun comes to the Point where they set out from together, 1 H. 55 M. 51 S. 15 T. (which wants but 4 M. 8 S. 45 T. of two Hours) before the Moon. But that the Julian Reckoning over-runs the Lunar, 3 M. 8 H. 45 T. more than an Hour and Half in every Cycle; which, (like the 11 Minutes Difference between the Julian and tropical solar Year) has been the Occasion of the *apparent Anticipation*; which has no Foundation in Nature, but owes its Existence entirely to a mistaken Computation.

Having premised thus much, I shall finish this Explanation with giving an Account of the Method used in the Lunar Calculations, and for that Purpose, shall explain the Calculation,

EXPLANATION

Of the Method made Use of in the foregoing Calculations.

culation, P. 94, where the total and central Eclipse of the Sun, which was observed in London, A. D. 1715, is calculated from the original Point of the Full Moon, the third Day of the Creation; to that very Point when it was observed at London; and from that Point, to the Full Moon next Thursday Morning, Sept. 27th.

The Year of the World answering to 1715, has been found to be A. M. 5722, from which we throw off One, as was observed in the Solar Reckoning, and then divide 5721 by 19, the Number of Years in a Cycle, which gives 301 Cycles, and leaves in Remainder $\frac{2}{19}$ of another; we then multiply the Remainder 2 by 12, the Number of Lunations in a Year; which make 24 Lunations.—And, as about one Month is intercalated every three Years, to make the Computation agree with the Solar, we add One to this Sum, which makes 25 Lunations.— We then multiply these 301 Cycles, by 235, the

EXPLANATION 109

Of the Method made Use of in the foregoing Calculations.

the Number of Lunations in a Cycle, which give 70735; to which we add the 25 remaining Lunations, these make 70760, which brings it to the Full Moon at the autumnal Equinox; but, as this Eclipse happened at a New Moon, near the vernal Equinox, we add Six Lunations to bring it thereto, and Half a Lunation to bring it from the Full of the Moon, (at which Point all these Lunations end, as they began at that Point at the Creation) to the New.—These make in the Whole 70766½.—We then divide these Lunations by twelve, (the Number contained in a Year) and that gives 5897 lunar Years, and leaves 2 Lunations and Half in Remainder. To bring these to Periods of 30 Years, we divide 30, which gives 196 Periods, and 17 Years of another Period.—We then add the Periods and Lunations together, which makes 2089774 Days, 11 H. 50 M. which is the Distance between the Full Moon at the Creation, and the Eclipse of the Sun, which happened in 1715, in the first Meridian; but in

Order

EXPLANATION

Of the Method made Use of in the foregoing Calculations.

Order to bring it to the Meridian of Greenwich Obfervatory, we add 10 H. 24 M. which makes 2089774 Days, 22 H. 14 M. for the New Moon at Greenwich.—Then, as the Calends of January are 297 D. before Oct. 24, we add that Sum to it, as we did 298 in the folar Computation, to bring from the Calends of Jan. to Oct. 25, which is one Day fhort of the Solar Reckoning, as the Moon was Full one whole Day before the Sun began to meafure Time at the Creation. With this Addition to the above Sum it makes 2090071 Days, 22 H. 14 M.—From which we fubftract the Number of Days of the Julian Reduction, for A. M. 5722, which leaves 111 Days, 22 H. 14 M. from the Calends of January; from thence, to the laft Day of March inclufive, are 90 Days, which we fubftract from the above Sum; and then find that the Point of Time, when the Moon interfected the Path of the Earth, in Conjunction with the Sun, was April 21 Days, 22 H. 14 M. P. M. that is April 22 D. 10 H. 14 M.

EXPLANATION

Of the Method made Use of in the foregoing Calculations.

14 M. in the Morning.—Thus it may be observed, that our Calculation differs only 23 Minutes from Mr. Whiston's; which, supposing Mr. Whiston's to be precisely true, is but a very little, considering the Length of Time of 70766 Lunations, or 5722 tropical solar Years.

In Order to know the Day of the Week when this Eclipse happened, we divide 2089774 Days, the Number of Rotations the Equator has made between the fourth of the Creation, and that Point, (when the Moon intersected the Earth's Path) by 7, the Number of Days in a Week, first adding 4 for the first 4 *extra* Days, before the Sun began to measure Time; and it will give 298539 Weeks, and leave in Remainder 5, *(Friday)* the fifth Day of the Week.

Between that Eclipse and the Full Moon which will happen next Thursday, Sept. 27, there will have passed $895\frac{1}{2}$ Lunations.—
We

112 EXPLANATION

Of the Method made Use of in the foregoing Calculations.

We therefore add the Quantity of these Lunations together, and find it to contain 2116219 Days, 13 H. 22 M. 5 S. We then add 297 Days, to bring it to Oct. 24. after substracting the Julian Reduction for this Year, A. M. 5794, it leaves 258 D. 13 H. 22 M. 5 S. from which we substract 243, the Number of Days from the Calends of January, to the End of August inclusive; and we shall have Sept. 15 D. 13 H. 22 M. 5 S. P. M. for the Full Moon this Year, in *Libra*, which is according to our Reckoning, Sept. 16 D. 1 H. 22 M. 5 S. P. M. O. S. to which we add 11, to bring to N. S. and then it will be Sept. 27th, at 22 Minutes, 5 Seconds past One in the Morning.

For the Day of the Week   2116219 Days
         Extra Days   .   4
            ÷ 7) 2116223 (302317 Weeks
                      (4) (Thursday

I now hope I have given *demonstrative* Evidence that what I asserted is true, viz. that

Moses

EXPLANATION 113
Of the Method made Use of in the foregoing Calculations.

Moses has given us an Account of the Place of the Sun and Moon at the Creation; which, according to his Chronology, happened at a Full Moon, at the autumnal Equinox, in the 706th Year of the Julian Period.

I am now willing to join Issue with the doubting Sceptic, and bring my Cause to be tried and determined by the discerning Public.—I shall beg Leave to sum up the Evidence of this last Calculation *only*.

The Matter at Issue is, whether Moses in his History of the Creation, has given us Instruction, where the Sun and Moon were placed at that Time —It appears to me that he has done it, and I postulate it as true, viz. that the Sun was placed in *Libra*, on Oct. 25, according to the Julian Reckoning, at Noon, in the first Meridian, on Thursday the fourth Day of the Week.—That the Moon was 15 Days old; that had she been in Being, she would have been directly in

P   Opposition

EXPLANATION

Of the Method made Use of in the foregoing Calculations.

Oppofition to the Sun, on Wednefday Noon, the third Day of the Week, and in her Node, Oct. 24, according to the Julian Reckoning, and that fhe would then be totally and centrally eclipfed; and that this happened in the Year 706, of the Julian Period.—This is the *firft* or *original* Root or Point from whence I begin all my Calculations.—The Point I meafure to is a moft certain One; and was obferved by many Thoufands of People.—It is the Eclipfe of the Sun which happened at London, on a Friday, April 22. The Middle of which, according to Mr. Whifton's Calculations, was at nine Minutes before Ten in the Morning.—This was in A. D. 1715, and we know this Year was in Connection with 6428 of the Julian Period. Now as the Mofaic Chronology places the Year of the Creation in A. I. P. 706; if we fubftract 706 from 6428, it will give 5722, the Number of the annual Revolutions which the Earth has made between thefe two Points; which this Eclipfe proved to be exactly true.

From

EXPLANATION 115

Of the Method made Ufe of in the foregoing Calculations.

From this Point to next Thurfday, Sept. 27, at twenty-two Minutes paſt One in the Morning, there will have paſſed 26444 Rotations of the Equator, and as much as meaſured 15 H. 8 M. 5 S. befides.—Now the firſt Point of this ſecond Calculation begins at London, at the central Point of the total Eclipſe, 1715, and ends at 22 Minutes paſt One in the Morning, on Thurſday, Sept. 27. Between theſe two Points, the Moon will have made 895½ Lunations—that is, from her Conjunction with the Sun, A. D. 1715, to her Oppoſition, 1787.—This is the lunar Meaſure between theſe two Points.— The ſolar Meaſure will be found to agree with it. Our firſt Point of ſolar Meaſure is Oct. 25, at Noon, A. I. P. 706, when the Sun entered *Libra*, in the firſt Meridian, on Thurſday the 4th Day of the Week.—Our next Point is this Day, Sept. 22, when the Sun will be found to enter *Libra* in the Meridian of Greenwich, at ten Minutes paſt Four Tomorrow Morning, A. I. P. 6500.—Between
theſe

EXPLANATION

Of the Method made Use of in the foregoing Calculations.

thefe two Points, the Earth will have made 5794 annual Revolutions through the Ecliptic, which fhe has performed in 2116214 D. 16 H. 10 M. and will end To-morrow Morning, the 7th Day of the Week or Sunday, at ten Minutes paft Four.

The firft lunar Calculation began at the original Point, at the Creation, and ended at the total Eclipfe of the Sun, A. D. 1715.— The fecond began at the Point where the firft ended, and finifhed at the Full Moon, Sept. 27, at 22 Minutes paft One in the Morning.—By comparing the Sum of thefe two lunar Calculations, we fhall find them to agree exactly with the folar Meafure, begun at the original Point, at the Creation, and ending To-morrow at ten Minutes paft Four in the Morning.———Here they follow.

	Days.	H.	M.	
Lunar Meafure	2116219	13	22	Sunday
Solar Ditto	2116214	16	10	Thurfday

$$4\ \ 21\ \ 12$$

It

EXPLANATION

Of the Method made Use of in the foregoing Calculations.

It may be obferved, that the Difference between the folar and lunar Meafure is 4 D. 21 H. 12 M. and wants but 2 H. 48 M. of five Days Difference between the lunar and folar Reckoning; but between Sunday and Thurfday, there are only four Days — It muft be remarked, that the Moon was Full one whole Day before the Sun began to meafure Time, therefore one Day muft be fubftracted from the lunar Computation, which makes the exact Difference to be 3 D. 21 H. 12 M. as appears by thefe Calculations.— Does not this prove to Demonftration, that what I have poftulated is true?

Advertifement.

Advertisement.

THE following Letters were occasioned by a Tour of Mr. Heaviside and Mr. Penrose, through Cornwall, A. D. 1783, to view and examine, the Nature of the Mines, Clifts, Druid Monuments, and other Antiquities found there:—This, as may be imagined, occasioned many Observations and Remarks, in Order to account for the different Phenomena seen.—Hence, Mr. Heaviside, in his Letter to Mr. Penrose, after his Return to London, from Plymouth, sent him some Observations he made as he passed over the Mendipp Hills, with some Queries.—The first Letter is an Answer to them.

LETTER I.

To JOHN HEAVISIDE, Esq.

An Answer to some Queries proposed by Mr. Heaviside; whether Ore, Metal, or Coal were ever found under Chalk?—Observations where Ore and Metals are found, with Remarks on the Formation of the terraqueous Globe.—How Metals, Salts, &c. were dissolved, and reformed at the Deluge; together with the Method by which the different Strata *were formed.—The Flood described.*

DEAR SIR,

YOUR Favour, with your judicious Observations on the Mendipp Hills, I received; with your *Quere* whether Ore, Metal, or Coals are ever found under Chalk?— In Answer to which, I observe, that I have not met with any Account that either of the above have ever been found under such a *Stratum*; Coals, as you remark, are found under *Strata* of Stone and Clay.—Ore and
Metals

Metals are generally (though not always) in Fissures of large hard Strata of Stone; which *Strata* were formed and *cracked before* the Metals were deposited in these Fissures and Cracks; indeed, Lead is often found in crumbling Ground; and Iron sometimes in Floats—the philosophical Cause of which require more Room to discuss, than can be contained in a common Letter.— Besides, Philosophers are not yet agreed, how, and in what Manner, or by what Agent or Agents, this terraqueous Globe was formed—therefore, it will be no easy Matter for me to explain it in such a Manner as to gain a general Assent; supposing my Theory to be true— and however satisfactory it may be to myself, it may not be so to others.—One great Difficulty is, that the *Stratum* of the greatest specific Gravity is not always the lowermost; but, when we suppose, that before these different *Strata* subsided, every Thing was in the greatest Confusion; and also, that the greatest Part of every *Stratum*, as deep as has been examined, (if not the Whole) was in a State of Solution; so it may appear likely,
that

that it remained in this Manner till it met with a Fluid, of quite a different Nature; (which from the great Disturbance and Confusion this would occasion,) it would let fall its earthly Contents, in the same Manner as we often see performed in Chymical Operations; particularly in the making of *Magnesia Alba*.—The acid Salt being dissolved in Water, is quite clear and transparent; as is also the Alcaline Salt dissolved in the same Manner;—these will continue clear and transparent nearly as long as you choose, if you keep them separate and apart, but mix them together, and they will immediately become very turbid, and let fall a large Sediment or *Stratum*; and after a Time, the incumbent Liquor will become clear again; but if this Liquor is not entirely freed from all its saline Parts, whether they be acid or alkaline, add to it a Solution of the other, they will again become turbid, and let fall their Contents, and this *toties, quoties,* as often as this is done, till all the earthly Parts are subsided. Operations of this Kind give us an Idea of the Solution of the earthly Parts, which were dissolved

dissolved at the Deluge, and again subsided in different *Strata*, as we observe them at this Day: Hence we may understand the Cause why every *Stratum* is not found to have settled *exactly* according to its specific Gravity. Hence also we must imagine, that if any *Exuviæ* of Animals or Vegetables were mixed with these Fluids, that they would be carried down together with the earthly Matter, and be mixed throughout the *Stratum*, in the Manner we find them at this Day.

From Observation we also find, that Metals of all Sorts will dissolve in particular Fluids, as Gold in *Aqua Regia*, other Metals in *Aquafortis*; there are also Solvents that will dissolve all Sorts of Salts and precious Stones; these Liquids, after the Solution, appear as clear as pure Water; but on being mixed with a Fluid of a different Quality, become turbid, and let fall their Contents.—Hence we may easily conceive how the different *Strata* of the Earth were formed, and by what Means some of the Strata of Stone, Clay, &c. were loaded and filled with the different

different Exuviæ of Animals and Vegetables. But then perhaps the following Question will be asked—if it was so? how comes it that Metals did not subside in the same Manner, and not remain suspended, till after the earthy *Strata* were so far hardened as to be cracked in different Fissures; after which the different Metals filled these Fissures together with Spar and other saline Concretions of the same Kind? To answer this Question we must again have Recourse to the different Effects produced by Chymical Operations; but it will be proper first to explain how these different Cracks were produced.—It appears by the Account Moses gives of the coming on of the Flood, that they were occasioned, in a great Measure, by breaking up the Fountains of the great Deep, and opening the Windows of Heaven. (a) Now it is observable, that God says to Noah, *I, even I,* (b) *do bring a Flood of Waters upon the Earth,* thereby letting him know that it would be a Miracle, performed by God himself,

(a) Gen. VII. 11.—(b) Gen. V. 17.

self, and brought about contrary to the *Mechanism* of Nature.—But then, notwithstanding it was brought on by his Order, and contrary to the Mechanism of Nature; yet, he would now, as he did at the Formation, make the material Agents perform it.—Thus he made the *internal* Expansion act with greater Power; and by this Means force out the Water of the great Deep, through the Fountains and Windows of Heaven; (c) by this Means the Place or Centre of Gravity being altered, and the Cause of the Attraction of Cohesion being taken away, they were made to dissolve and cover the Earth.— Now the Power of the internal Expansion being ordered by God to be of a *just Strength, to throw out the Waters, so as to cover the Hills fifteen Cubits upwards, and no farther.* And being then restrained by the Agency of the outward Expanse or Pressure of the Ethers and Air—these two Powers acted much in the same

---

(c) These Windows of Heaven, according to the Hebrew, are the Cracks and Holes in the Earth, which, before this Event happened, were filled with the same Ethers as fills the Heavens, but were now so enlarged, as to admit the Water through them.

same Manner they did at the Formation.—And the Power or Effect of Gravity was made to act both within and without the Waters, which were then a compleat Globe, covering all the earthy Parts.—The internal Expansion, acting in this Manner, in the Midst of the Globe, forced Gravity to effect the same outward, from the Centre, as it did on the Outside towards the Centre; by these Means a solid Shell of the earthy Parts was formed between the outward Surface of the Waters, and the inward Surface.—After this the internal Expansion still increasing, and by the Closeness of the earthy Shell, being prevented from finding its Way outward, its expansive Force gradually distended, the incumbent *Strata*, (like a Bladder forceably blown) and opened the Cracks and Fissures more and more, till a violent Explosion ensued, which tore the Globe into Millions of Fragments, and threw them into every possible Degree of Confusion; some of them more elevated, and others more depressed: Hence arose an indefinite Number of subterraneous Caverns, for many Miles, and some for many Hundreds

Hundreds of Miles.—After this *God remembered Noah*, (d) (and used the same Agent then as he did at the Formation) and *caused a Wind*, or Etherial Spirit to pass over the Earth, which quieted the Waters, and *made them recede*, (e) and by this Agent he also made Gravity to act again, towards the Centre, till the Waters were forced to their proper Place, where the gravitating Ethers, (as God commanded) (f) *shut the Sea with Doors, when it brake forth, it had issued out of the Womb; when he made thick Darkness a swadling Bond for it;* and said, *hitherto shalt thou come, and no farther:* Here *shall thy proud Waves be stayed:* Here *is a Bound sat that they may not pass over; that they turn not again to cover the Earth.*

Having in short explained the coming on the Waters of the Deluge, the Destruction of the Earth thereby, and its Reformation; I shall now endeavour to answer your Question, why the Metals did not subside with the earthy

---

(d) Gen. VIII. 1.—(e) This is a literal Translation of the Hebrew.
(f) Job. XXXVIII. 8, 9.

earthy Matter, but were placed in the Fiffures we now find them, which must have been done after these Fissures were formed?

In the first Place it must be observed, that Metals require a stronger *Menstruum* than mere Water, to dissolve and take up their Parts; and also that they are separated from one another with greater Difficulty; and Salts or Gems, require some of the watery Parts to be evaporated, before they will run into Chrystals, or separate from the Liquid; besides as they require a *Menstruum saturated with proper Salts*, before they will be dissolved, and sustained in them; so they must also meet with another Menstruum, well stocked with Salts of an opposite Nature, before they will let their Contents fall again, and perhaps might require the additional Heat which the Waters received from the internal Fire to do it.—Hence the metalline and chrystalline Particles, might not separate till the greater Part of the Water was run off the Earth, when they were forced into the Cracks and Fissures.— Thus, we observe, that

that Gold is diſſolved by *Aqua Regia, a particular ſaline Fluid!* whilſt all other Metals are diſſolved by *Aqua-fortis*.—Hence, Gold is found often in the Earth or Sand, pure, and without the Mixture of other Metals; but Silver, Tin, Lead, Copper, &c are often found mixed, and incorporated in the ſame Maſs; to which generally is added Spar, which from its Tranſparency, angular Form, &c. appears to have Shot, and to be formed in the ſame Manner as (other) Salts.—Quere, Are not Diamonds formed after the ſame Manner?—Now, if the different *Strata* of the Earth were formed as above deſcribed, it ſeems natural to imagine, that they would carry down with them the different *Exuviæ*, as Shells, Vegetables, Wood, Bones, &c. which were contained therein, though of different ſpecific Gravities to the S*trata when formed*; and there remain mixed with the *Strata*, in the ſame Manner as they are now found.

According to your Deſire, I have ſent you ſome ſhort Hints of my *Ideas* concerning the Deſtruction

Destruction and Reformation of this terraqueous Globe; the Errors you find therein, your superior Judgment will easily correct; and what they are, let me know in your next Epistle.

I am,

Dear Sir,

Your obliged,

And obedient,

Humble Servant,

J. Penrose.

Stonehouse,
Aug. 1, 1783.

To F. PENROSE, Esq.

Mr. Heaviside's Answer to the former Letter, with his Remarks thereon; together with his Theory of the Deluge.—That he cannot think that the Earth underwent a general Dissolution, at that Time; that he believed the central Nucleus *was Fire; with Objections to the Dissolution of the Earth at the Deluge.*

DEAR SIR,

I Am much obliged to you for your Answer to the Quere in my last; it was a sudden Question which arose in my Mind on seeing those Hills; and I neither did, nor do, recollect ever to have met with it in the Course of my reading; and if it has never been touched upon by any Naturalist, it seems very surprising, for it appears to me to be well worthy the Observation of one.—To give a Reason why Metals may not be equally found under Chalk, as under Stone, may not indeed be so easy, as 'tis to make the Observation.—

I

I must also thank you for the Trouble you suffered that Quere to cause you, by explaining your Theory of the Earth, and desiring my Opinion of it.— But, really, Sir, my Opinion in these Matters is of very little Value; for to tell you a Truth, my reading has always been desultory and varied; for as Objects presented themselves to my Mind, I pursued them either till I was tired of them, or new ones started to turn the Current of my Thoughts another Way: But I never studied any Science methodically or scientifically, nor ever had any one to encourage or assist me in any Pursuit I entered upon; so that you must not expect any regular, well-digested System from me: However, as you desire it, I will give you my Thoughts just as they arise at this Moment of my Writing; but, not having Leisure to digest them, will probably be confused enough.—First, then, I must tell you, that I agree to your Theory *in Part*, but not wholly; because I do not think that the *general* Dissolution of the Earth, at the Deluge, (which you suppose) either did or could take Place; nor could it have

have produced the prefent Appearances, if it had.—But that a partial Diffolution of the *earthy* Parts, Sand, Gravel, &c. &c. was caufed by it, I readily affent to; yet I cannot think that the immenfe Bodies of Rocks that now exift in the World, were ever *in fluore* fince they were firft formed at the Creation. My own Idea is in fhort this; when the World was firft formed out of the chaotic Matter, the central *Nucleus* was Fire, and that it was enclofed in a Shell or Cafe, formed of fome of the heavieft Particles, fuch as Marble, Stone, &c. and that the other component Particles took their Places, not indeed exactly according to their fpecific Gravities, but perhaps nearly fo; that the Waters drained off into the hollows, or loweft Parts of the Surface, and formed the Sea.—That at the appointed Time, this central Fire burft its *ftony Shell*, with a violent Explofion, and was *one* great efficient Caufe of the Deluge.—And as this Earth or Cruft muft neceffarily have been *thinneft*, where thofe deep Hollows had been made to receive the *Sea*, fo probably thofe Parts would

firft

first yield to the Force of the Explosion, and be thrown farthest from the Center, as being lightest, and consequently form the *highest* Parts of our present Globe, such as the Andes, Alps, &c. and (if you please) the Mountains of Cornwall; all of which are of Rock. That the violent Agitation of the Waters, caused by this Explosion, would, *in many Parts*, wash much of the earthy Particles which covered these Rocks in their pristine Situation, from them; and thereby leave them in the naked State we now see them *in many Places*: but that in others, where the rocky Shell was not forced up quite so high, it remains covered with the different *Strata* of Sand, Shells, &c. much in the same Manner as it did when it originally made a Part of the great Bason which contained the Sea; which seems to me to be a very natural Solution of the Phenomenon of Shells, &c. being found even on very high Mountains; and different Sorts of them in different Places; as we now find that the different Sorts of Shell-fish, as well as others, are found in much greater Quantities in some Parts of our Seas than in others. On

On this Principle it is likewise easy to conceive, how those Fissures were caused in the hard Rocks of Cornwall and Derbyshire, &c. which are now filled with what they call the (Metallick) *Load:* but whether that *Load* was originally in the State it is now found, I very much doubt: My own Opinion being rather that they have been gradually formed by the Admixture of certain impregnated Fluids, with earthy Particles properly adapted to receive them, and become the Basis of Mineral Substance.

And what inclines me to this Opinion, and confirms me in it, is my own Observation of the Formation of what are vulgarly called Plumb-pudding Stones; which I have seen in the State of *loose Gravel*, and watched it through all the Gradations between that and the hardness of a Granite: I have also seen a small *Ruby*, in the Center of a *Diamond*, which incontestably proves that the Ruby was formed before the constituent Parts of the Diamond, which must then have been in a Fluid or soft State, for otherwise they could not have surrounded and enclosed it.

But to return, and give you my Objections to *Part* of your Theory; if, as you suppose, all the terraqueous Globe was in a State of Solution at the Time of the Deluge, how could the Rocks of Marble and Granite, acquire such great Hardness and Solidity, in so short a Space as one Year, to admit of being cracked and split as we now see them.— Would they not rather have admitted of being arched or bent, as being in a *softer* State? But, admitting for Argument's Sake, that they could have acquired sufficient Hardness, what Force, or what Cause could have been applied to them *since then*, sufficient to crack, break, and tumble them about in the wonderful Manner we now see them? You will observe, that we so far agree about the Formation of Ores, in these *Cracks*, as to suppose them formed there, subsequent to those *Cracks:* But whether you will agree with me, that they were formed upon a Matrix of earthy Particles, by Impregnation from Fluids, I know not; but rather think you will, from the Instance you properly bring of Spars being found among them, which

every

every one knows are formed from aqueous Particles, loaded with what may properly enough be called Saline ones.

Thus, my Dear Sir, you have a hasty Sketch of my Philosophy, the Product of the first leisure Hour I have had since my Return to Town.

I am,

DEAR SIR,

Your very obedient,

And much obliged Servant,

J. HEAVISIDE.

Prince's-Street, Oct. 10, 1788.

LET. III. *On the* DELUGE.

To JOHN HEAVISIDE, Esq.

Facts which prove that all Parts of Europe, Asia, Africa, *and* America, *the* Exuviæ *of Animals and Vegetables, particularly Sea Shells, are found in different* Strata *of Stone, both on the Tops of the highest Mountains in the World, and also at the greatest Depths that have been dug below the Surface of the Earth.—Some farther Account of the Deluge.*

DEAR SIR,

THOUGH we cannot *exactly* agree in our Ideas about the Formation of the Earth, *at the Creation*, and the Destruction (as I suppose) and Reformation of it at the Deluge; yet the genteel and impartial Manner in which you mention your Objections, shews that Truth is your Object.—And, I am sure, that no one, who reads your Observations, but must think (notwithstanding what you say) that you have made some Proficiencies in the Study of Natural Philosophy,

I believe you have been teazed enough already, to know that it is my Hobby-Horse. As Uncle Toby had his, so I have mine; for when Philosophy is once made the Subject of Conversation, I dont know when to have done with it; and therefore, I suppose, you will desire no more on the Subject; if so, throw this in the Fire, and trouble yourself no more about it.

It gave me great Satisfaction to find that your Ideas agreed in Part with mine; but you say you cannot think with me, " that " there was a *general Dissolution* of the Earth " at the Deluge, and that the immense Bo- " dies of Rock that now exist, were ever in " a fluid State, since they were first formed " at the Creation."

The Way to come at the Truth of what we have not seen, or don't know for certain, is to apply to Matters of Fact, Experiments, and the natural *Phenomena* of Nature.—On examining this Earth, in *all Parts* of the World, in *America* as well as *Europe*; *Asia*, and

and *America*; from the Tops of the higheſt Mountains, to the deepeſt Places that have been dug in the Earth; we find it is compoſed of different *Strata,* as Sand, Gravel, Stone, Clay, &c.—In all *theſe Strata* are found *Exuviæ* of Animals and Vegetables; particularly Sea Shells, in large Quantities.— Does not this prove, that theſe Shells, &c. *were mixed* with the Subſtance of the Stone and other *Strata,* when they were in a fluid State?

This could not happen at any Time, but at the general Deluge.—And (as was obſerved before) that, as they are to be found in great Part of the *Strata,* from the Tops of the higheſt Mountains, to the greateſt Depths in the Earth; all muſt be diſſolved.—The finding Skeletons of Elephants, and the Horns of the Mouſe Deer, here in England, ſeems to prove that theſe *Strata,* wherein they are found, were in a State of Solution when theſe Relicks were there depoſited; and alſo that the Deluge was univerſal.—How is it poſſible for a Flood of Water, many Feet
deep,

deep, to be partial on any Part of the Earth; it is well known that Water will give Way to Pressure, as may be observed by Pumps and Hydrostatic Machines, &c.—Therefore, as the Pressure of the Atmosphere is universally alike all over the Globe, (allowing for the Difference between the Heat at the Equator, and the Cold at each Pole) the Water must be forced equally round it.—This being the Case, we may reasonably suppose, that these Relicks must be brought from other Climates, to this Place; neither one of them being an Inhabitant here.—Large Trees are also found in some of the Northern Latitudes, which are so cold as not to admit a Shrub to grow.

Moses, in his History of the Flood, as before observed, tells us, that God said, *I, even I, do bring on a Flood of Waters on the Earth.*—Hence we are informed, that it was brought on by *the immediate Act of God himself*, and *not according to the Agency of Nature.*

Nature.—Now though God brought it on *contrary* to that Agency, which he had established; yet he made Use of his material Agents, both to bring it on, and to carry it off.—Thus we find that Moses, in his History tells us, that the Method God ordered was *to break up the Fountains of the great Deep, and open the Windows of Heaven.* (3)

The literal Translation of the above Passage is, That all the Openings of the great Deep, through which the Fountains flowed, and the Holes and Cracks through which Air, Steam, or the internal *Expansion* or *Heaven* passed, were enlarged, spread abroad, and broke up.—Also that there was a very great Rain.—From all which it may not be improbable, but that the Shells, and different Parts of Animals and Vegetables, so found, were appointed as an undeniable Evidence, to the *latest Posterity,* that Moses's History of the Flood is true.

The Method made Use of was, (as he informs us) to increase the internal Expansion and

(3) Gen. VII. 11.

and Rarefaction, so as to force out the Water from the Deep, through those Openings which became larger continually, and resisted less, as the Centre of *Gravity* was altered, by lessening the compressing Force without, and increasing the expansive Force within.— Thus the *Attraction of Cohesion* was taken away; hence the Parts of Stone, &c. became loose and easily dissolved, and were moved, and *by the Force of the Water below*, mixed with it and carried away.—The *Expansion* below continuing and increasing, till it had forced the Water fifteen Cubits upwards, above the highest Hills, which were covered and hid.

By this Description of the Agents, you may observe, that I agree with you in thinking, that there is a central Fire within this Globe, which I take to be the first Agent in all the Operations of Nature.— The late Earthquakes have shewed us something of its Effects, by which were thrown out hot Water, and burning Sand, &c.—Is it not probable that this central Fire may be made, by God,

God, the Agent, which, at the laſt Day, may deſtroy this terraqueous Globe, with its Inhabitants?—Indeed this central Fire, which you mention, appears to be the cauſe of our Lakes and Springs, (h) both hot and cold — Is it not probable that it aſſiſts to increaſe the Fertility of the Earth in ſome Places more than in others.—The Parts of Italy ſo much damaged by the late Earthquakes, as well as by former ones, are allowed to be ſome of the moſt fertile Places on Earth:— Can there be a Doubt but that Earthquakes are brought on by Steam ariſing from this central Fire. (i) It is obſerved, that after long continued Froſts, that the Thaw, generally, if not always, proceeds from below:—Do not theſe *Effluvia* from below, cauſe the Drains, &c. to ſmell before Rain? Has it not alſo an aparent Effect in ſinking the Quickſilver of the Barometer, by its Force upwards, abating the Preſſure of the Atmoſphere? Without this, how will you account for the Difference of Cold under the ſame Latitudes, as *Newfoundland, Hudſon's Bay,*

(h) See Letter. XVI. (i) Michel, on Earthquakes, Part 2.—Whithurſt, C. XII

Bay, &c. which are in the same Latitude as England, and yet the Cold much more intense?— Unless you will suppose that the Shell of the Earth, under these Places in *America*, is thicker and closer than it is here in England, and thereby the Heat of the Fire and Steam below, are prevented from having so great an Effect on it.

I have now given you a short Narrative of my Theory of the Deluge, and how it was brought on.—Moses in his History gives but a short Relation about its going off, and the Reformation of the terraqueous Globe; which indeed he had no Occasion to do, as he had been so particular before in his History of the Creation and Formation of the antidiluvian Earth; which I shall explain in my next Letter, as I have already run this to a great Length.—He only lets us know that God did not forget Noah, or suffer him to be destroyed, but that he caused a *Wind or gravitating Ether* to pass over the Earth, by which the Waters were assuaged, or as it is in the Hebrew, the Waters were *forced down*.

Adieu,

Stonehouse, Sept. 27, 1783.

F. PENROSE.

To JOHN HEAVISIDE, Esq.

Original Names ideal.—The Reason why it has been asserted, and generally believed, that the Scriptures do not speak strictly true, *with Regard to Philosophy, on the Motion of the Sun, Earth, &c. but is accommodated to vulgar Apprehensions.—The Mosaic Account of the Creation, and Formation, of this System; describing the Agents, which carry on the mechanical Operations of Nature; together with some Extracts from* Sir Isaac Newton, *to shew that he supposed the Agents of Nature to be the same as those revealed in the Scriptures.*

Dear Sir,

ACCORDING to the Promise in my last Letter, I have herewith sent you my Theory of the Creation and Formation of this terraqueous Globe.— The Instruction for doing it, I have taken from the Mosaic History, which Moses tells us came from *Jehovah* himself.—Indeed we have no other

Account of this grand Affair, therefore let us examine it with the same critical Strickness we would any other History.—If we find this History confirmed by all the Parts of the terraqueous Globe, and also by all the Phenomena of the Sun and Moon, &c. why shall we not believe it? *

It is agreed by the learned in general, and by Antiquarians in particular, that original Names, (in all Languages) were ideal, and gave an emblematical Representation of the Thing signified thereby.— Thus in Latin, Candelabrum signifies a Candlestick.—This Word is compounded of *Candela,* a Candle, and *Labrum,* a Cistern or Socket to contain a Candle; so that it was expressive, that this Instrument was to contain a Candle:— In English it is a *Candle-stick,* denoting that it was then made of a *Stick* or *Wood,* and not of Silver or other Metal as it is now.—We are informed by Moses, that the Names given by God, by Adam, by the Patriarchs, or by
Himself,

---

* See Introduction.

Himself, were all *ideal,* and expressed the Reason why the Name was given.

Thus, when Moses asked the Lord, what he should say was his Name, (k) *God said unto Moses, I am, that I am; thou shalt say, I AM has sent me unto you,* JeHoVaH.—This is the incommunicable Name given by God himself; and though it contains but four Letters in the Hebrew, (the small Vowels being added to assist the Sound) yet it is so comprehensive and expressive, as to require a Sentence to explain it, which, with all Humility, I shall endeavour to do, viz. *The eternal self-existing Being, who was, and is, and is to come.*—Moses also informs us, that Adam called his Wife's Name HoVaH, *Eve.* This is a Participle passive, from HIaH *vixit*, to live, signifying *Life giving,* or, as we are told, because she was to be the Mother of all Living; or the Person from whom all Posterity were to derive their Being.—We also find, that God not only gave ideal Names, but also that he ordered those Names to be changed

(k) Exod. III. 13, 14.

changed on particular Occasions, when the Alteration in Condition required it.—Thus *Abraham* from *Abram*, that is, from high Father, to the Father of a *great Multitude*, to express and be a Memorial of the Promise which God made him.—That *He should be the Father of many Nations.* (l) God also altered the Name of Jacob to Israel, &c. (m) If these Examples are not sufficient to satisfy any Inquirer, let him consult the Scripture Names at the End of *Cruden's* Concordance, and, I believe, he will want no more Examples?

For the above Reason, I shall give, (together with the Mosaic History of the Creation) a literal Translation of the Meaning of the Hebrew Words as they occur.—If it don't give you Instruction, I think it will add to your Amusement.—But before I do this, it will be proper to take Notice of a general Notion which has prevailed for about the three last Centuries, viz. That Moses, when he gives an Account of the Creation, Deluge, or Motions of the Heavenly Bodies,
does

(l) Gen. XVII. 5.—(m) Gen. XXXII. 28.

does not speak philosophically true, *but accommodates himself to the vulgar Apprehensions of Men, to such Points of natural Philosophy as they were not able to comprehend.*

Now, in Answer to this, it is confest, in general, that there is a great deal of *Geography*, of authentic *History*, and *Chronology*, in the Bible.—Its History, its Chronology, or Philosophy, must be in Fact as true as its Theology; for to speak false in any Case whatsoever, or, if we suppose that any Part of the divine Word to be erroneous, it so far shakes the Authority of the rest.—If we believe his History of the Israelites to be true; why should we disbelieve his History of the Creation? especially if the Phenomena of the Sun and Moon, and all Nature confirm it.

Let us now enquire, why it was supposed that the Scriptures did not speak strictly true, with Regard to Philosophy.—By this Inquiry we shall find, that about Three Hundred Years ago, *Copernicus* published his Account

count of the Solar System, (which was no other than a Recovery of what was before maintained by *Pythagoras*, and other ancient Philosophers.)—For some Centuries before this, there had reigned an universal Ignorance, with Regard to the Sciences.—The Church, which was then that of Rome, had not, neither did they understand any other Scriptures but the vulgar Latin; which, according to their Apprehensions, asserted, that the Earth stood still, and that the Body of the Sun moved, rose, and set.—*Copernicus* and his Followers proved beyond Dispute, that it was not the Sun, but the Earth which moved. This being the Case, and these *learned Ecclesiasticks not being able to read and understand the original Hebrew*, (which spoke the contrary) were forced to give up the Cause, and to save Appearances, to cover their Ignorance, and to prevent farther Inquiry, they contrived to get it asserted, and preached from the Pulpit, that the Scriptures did not speak philosophically true, but that Moses did accommodate himself to the Apprehensions of the Vulgar.—Mankind being thus educated and

and taught with their firſt Ideas, no Body ſeemed to doubt it. *

Moſes, in the firſt Chapter of Geneſis tells us, that the World was not *eternal*, but that in *the Beginning* God created the Heavens and the Earth.—After this he goes on to let us know, what Time God was forming it, and what material Agents he made uſe of for that Purpoſe.—He tells us that the Earth was created *without Form*, and had a *Void* or *Hollow* in the *Midſt* of it.—That the Faces, (plural) or Outſides of it were covered with *Darkneſs*.—That the firſt Thing which God did, was for RUaCH, his Spirit, to cauſe a Motion, or Wind, or Preſſure, amongſt the Darkneſs on the Outſide of the Waters.—The next Word, MeRaCHaPHeT, deſcribing the Motion to be of the vibrating Kind, backwards and forwards, like the Waves of the Sea, preſſed by Wind, or the Breath of an Animal, or the Hovering of a Hawk over his Prey; and God *ſaid let there be Light*.—

Here

---

* Hence appears the Abſurdity of Perſons explaining written Laws they cannot read and underſtand.

Here it may be obferved, that it was not a *new* Creation, but God faid *let there be Light*; or let this expanfive Struggle or Conflict continue till it produced Light—and there was Light; and God faw that the Light was good, or according to the Hebrew Signification, *that it was compleat*, and fit to anfwer all the Purpofes it was defigned for.— The Hebrew Name is AUR, a Particle paffive from JAR, to flow like a River, to irradiate, to expand; as a Subftantive a Splendor, an Irradiation, a continual Flowing or Motion.—Thus we find that the Name given to this Subftance, (which was before called CHeSHeC, *Darknefs*, Stillnefs, Inertnefs, Sluggifhnefs) was of a quite different Quality to what it had been before, which was Stillnefs, Inertnefs; but this, a continual Flowing, like a River, *Motion itfelf*, or the moving Agent.—Hence it may be obferved, that the Darknefs which furrounded the terraqueous Globe, was divided into two Parts, viz. RUaCH, Spirit, Wind, or Air, in Motion, which caufed Gravity and Compreffion, and AUR, Light, which gave Motion, and irradiated.

diated.—That God placed the Earth between the Light and Darkneſs, ſo that Light was on one Side of the Earth, and Darkneſs on the other.—That God called the Air on that Side of the Globe which was covered with Light, JOM, *Day*, or *Tumult*, from the violent Agitation or Struggle there carried on between the two Parts, Light and Darkneſs.—The State of the Air, on the oppoſite Side of the Earth, he called LaILaH, *Night*, *Inactivity*, *Laſſitude*: Hence, on that Side of the Earth which was Day, there was a continual Struggle, or Conflict; and on the contrary Side, Night, or *Inactivity*.—That by cauſing the Globe to make a Rotation all round, there was Evening and Morning, or one Day.

On the ſecond Day we are told that God ſaid, " Let there be a *Firmament* or *Expan-*
" *ſion* in the Midſt *(void)* of the Waters, and
" let that be an Inſtrument and Cauſe to di-
" vide between the Waters and the Waters."
Thus let the Motion between the Light and Darkneſs increaſe, and by their Struggle and Conflict,

Conflict, cause an Expansion or Firmament; which Expansion, we are told, was the Instrument God made use of to separate or make to *gravitate* the earthy Parts from the Waters, and so form the Shell; which Shell of Earth when formed, separated and made a Division between the two Waters, viz. those on the Outside, under the outward Firmament, and these Waters on the Inside of the Shell, above the internal Expansion, in the *Midst* of the Waters.—After the Expansions between the Light and Darkness had begun to perform the Office they were designed for, God gave them new Names to denote their Office.—He now called them *Heavens*, (n) SHeMIM, that is the *Placers*, the *Disposers*, the *Agents*; also SHeCHeKIM the Conflictors.—These were God's Agents under him, whose Power he lets us know their Names represented.—Thus ended the second Day.*

(n) Psalm 89, 37.

* Saint Paul tells us, Rom. I. 20. *That the invisible Things of him from the Creation of the World, are clearly seen, being understood by the Things that are made, even his eternal Power and Godhead.*

On the third Day the Action of the Expansion or Firmament, in the Midst of the Waters, still continuing and increasing by being surrounded and pent up within the Shell

●

head.—In the Margin of our Bible, the Translators have referred us to the XIX Psalm, as the Place where the Scriptures have pointed out to us those Parts of *created Nature* which do it: I shall therefore give the first six Verses of that Psalm, which differ little from the English Translation, except being more literal.

Verse 1st. " The Heavens, *as Books, represent to us, by* " *their Numbers in Circulation,* (a) the Glory of God; and the " Firmament sheweth his handy Work, or his Strength and " Power."—(Thus, Job XXXVII, 18, we are told, that " the Skies or Heavens *are strong as a Molten Looking-Glass.)*

2d. " Day unto Day causes his Decree to be spread abroad, " and Night unto Night *the Knowledge of Jehovah.* *

3d. " Neither Words or Speech are in them; let their Sound be attended to!"

4th. " Their *Ordinance* goes out over the whole Earth, and " their *Fulness* (b) unto the End of the World.—The Place " or Tabernacle for the solar Light (c) is spread out in them.

5th. " Which like a Bridegroom coming out of his " Chamber,

Shell of Earth and Waters, *it burſt the Shell, and got Vent,* by which *the outward Waters,* (after the Rupture) were preſſed down by the Firmament, to join thoſe below, *within the Shell*

" Chamber, and triumphs as a ſtrong Man, *(like the great* " *Man)* to run a Courſe."

6th. " His going forth is from the End of the Heavens, " and his *Circuit* unto the Ends of it ; and there is no *Thing* " nor *Place* hid from the Heat thereof."

Obſervations on the Words which differ from the Engliſh Tranſ-lation.

(a) The Hebrew Word tranſlated *declare,* is MeSePRIM, not a Verb, but a plural Noun, agreeing with SHeMIM, *Heavens,* and derived from SareR, which according to *Avenarius's* Lexicon, ſignifies " *numeravit ordine, recenſit per Gyrum, et Circulum ;*" to number according to Order, to declare, as in a Book, to number by a Circle.—As a Noun, a Book, a Numeration, a Scribe.

(b) MeLIHiM, tranſlated Words are derived from MeLaH, which ſignifies *Fulneſs,* not Words.(*)—The Hebrew Words are DaGNoTH, JeHoVaH, which is literally the *Knowledge of Jehovah ;* but in the Engliſh Tranſlation it is, *ſheweth* Knowledge.

(c) SHeMoSH in the Engliſh Tranſlation is often rendered

Shell of the Earth, which was before occupied by the Expanſion, and thus, as Moſes informs us, the Waters were gathered to *one Place*; the Abyſs, but not to the Centre of the

dered *Sun*, as it is in this Place, though it never ſignifies the Body of the Sun throughout the whole Bible; but the Sun-Beams or Light proceeding from the Sun.—Whenever the ſolar Fire or Body of the Sun is mentioned in Scripture, it is called CHaMaH, and the Body of the Moon is called LIBNaH. Thus, Iſaiah XXX. 26.—" The Stream of Light " of LIBNaH, *the Moon*, ſhall be as the Stream of Light of " CHaMaH, *the Sun*, and the Stream of Light of CHaMaH " ſhall be ſevenfold."—The not making a proper Diſtinction between theſe two Hebrew Words, has been the Occaſion of great Confuſion, by attributing Motion to the Sun, and not to the Earth, (which is contrary to the Words of the Scriptures) and has given an Opportunity to the ſelf-ſuffic ent and conceited Deiſt, to ridicule them.—Thus in the Engliſh Tranſlation, the Sun is ſaid *to riſe* and *ſet;* but this is not found in the Hebrew; in thoſe Places it is SHeMoSH,- the *Solar Light*, which is ſaid to *ſpring out*, and the *Solar Light* to *go off*.—Thus, *Joſhua*, X. 12. The SHeMoSH, the *Solar Light*, is ſaid to be ſilent, or not to go off, but to remain ſtill on Gibeon.—And IaReCH, the Lunar, or *reflected* Light (this Word ſignifies *Effluvia, Odour*, or reflected Light, from a Body, as Canticles II. 13—V. 10, and 1 Sam. XXVI. 19, is the very ſame Word, of the ſame identical Letters, which in the Margin of the Engliſh Bible is tranſlated *Smell*) from the Moon, in the Valley of *Ajalon*.

Hence,

the Earth, which Place (I think with you) was and is always occupied by Fire.—Hence, as Moses informs us, by the going down of the Waters, the dry Land appeared.

- I

Hence, we find, in this Miracle, that neither the Motion of the Sun, Moon, or Earth is mentioned, or at all concerned about it: It was only the *Solar Light* and the *Lunar Light* which remained in both those Places, till *Joshua* had destroyed his Enemies.—It was a supernatural Light that remained there! as a supernatural Darkness had before remained in Egypt for three Days, (a *Darkness that might be felt!)* whilst the Children of Israel had Light in their Dwellings, Exod. X. 21, 22, 23. Yet we have not the least Reason to suppose that the Earth stood still all this while.—We are told the contrary, that this Miracle of Darkness remained three Days, or whilst the Earth made three Rotations round its Axis —As the Earth did not remain still or stop her Motion, whilst this Miracle of Light and Darkness was performed in Egypt, why should we suppose it did while a Miracle of the same Kind was performed on *Gibeon?* Had that been the Case, the whole Solar System must have been disordered! which would have answered no End; it was as much a Miracle without it.—That it did not is evident from our Astronomical Calculations of Eclipses, Equinoxes, &c. for there is not one Minute of that Day deficient.

Thus we find that SHeMoSH, the solar Light, and IaReCH, the Lunar, or reflected Light, remained *still*, without Motion, in both these Places, in a miraculous Manner,

contrary

I shall now recapitulate what has been observed, from which it may be remarked, that this terraqueous Globe was created in a confused Mass or a *Chaos*; that it had a *Hollow* or *Void* in the Midst of it.——That this *Void* was filled with Darkness, and the Outside of it was also covered with the same Substance.——That this Darkness was *inert* or *inactive Matter*, which afterwards had different Names given it by God, expressive of their Agency, till it was quite *good* or *compleat*, when it received the Name of *Heavens*, or the *Placers*, the *Agents*.——Thus God first caused a *Wind* Weight, or vibrating Motion or Agitation amongst the Darkness, by which *Light*

contrary to the Mechanism of Nature.——But that CHaMaH, the solar Fire, or Body of the Sun, and LiBNaH, the Body of the Moon, were at the same Time in their Places in the Heavens; and that the Earth continued her usual Motions, and no Difference was occasioned on other Parts of the Globe, besides upon *Gibeon*, and in the Valley of *Ajalon*.—— And Verse 13 it is said, that " the SHeMoSH, the solar
" Light, remained in that *Part* of the Heavens, (viz. over
" *Gibeon)* it did not go off, (or *set)* it was like an entire or
" perfect Day, and there was no Day like that before it or
" after it."

Light sprung out, to which he gave the Name of *Light*, *Iradiation*, Splendor, or flowing *Motion*.———That the Globe had Light, Day or Tumult on one Side, and *Night*, a *Lassitude*, or a Decay of it, on the other Side.—That the terraqueous Globe was a Division between them.—That by one Rotation there was Evening and Morning on all Parts of the Globe, which made the first Day.—That on the second Day God caused an Expansion amongst the Darkness, in the Midst of the Globe; which Expansion caused a Separation of the earthy Parts from the Waters, and forced them outwards to join those which were pressed towards the Centre, by the outward Expansion, and thus a firm Shell of Earth was formed, which was a Division between the outward and the internal Waters.—On the third Day the internal Expansion continually increasing, and being confined by the Shell of Earth, it arrived to such a Strength as to burst the Shell, and get Vent; after that mixing with the outward Expansion, the Waters were pressed down into the Place lately occupied by it, by which Means

LET. IV.   *On the* CREATION.   161

Means the Waters were in *one* Place, and the dry Land appeared; after they had performed this Action, God saw that they were good, or capable to perform the Agency he appointed for them; and he then gave them the Name of *Heavens*, the *Agents*, *Placers*; and deputed them to act.—And we find that they caused Vegetables, Trees, &c. to spring out of the Earth and grow.

Having now given you an Account of the Formation of this terraqueous Globe, as given by Moses, who tells us that the Earth now brought forth Vegetables, Trees, &c. I shall endeavour to explain how the natural Agents performed these Operations, which the Scriptures tell us they do; but before that, I take the Liberty to make some Extracts from *Sir Isaac Newton*, to shew that he supposed they did the same; and also that the *Phenomena* of *Projection* or *centrifugal* Force, together with the *Centripetal Gravity*, and all Kinds of Attractions are performed by the same Agents, *the* HEAVENS, *the* ETHERS; the Fluid which fills them.—This
X   will

will be a Confirmation, that he has properly applied his geometrical and mathematical Demonstrations of these Effects, or *Phenomena*; which Demonstrations, I doubt not, will stand the Test of Ages, as *Euclid's* has already done.

Sir *Isaac Newton's* great Judgement and Skill in Geometry, was the principal Cause of excelling his contemporary Philosophers, for God *comprehended the Dust of the Earth in a Measure, and weighed the Mountains in Scales, and the Hills in a Ballance*. (o) Hence the most certain Method to ascertain the Truth of an astronomical or philosophical Hypothesis, is by Geometry, by Numbers, Weights, and Measure.—This was the Method that great Mathematician pursued his Studies; for in a Book of *Des-cartes*, which he made use of when at College, there still remain in many Places in the Margin, the following Remarks.—*Error,* not *geometrical*. But then great Care should be taken in their Application, not to apply them to improper Subjects,

(o) Isaiah XL, 12.

Subjects, for if applied improperly, we shall be mislead by them.—Sir Isaac himself has been guilty of this Error.—The Science of Geometry is derived from the System of Nature, which is a perfect *Automaton*, or a mechanical Machine, that has the Power of Moving within itself; but it was formed and set a going by the Creator, who saw that it was good, perfect, and compleat, and capable to perform all the Operations he designed it for, many of which are secret and wonderful.

Now let it be observed, that what Moses calls HEAVENS, or the *material Agents* under God, *Sir Isaac Newton* calls ETHERS, of which he gives the following Description. " This Medium (says he) pervades all Bo-
" dies, and that there is *no Vacuum* but what
" it fills; that it readily pervades all Bodies,
" and by its elastic Force, is *expanded through*
" *the whole Heavens.* (p) And (q) that it is
" rarer within the Body of the Sun, than at
" its Surface; and rarer there than in the ce-
" lestial

(p) Opt. P. 323.—(q) Opt. P. 325.

"lestial Spaces; so that if the elastic Force of this Medium be exceeding great, it may suffice to *impel* Bodies from the denser Parts of the Medium, towards the rarer, with all that Force or *Impulse* which we call GRAVITY."—At the Conclusion of his *Principia* he tells the same. (r) He farther says, "We might add something concerning a certain most *subtile Spirit*, which *pervades* and lies *hid* in all Bodies; by the *Force* and *Action* of *which Spirit*, the Particles of Bodies mutually *attract* one another, at near Distances, and where, if contiguous, the elastic Bodies operate at greater Distances, as well repelling as attracting the neighbouring Corpuscles, and Light is *emitted*, refracted, inflected, and heat Bodies; and all *Sensation* is excited, and the *Members of animal Bodies move at the Command of the Will*, namely, by the Vibrations of this *Spirit*, mutually propagated, along the solid Filaments of the Nerves, from the outward Organs of Sense, to the Brain, and from the Brain to the Muscles."

Then

(r) Pemberton, P. 406.

Then in his *Opticks*, in Order to convey to us a Notion how this Agency was performed between the *Light proceeding* from the *Sun*, and the *Spirit* descending from the *Extremities.*— He has these Words. " The same " *great Weight* (or Spirit) may condense " those Vapours and Exhalations, as soon as " they shall at any Time begin to *ascend* from " the *Sun*, and make them presently fall " back *again into him*, and by that Action, " increase his Heat *much after the same Manner* that in our Earth the Air *increases* the " *Heat of a culinary Fire.* (f) But, says he, " it is difficult to explain how Rays can be " alternately in Fits of easy Reflection, and " easy Transmission; unless perhaps one " might suppose, that there are in *all Space*, " TWO, (*Light* and *Spirit* as he mentions " before) ethereal, vibrating Mediums."— Perhaps we may not get a more clear Description of the Agency of Nature than the above, from *Sir Isaac Newton*; the Truth of which all the *Phenomena* of Nature confirm, as well as the Scriptures; hence I shall
take

(f) Opt. P. 339.

take the Liberty of adopting his two Agents, *Light* and *Spirit*; and, note, that whenever I make Use of either, I may be understood to mean the same by them, as has been above described from Sir *Isaac Newton*.

Having now extended my Letter to a Length, that I think, will tire your Patience, and the next Thing coming on to be explained being Vegetation, which will require another long Letter, I shall now conclude this, with a Promise that you shall receive another in a few Days.

I am,

Dear Sir,

Your Friend,

And humble Servant,

F. PENROSE.

STONEHOUSE,
Oct. 4, 1783.

To JOHN HEAVISIDE, Esq.

Vegetation when it first began:—The Agents which carry it on described; together with the Method Nature makes use of for that Purpose.—The Vegetation of a Seed and Bud. Experiments from Dr. Hales, to ascertain the Effects of Heat and Cold on that Operation of Nature.

DEAR SIR,

MY last Letter I finished with the Waters being gathered together in *one Place*, and the dry Land appeared; and God said, let *the Earth bring forth Grass, the Herb yielding Seed, and the Fruit Tree yielding Fruit after his Kind, whose Seed is in itself, upon the Earth: and it was so. And God saw that they were good.*—On this the third Day ended,

It may be observed, that God, on the first Day, caused a *Splendor*, an *Irradiation*, amongst the Darkness, which covered the

Faces or Surfaces of the Waters. These *Sir Isaac Newton* observes, were the Agents, (which we find *afterwards* God called Heavens) to which he gives the Name Ethers, and filled all the celestial Space from the Sun to Saturn, and beyond.—These Agents, by their continual Conflict, caused an Expansion, and formed the terraqueous Globe.—Thus the Light by entering, opens and expands—and the Spirit, by pressing, forces every Thing closer together.—We are now told, that these Agents had a free Access to the Surface of the Earth, which by their Agency brought forth Grass; the Herb yielding Seed, &c. whose Seed was in itself.———Thus we find that Vegetation was the first Operation these Agents produced, after the forming of the terraqueous Globe.—And, perhaps, it is the *first in Dignity* that we shall be capable to understand—therefore, as it must be allowed, that the *Phenomena* produced by Nature, are much more *certain* and *less equivocal*, than what are obtained from Experiments of our own devising; so I shall endeavour to explain, in the best Manner I can,

can, the Agents employed to perform it. Now let it be remembered, as we have already observed from Sir *Isaac Newton*, that *Light*, and its perceivable *Effect*, *Heat*, and *Spirit* or *Cold*; together with the *Atmosphere, Water and Earth*, are the Things required to produce and carry on Vegetation.

Boerhaave says, that *Fire* and *Motion* are synonymous Terms; which, as he observes, is proved thus; Fire by its entering Bodies, and producing *Heat*, their Parts are dilated, and must necessarily be moved farther asunder; whether they be Solids or Fluids.—Thus, an Iron Bar, being heated, increases in all Dimensions, and the more so as it is farther and farther heated; but on being again exposed to the *Cold*, it contracts, and its Parts are forcibly *pressed* together, and return through all the Degrees of Dilatation, till it comes to its first Bulk, or to the same Degree of Heat which it had when that additional one was first applied; being *never two Minutes of the same Dimensions.*— Hence, says *Boerhaave*, " If there were the greatest Degree of Cold, " and

" and all Fire were taken away, all Nature
" would grow into one concrete Body, *folid
" as Gold, and hard as Diamond.*--But, up-
" on the Application of Fire, it would *re-
" cover its former Mobility.*—Confequently
" every Diminution of Fire is attended with
" a proportionable Diminution of Motion,
" and *Vice Verfa.*"—Now, as we have the
Authority of *Sir Ifaac Newton* and *Boerhaave,*
to affirm that the Heavenly Spaces, and all
Matter, are filled with an ethereal Fluid,
which acts in two Capacities, viz. by *Light* or
Heat entering their Parts, and expanding
them, and by *Spirit* or *Cold compreffing and
forcing them together;* we fhall endeavour to
trace out the Method Nature makes ufe of to
caufe Vegetation from a Seed to a perfect
Plant or Tree.

Every Year, nay every Day, Experience
confirms us, that *Heat* and *Cold,* which are
the *Signs* of *Light* and *Spirit,* are the operat-
ing Caufes of Vegetation.—Thus, on the
coming on of Winter, as the Heat of the
Sun decreafes, Vegetation languifhes in Pro-
portron

portion as he withdraws his Warmth.——
.Thus, if the Autumn proves warm, Vegetation is carried on with greater Vigour, and longer, than when, on the contrary, cold prevails.—And in the greateſt Cold, in our Winter, it is quite ſtop'd and at a Stand; and thus it continues, till by the Increaſe of Heat in the Spring, the vegetable Juices are again put into Motion, when Seeds, Plants, and Trees begin to vegetate.—Therefore, in Order to explain this Operation, I ſhall take the following Method.—1ſt I ſhall examine, after a Seed is put into the Ground, what are the Cauſes which make it vegetate, and to become a Plant:—2dly, what are the Cauſes, when Spring comes on, that make Plants and Trees to vegetate, and puſh forth their Buds and Leaves; and 3dly, when Summer advances, what occaſions Trees to grow, to bring forth their Fruits and Seeds to Perfection.

Thoſe Perſons who have been moſt converſant with, and who have made the greateſt Diſcoveries in microſcopical Obſervations, aſſert,

assert, that every Herb and Tree bear their own proper Seed, after their Kind.—These, on being thrown into the Earth, which is of a proper Heat, Moisture, &c. spread forth their Roots, and receive from thence their Nourishment and Support.—That the Lineaments of the future Plants, of every particular Kind, are in the Seed itself.—So is the Form of every Shoot of a Tree in the Bud, before it is forced open, and made to grow by the natural Agents acting thereon. These Buds, on the coming on of the cold Weather in Autumn, are covered close, and defended therefrom, by a thick mucilaginous and gummy Juice, very observeable in many Trees, especially the Horse Chesnut, Ash,&c. and those Trees which shed their Leaves first, and are latest in the Spring before they Shoot. This gummy Substance continues thereon, till the Warmth of the Spring, or *some artificial Heat*, dissolves it, and frees the Bud from this obstructing Matter.— The same Heat which dissolves the Gum, penetrates the Bark of the Tree, thins and makes fluid the Juices contained in the *vascular Series* of Vessels,

Veffels, between the Bark and the Wood, and expands them.—The Manner and Power of which may be underftood by the Effect Warmth has on a Bottle of Ale, or other Liquor, which it expands with fuch Force, that unlefs it finds a Paffage by the Mouth of the Bottle, or fome other Way, it burfts the containing Bottles.——This expanfive Force continually increafing by the frefh addition of Heat, enters the Bud; (a Paffage being made through the Rind for that Purpofe;) where the Reffiftance of the gummy Subftance being taken away, it expands his Parts, and fpreads open its Leaves.—When this is done, it becomes in a growing State; the Method, of which will hereafter be explained; but before we do that, it will be proper to examine the Make and Form of the different Parts of a Plant or Tree which I fhall now defcribe.

1ft. There is a thin outer Rind. 2dly. The *inner Rind* much thicker than the former, though both thefe Rinds are in general but thin, and of a *reticular* Form, with a Series of of Veſſels between them; all theſe expand and dilate as the Tree increaſes in Size.—— Their Uſe ſeems to be for the ſame Purpoſe as the Skin of Animals, either to inhale or exhale, according to the Alterations of the Weather, and alſo to dilate for the Enlargement of the Tree.—The 3d is the *Blea*, of a *ſpungy Nature*; it is of a conſiderable Thickneſs, and Uniform in its Texture, compoſed of hexagenal Cells, which appear to be deſigned for Reſervoirs, for containing the watery and nouriſhing Particles, abſorbed from the Atmoſphere, under which lie the 4th Subſtance, called the *vaſcular Series*.— Its Structure is extremely Simple, being a ſingle Courſe of greeniſh Veſſels, lodged between two Membranes.—Theſe Veſſels have a free Communication with the Wood and *Blea*.—Here are found the greateſt Part of the Juices for the Support of the Plant or Tree, all theſe paſs upwards or downwards, according as the Heat or Cold, Moiſtneſs or Dryneſs prevail.—Here the Weather has a great Influence, for as the Heat from the Sun gets Strength, in the Spring of the Year,

Year, it thins and expands the mucilaginous Juices here contained, and forces out the Bud. On the contrary, as the Cold of Winter advances, thefe Fluids are condenfed, thickened, and become mucilaginous.—We come next to the 5th, the Wood, and 6th, to the pyramidal Veffels contained therein; thefe pyramidal Veffels are not continued Tubes, are feldom found many Inches long, (as may be obferved in Oak, Elm, and Horfe Chefnut, &c.) and refemble thefe in the Bones of Animals.—A new circular Ring of thefe Tubes are formed every Year; thefe which are formed in Summer, are larger than thofe formed in Winter.—Thefe Rings of Tubes, facing the South, are alfo larger than thofe towards the North; fo that moft Trees are *eliptical* inftead of round, with the moft prominent Side towards the South.—A new Root, a new Branch, and a new Circle of Fibres are formed every Year: Thus it may be obferved, that a Root or Branch of the laft Year, has only one Circle of Fibres, whilft the other Roots and Branches, as well as the Trunk, have as many Circles as they

are

are Years Growth.—The Roots are pushed forward, and formed from a Substance, found at the Extremity of every fibrous Root, in Form of a spungy Nipple.—The 7th is the *Pith*.—Whatever Part of the Plant we examine, we find these *seven* and no more.—The Root, the ascending Stalk, and descending Fibre, are one and the same, and not three Substances.— The Fibres of the Root *are supposed to be simple, capillary, Tubes;* but, upon a minute Inspection, we discover them to consist of the same component Parts of the Plant.

The only Part remaining necessary to be described are the Leaves, which are found to be formed of a Number of Vessels, interwoven amongst each other, in a net-like Form, very much resembling the Anastomosis of the Blood Vessels in the Lungs of Animals, and appear to be of the same Use to Vegetables, that the Lungs are to Animals, viz. to throw off the superfluous Moisture; these have innumerable Openings, which answer both for the Discharge of the superfluous Moisture,

Moisture, and also for receiving the nutritious Particles from the Atmosphere.—The Leaves are formed by the expanding and unfolding the Buds: these Buds make a Perforation through the several Integuments, whereby an easy Passage is given for the expanding Sap, to enter, to enlarge, and unfold the Leaves, which are spread out thereby, and being full of Pores, the Heat from the Sun has an easy Passage through them, and thereby to enter their Fluids, and expand them, till they are *specifically lighter* than the surrounding Atmosphere, and are forced off by it.—These Pores also admit the descending Dew, when the Coldness of the Air is so far increased as to overpower the internal Heat of the Juices contained in the Plant.—Having given an anatomical Description of the different Parts of a Tree or Plant, if you desire any Thing farther on this Subject, I would advise you to consult *Malpighi* and *Grew*, or a more late Author, the ingenious Dr. *Hunter*.

In Order to prove my Theory on Vegetation, it may be thought necessary to produce some Experiments, as well as the *Phenomena* of Nature, to confirm it.—As I cannot make, or find any more fit for this Purpose, than these already made by Dr. Hales, who, (as will be allowed by all) was accurate in making, and faithful in relating them, and had no farther Intention to answer, but that Truth might appear; for the above Reasons I shall take the Liberty to transcribe some of them in his own Words.

Dr. Hales tells us, that in Order to be informed how far Heat and Cold answered the different Purposes of Vegetation, " He " made use of six Thermometers, the first of " which was above Ground, in the open Air; " the second two Inches under Ground, in a " South Aspect, the other four at different " Depths, till the sixth was two Feet under " Ground; (he tells us) that he kept a " Register of their Rise and Fall, during the " Month of August, and observed, that in " the greatest Noon-Tide Heat, the Spirit " in that Thermometer, which was exposed " to the Sun, was risen, since early in the
" Morning,

" Morning, from 21 to 48 Degrees.—The
" second Thermometer, whose Ball was two
" Inches under Ground, was at 45 Degrees,
" and the 3d, 4th, and 5th Thermometers
" were gradually of less and less Degrees of
" Heat, as they were placed lower in the
" Ground, to the sixth Thermometer, which
" was two Feet under Ground, in which the
" Spirit was 31 Degrees high; the 5th and
" 6th Thermometers, kept nearly to the
" same Height both Night and Day, till to-
" wards the End of the Month; when, as
" the Days grew shorter and cooler, they
" then fell to 27 and 25 Degrees. (t)

" When in the coldest Day in Winter,
" the Frost was so intense as to freeze the
" Surface of the stagnant Water, near an
" Inch thick; then the Spirit in the Ther-
" mometer, which was exposed to the open
" Air, was fallen four Degrees below the
" freezing Point; the Spirit of that Ball
" which was two Inches under Ground, was
" four Degrees above the freezing Point;
" the

(t) Hales's Staticks, Vol. I. Ex. XX.

"the 3d, 4th, and 5th Thermometers were
"proportionally fallen, lefs and lefs, as they
"were deeper to the fixth Thermometer;
"which being two Feet under Ground, the
"Spirit was ten Degrees above the freezing
"Point.—In this State the Work of Vege-
"tation feemed to be at a ftand, at leaft
"within the Reach of the Froft.—But when
"the Cold was fo far relaxed, as to have the
"Spirit in the firft Thermometer, but five
"Degrees above the freezing Point, the fe-
"cond eight, and the fixth thirteen Degrees,
"though it was ftill very cold; yet this be-
"ing fome Advance from Freezing towards
"*Warm*, and *there being confequently fome
"Expanfion in the Sap*, feveral Evergreens
"and hardy Plants grew."

The above Experiments of Dr. Hales, on the fix Thermometers, from that in the Air, to that which was two Feet under Ground, fhow us the different Degrees of Heat at the different Depths, and alfo the Manner in which they retained it.—It muft alfo be remembered, that Solids and Fluids acquire

their

their Heat fooner, and retain it longer, in Proportion to their Denfity.—Thus, put a Piece of Metal in Water, and place it on the Fire; the Metal will be fo hot as not to be touched, by the Time the Water is warm:— Alfo, if you fit near the Fire, with a Key in your Pocket, the Key will be hot, and your Cloths hardly warm.

The fame Thing may be obferved, where the Sun fhines upon a Piece of Metal; this, in a ftrong Sun-fhine, will be found to be much hotter than the furrounding Atmofphere.—The fame Effect may be obferved with Regard to Cold, as has been by Heat, viz. by expofing a Key to the *Cold Ether*, in a Froft, it will be found to acquire a Degree of Coldnefs, much exceeding that of the Atmofphere.— Hence, (as will be explained hereafter) as the Earth is 1500 Times denfer than the Air, fo it will be found, by that Means, to be very ufeful in carrying on Vegetation.

From the above Facts, I fhall endeavour

to draw proper Conclusions: In Order to do this, I shall observe the different Changes a Vegetable undergoes, from the Seed to a perfect Plant.—For this Purpose I shall make Choice of a Kidney-Bean; as in that, these different Changes, which the Seed undergoes, will be more perceivable than in some others.

By putting a Kidney-Bean into the Ground, and covering it with a proper Quantity of Mould, at a proper Season of the Year; in a few Days, the warm ascending Vapour from the Earth enters its Pores, and forcibly expands the Lobes of the Bean:—This expanding Vapour, (from the make of the Bean,) is forced from these Lobes into the capillary Vessels of the Radicle, which, by continually receiving a fresh Supply, is forced out and elongated, which when extended to a certain Degree, resists more than the Power from above; at this Time, still receiving additional Nourishment from the Earth, the expanded Seed Leaves are forced out of the Ground; after this the *Plume* being uncovered, by the opening of the Lobes, the expansive

pansive Force opens and unfolds its Leaves, and when they are sufficiently enlarged, so as to throw off the superfluous Moisture, becomes a perfect Plant, an hydraulic Machine, *Sui Generis,* and wants no more Assistance from the Lobes, which now drop off as useless.

Having now, according to my Proposal, explained the Method whereby a Seed becomes a perfect Plant, and, as my Letter is already extended to a greater Length than, perhaps, you will like to read at one Time, I will leave the Consideration of the Means and Causes of its Growth and Support, to my next Letter, which you may expect to receive soon after this.

Adieu,

F. PENROSE.

STONEHOUSE,
   Oct. 11, 1783.

To JOHN HEAVISIDE, Esq.

Experiments from Dr. Hales, which prove that Vegetables inspire and expire according to the Dryness and Moisture, and the Heat and Coldness of the Air.—The Method Nature makes use of to perform Vegetation.—Trees and Vegetables grow in the Form of a Pyramid, unless prevented.—The Cause assigned why Plants in a Green-house, or other Room, point towards the Window.—The Juices of Vegetables always in Motion, but do not circulate like the Blood in Animals.—Some more Experiments from Dr. Hales, to explain the Method Nature makes use of in the Bleeding Season, (in the Spring of the Year) to force out the Buds and Leaves.

DEAR SIR,

I Finished my last Letter with the Account of the Progress of a Vegetable from a Seed to a perfect Plant; and according to my Promise, I have sent you an Account of the

Methods

Methods Nature makes ufe for its future Growth and Support.

Having received the greateſt Information for doing it, from the Experiments of the judicious Dr. Hales, I ſhall now take the Liberty to make Uſe of ſome more of them, for confirming what I ſhall now ſend you.

The following Experiments were made in Order to obſerve the different Effects produced by the different Degrees of the Heat by Day, and the Cold by Night;—on the Growth of Vegetables; and alſo, the different Effects produced on them, by the different Changes of the Weather.—For this Purpoſe he planted a Cabbage and a Sunflower, each in a Pot, which he conſtantly weighed every Day, for a Month.—He found, "that ſome Days the Cabbage perſpired, "when the Weather was hot and dry, more "than a Pound and Half.—That the Sun- "flower, in twelve Hours, of a very warm "Day, perſpired one Pound and fourteen "Ounces; the middle Rate one Pound four "Ounces;

"Ounces;—The Perspiration of a warm, dry
" Night, without any sensible Dew, was a-
" bout three Ounces; but when any sensible
" but small Dew, then the Perspiration was
" nothing.—When a large Dew, and some
" little Rain in the Night, it increased in
" the Weight two or three Ounces. (u)

From the above Experiments, it may be observed, that these Vegetables perspired more or less, according to the State of the Atmosphere which surrounded them, whether it was warm or cold, moist or dry;— That they *perspired* most in a warm and dry Air; on the contrary, in moist Weather, or a large Dew, they *inspired* very considerably from the Atmosphere, as their Increase of Weight demonstrates.

Hence it is clear, from the foregoing Experiments, that the Leaves of Plants are serviceable towards carrying on the Work of Vegetation, in bringing Nourishment from the

(u) Hales's Staticks, Vol. I. Exp. 1.

the lower Parts and Roots;—Plenty of Dew is imbibed by them, by which Means they receive a great Part of their Food from the Atmosphere, which is always stocked with vegetable Nourishment.— Hence we find, that after the Plume of the Seed, and the Leaves are pushed out, they perspire or inspire, *according to the Heat*, the *Coldness*, the *Dryness*, or *Moistness* of the Air; in the Day-Time, when the Air is hot and dry, it dilates, and expands their Pores, (more especially when the Sun shines) and rarefies their Juices, whereby it ascends in the Atmosphere; thus a *Vacuum* is made, and Room is given, for the Sap ascending from the Roots!

The small fibrous Roots act the Part of *Syphons*, and the moist Vapour, ascending from the Earth, is absorbed or sucked in, by the Roots, faster or flower, more or less, in Proportion to the Number of Roots, and the Rarefaction of the Fluids in them; for these Juices will *recede* and *accede* according to the Heat and Rarefaction, or Cold and Compression, till an Equilibrium is formed:—When
that

that happens to be the Cafe, and every Pore and Veficle is filled, then the Moifture, Dew, or Rain will remain on the Leaves, in the fame Manner as it may be obferved to do on oiled Paper, when every Pore of the Paper is filled with Oil.—This may often be obferved in a growing Seafon, in the Morning, in the Spring of the Year.

Thus, fo long as the Heat proceeding from the Sun, is powerful enough to rarefy the Juices, in the Leaves of the Plant, to a fufficient Degree, they continue to perfpire the fuperfluous Juices, afcending from the Roots, and what they fend up, as regularly continue to fupply the Place of thofe perfpired; unlefs (as it fometimes happens) in a hot and fultry Day, that there is more Moifture perfpired by the Leaves, than the Roots can fufficiently fupply, during that Time.—When this happens to be the Cafe, we obferve the Leaves of the Plant to flag, and to continue in that State till the Coldnefs and Moiftnefs of the Air is fo far increafed as to prevent the Heat from rarefying more Juices than can be fupplied in the fame Time from the Roots.

As the Heat of the Sun goes off in the Evening, and the Air becomes colder, and loaded with Dew, the Perspiration of the Leaves abates, till the Coldness and Denseness of the Atmosphere, together with the descending Dew, fill up the Pores of the Leaves, stop the Motion of the Sap upwards, and by its Increase of Gravity, makes the Sap to descend towards the Roots, and carry with it from the Dew, such nutritious Particles of the Atmosphere, as it may contain: thus it finds its Way to the most capillary Roots, forces out the Sap that Way, and elongates them!

The Difference of Density between the Earth and the surrounding Atmosphere, adds greatly to the Growth or Elongation of the Roots of Trees and Vegetables: The Earth being so much denser than the Atmosphere, it retains the Heat, it receives from the Sun, a considerable Time longer; neither is it subject to the sudden and great Changes often occasioned in the Atmosphere; indeed some little below the Surface (as was proved by the

the Thermometers) it retains the same Heat great Part of the Summer, Night and Day.

It is the Nature of Trees and Vegetables, (if their Growth is not prevented by other Trees or Vegetables standing too near them) to take the Form of a Pyramid; the lowest lateral Branches being longer than those immediately above; and, as the Tree advances, the lateral Branches succeed in first, second, and third Order, &c.—Thus they continue to grow in this Manner, unless the Rarefaction and Perspiration of these lateral Branches are prevented by others growing too near them, as may be observed to be the Case in thick Woods, Groves, Corn, and other Vegetables, which stand so thick and close to each other, as to shade and hinder the Expansion and Condensation by the Heat and Air, and of Consequence the Perspiration of the lateral Branches.—When this happens to be the Case, the Rarefaction and Perspiration can only be carried on in the upper Part of the Tree or Plant:—Hence, by the Sap being perspired from the top Branches only,

the

the Tree is enlarged in no other Part, and grows in Height only; thus, by the Perſpiration being carried on no where but the Top, moſt, if not all, the lateral Branches, periſh for want of Perſpiration, and of Conſequence Nutrition.— Hence, the Reaſon why Trees grow upwards, for the Sun-Beams deſcend in ſtraight Lines to the Earth, and enter the Tree at its Top, whereby the greateſt Rarefaction will be there, and the Juices in the Tree, aſcending from the Root, will be forced thereto, and the Branches will there be enlarged and lengthened; but when Plants ſtand ſingle, or at a proper Diſtance, and ſurrounded with a Freedom of Air, the lateral Branches grow in a juſt Proportion to the Top, as *the Atmoſphere, and all Fluids, preſs equally every Way.*

Hence alſo is the Reaſon why Plants, in a Room or Houſe, where there is but one Window, (eſpecially if that Window faces the South;)—the Plants placed therein will always grow towards the Window, where the Sun-Beams and Light enter: Thus,

Plants

Plants which perspire very plentifully, as the Sun-flower, may be observed in Height of the growing Season, to follow the Sun, with their Tops pointing to him; in the Morning they bend towards the East, at Noon South, and in the Evening towards the West.—By the same Cause, Trees or Plants, near a Wall, always grow from it, pointing towards the Sun; nay if a Plant is placed in such a Situation, that no Sun-Beams are sent on it, its Growth will tend to the Place from whence the Light proceeds

Thus, during the Summer Season, when there is Heat enough to make Vegetables grow, their Juices are in continual Motion, as well as the Blood in Animals, but with this Difference; that the Blood in Animals undergoes a continual Circulation, but the Motion of the Sap in Vegetables, is only from their Roots, through their whole Substance, where, at particular Places, the *plastick* Make of those Parts absorbs and retains such Portions of the nutritious Juices, as are proper for their Support and Increase.—Thus it may

may be observed, particularly in a Grain of Wheat, which puts forth three different Succeffions of Roots, for the different Periods of its Growth; firft, after putting a Grain of Wheat in the Ground, three Fibres are fhot from the Radicle; upon the Wheat fpearing, frefh Fibres are ftruck out; foon after they are eftablifhed, the three firft Fibres, with their Branches, gradually decay.—As foon as it comes in Ear, frefh Fibres make their Appearance, foon after which the fecond decay. The above Account of thefe *three* Sorts of Roots, made by *culmiferous* Plants, are given us by the ingenious Dr. *Cullen*, who tells us it was a Difcovery of *Bennet's*, and are termed by him, the *Infancy*, the *Adolefcence*, and *Maturity* of the Plant.

Now let the Unbeliever, who makes an *Idol* of his own Underftanding, meditate on the Power given by God, to a Vegetable, to enable every Part thereof to cull and appropriate fuch Parts only, of the nutritious Juices they receive, as are fitted for the Growth and Support of thefe only, whether it be for Leaves,

B b Roots,

Roots, Stalks, Flowers, or Seeds.— If he cannot understand the Actions of this *simple Machine*, let it humble his Pride so far as not to be Wise above what is revealed!

Having explained the Method Nature makes Use of to cause the Vegetation and Growth of Plants, I shall now, as I proposed, endeavour to explain the Means whereby Trees push forth their Buds, Leaves, Fruit, and Seeds.—In Order to do this, I shall again take the Liberty to make use of some more of Dr. *Hales*'s Experiments, which he made on Vines, to ascertain the Strength of the Expansion of the Sap, at the Bleeding Season, in the Spring of the Year.—" April 6th, "at nine, A. M. Rain the Evening before, " he cut off a Vine, on a Southern Aspect, " two Feet nine Inches from the Ground; " the remaining Stem had no lateral Branches; " he fixed on it a mercurial Gage.—At 11, " A. M. the Mercury was risen 15 Inches.— " at 4, P. M. it was sunk an Inch." (v)

" April 7th, at 8, A. M. risen very little,
" a

(v) Hales's Staticks, Vol. I. Exper. XXXVI.

"a Fog:—At 11, A. M. 17 Inches high, "the Fog gone."

"April 10th, at 7, A. M. Mercury 18 Inches high; he then added more Mercury, so as to make the Surface 23 Inches high: *The Sap retreated a little into the Stem,* upon this additional Weight, *which shews with what an absolute Force it advances.*—At Noon it was sunk one Inch."

"April 11th, at 7, A. M. 24¾ Inches high, Sun-shine.— At 7, P. M. 18 Inches high."

"April 14th, at 7, A. M. 20¼ Inches high; at 9, A. M. 22½ fine warm Sunshine.—*Here we see that the warm Morning Sun gives a fresh Vigour to the Sap.*—At 11, A. M. the same Day, 16½—*The great Perspiration of the Stem makes it sink.*"

"April 16th, at 6, A. M. 19½ Rain.— At 4, P. M. 13 Inches."—Though it had sunk since Morning, he found by Exp. 34, that

that it had rifen fince Noon two Inches.—*This Difference he fays was accafioned, in the firft, by the Perfpiration of the Sap.*—The other Stem being *fo very fhort,* there was little Room for it."

" April 17th, at 11, A. M. 24¼ high, Rain and Warm; at 7, P. M. 29½ fine warm rainy Weather, *which made the Sap rife all Day, there being little Perfpiration by Reafon of the Rain.*"

" April 18th, at 7, A. M. 32½ Inches high, *and would have rifen higher, if there had been more Mercury in the Gage.*—From this Time, to May the 5th, the Force gradually *decreafed.*—The greateft Height of the Mercury being 32½ Inches, *the Force of the Sap was equal to* 36 Feet, 5⅓ Inches Height *of Water.*

" Here the Force of the rifing Sap in the Morning, is plainly owing to the Energy *(of the Sap)* in the Root and Stem.—In another mercurial Gage, (fixed under the Bottom

tom of the Vine, which ran twenty Feet high). the Mercury was raised by the Force of the Sap, 38 Inches, equal to 43 Feet, 3 Inches ½ of Water.—— As the greatest Height the Atmosphere will rise Water is thirty-two Feet, so this Force was about *one Third greater* than the Pressure of the Atmosphere."

Dr. Hales tells us " That the Mercury constantly subsided in a Gage, fixed on a Branch of a large old Vine, by the Retreat of the Sap, about nine or ten in the Morning, when the Sun was hot; but in a moist, foggy Morning, the Sap was later before it retreated viz. till Noon, or some Time after the Fog was gone."— About four or five o'Clock, P. M. when the Sun went off the Vine, the Sap began to push afresh into the Gages, but it always rose fastest from the Sun Rise, till nine or ten in the Morning.— The Sap on the Branch of a large old Vine played the most freely to and fro, and was therefore soonest affected with the Changes from hot to cold, or from wet to dry, and
Vice

Vice versa."(w)—He obferves that the great Force, exerted by the Branch of this large old Vine, " was not from the Root only, but muft alfo proceed from fome Power in the Stem and Branches."—After the Leaves are pufhed out, no Trees will then bleed, neither have they any Force to pufh out their Sap; *all* is then perfpired by the Leaves.— " Moifture and Warmth made the Sap moft " vigorous, Ex. 38, but the Vigour of the " Sap would immediately be greatly abated " by cold Eafterly Winds." (x)

" If, in the Morning, while the Sap is in a rifing State, there was a cold Wind, with a Mixture of Sun-fhine and Cloud; when the Sun was clouded, the Sap would immediately fubfide, at the Rate of an Inch in a Minute, for feveral Inches, if the Sun continued fo long clouded: But as foon as the Sun-Beams broke out again, it would immediately return to its then rifing State, juft as any Liquor in a *Thermometer* rifes and falls with the Alternacies of Heat and Cold; whence, fays he, it is probable, that the plentiful

(w) Hales's Exp. XXXVI.—(x) Exp. XXXVIII.

plentiful Rise of the Sap, in the Vine, in the Bleeding Season, is effected in the same Manner.—When, says he, three Tubes were fixed at the same Time to Vines on an *eastern*, a *southern*, and *western* Aspect, round my Porch, the Sap would begin to rise in the Morning, first in the eastern Tube, next in the southern, and last in the western Tube: and towards Noon it would accordingly begin to subside, first in the eastern Tube, next in the southern, and last in the western Tube."

" Rain and Warmth, after cold and dry, would make the Sap rise all the next Day, without subsiding, though it would rise then slowest about Noon.—The Sap begins to rise sooner in the Morning, in cool Weather, than after hot Days."

" When at the Distance of four or five Days, Tubes were fixed to two different Branches, which came from the same Stem, the Sap would rise highest in that which was last fixed; yet, if in the fixing the second

Tube,

Tube, there was much Sap loſt, the Sap would ſubſide in the firſt Tube."

" In very hot Weather, many Air-bubbles would riſe, ſo as to make a Froth an Inch deep, on the Top of the Sap in the Tube."

" But when towards the latter End of *April*, the Spring advances, and many young Shoots are come forth, and the Surface of the Vine is greatly increaſed and enlarged by the Expanſion of the ſeveral Leaves, whereby the Perſpiration is much increaſed, and the Sap more plentifully exhauſted, it then ceaſes to flow in a viſible Manner, till the Return of the following Spring."

" And as in the Vine, ſo is the Caſe the ſame in all the bleeding Trees, which ceaſe Bleeding as ſoon as the young Leaves begin to expand enough to perſpire plentifully, and to draw off the redundant Sap.

Exp. 44, " Since by other Experiments it is

is found, that the greatest Part of the Sap is raised by the Warmth of the Sun on the Leaves, which seem to be made broad and thin for that Purpose; for the same Reason it is probable, it should rise also, in those Parts which are most exposed to the Sun, as the Bark is" ——— " It is found that the Trunk and Branches of Vines were always in an imbibing State, *caused by the great Perspiration of the Leaves, except in the Bleeding Season."* (u)

Therefore to prove the great Power Seeds receive, (when sown) from the expansive Power of a warm Vapour — Dr. Hales put some Peas into an Iron Pot, with some Water, and then fixed on it a Cover, and on that 184 Pounds Weight, which the dilating Peas lifted up; he also found they would lift up any Weight that was not sufficient to press them together. (w) " We see, says he, by this
" Experiment, the vast Force with which
" swelling Peas expand; and 'tis doubtless
" the same *Force* which is exerted, not only
" in *pushing* the Plume upwards into the Air,
" but

(u, Hales's Staticks, Vol. I. Exp. XLVI.— (w) Vol. I. Exp. XXXII.

"but also in enabling the first Shooting of the Radicle of the Pea, and all its subsequent tender Fibres, to penetrate and shoot into the Earth."

Having now given the Experiments I proposed, with Regard to Vegetation, with some Observations thereon, in my next Letter, I shall endeavour to explain that Operation in as short and easy a Manner as I can.

Adieu,

F. PENROSE.

STONEHOUSE,
Oct. 18, 1783.

To

LET. VII. *On* VEGETATION.

To JOHN HEAVISIDE. Esq.

A Recapitulation of the Method Nature makes use of to carry on Vegetation.—The natural Agents hot and cold Ether.—Fire and Motion synonimous.—The Phenomenon of Vegetation a proper one to explain the Agency of Nature.—The Cause why Trees shed their Leaves in Autumn; and the Means made use of to push forth their Buds and Leaves in the Spring.—The Scripture Account of Vegetation perfectly agreeable with Nature. Cold and hot Ether, the Agents which support and carry on Animal as well as vegetable Life.

DEAR SIR,

IN my three former Letters, I described the Agents, and the Method Nature made Use of to carry on Vegetation, which were long, and which, I imagine, you thought tedious, on Account of the many Phenomena and Experiments there related, to prove that
what

what I said was confirmed by Nature.—I shall now, in Order that you may have a more clear Perception of it, recapitulate that natural Operation in as short and clear a Manner as I can.

A Recapitulation of what has been observed.

In the first Place I shewed from Sir Isaac Newton's own Words, that he supposed there was an *ethereal Fluid, which filled the Pores of all Bodies*; and also that this Fluid filled all Space, from the Sun to the Orb of Saturn, and beyond.

Secondly, That this Fluid acted in *two* Conditions, one of which he called *Light* or Heat, and the other *Spirit* or Cold.—That these two were in continual Circulation and *Struggle*, from the Sun to the Extremities of the System.—The Light or Heat, ascending from the Sun, *opening* and *expanding*; and, the Spirit descending to the Sun, *contracting* and *compressing* every Thing.— After this I gave *Boerhaave*'s Account of what were the Agents Nature made Use of

in

in her Operations, which was "That Fire
" or Motion were *synonimous*," for, says he,
" let an Iron Bar be heated, it increases in
" all its Dimensions, and the more so as it is
" farther and farther heated; but on being
" exposed to the *Cold*, it contracts, and its
" Parts are forcibly pressed together, and re-
" turn through all the Degrees of Dilatation,
" till it comes to its first Bulk, or to the
" same Degree of Heat which it had when
" the additional one was applied, being never
" two Minutes *of the same Dimensions*.——
" Hence, says he, if there were the greatest
" Cold, and all Fire were taken away, all
" Nature would grow into one concreate
" Body, *solid as Gold*, and *hard as a Diamond*.
" But upon the Application of Fire *it would*
" *recover its former Mobility*."

Finding that these two great Philosophers, as well all the Ancients, attributed the first Agent in Nature to be Fire; and that all Nature were filled with an Ether, which acted in two Qualities, viz. Light and Heat, or Spirit and Cold; and imagining that the
Phenomina

Phenomina produced by natural Operations, were more fimple, expreffive, and lefs equivocal than Experiments produced by Art; I endeavoured to find one that would anfwer our Purpofe; accordingly, that of Vegetation appeared to be moft likely to do it.—Therefore I examined the Obfervations and the Explanations of different Philofophers thereon; and found little Affiftance from any but the ingenious Dr. Hales, who, from a Set of well chofen Experiments, accurately performed, and faithfully related, hath cleared this fimple Operation from its Intricacy.

By which it appears, that a Seed is covered with an outward Shell, which is of fuch a clofe Contexture, as to prevent the common Atmofphere from entering.

The Seed, by being put into the warm Ground, is acted upon by the *warm Vapour*, which is continually afcending into the outward Atmofphere.—The *Light* or *Heat* of this active Vapour enters the outward Shell, penetrates and expands the Lobes of the Seed

Seed (which Lobes anſwer the ſame Purpoſe to Seeds, that the *Placentia* does to Animals) expands and enlarges them; from hence, by the *plaſtick* Make of the Seed, it is forced into the Radicle, which it alſo extends and elongates, and puſhes into the Mould, and by being continually acted upon in the above Manner, it continually increaſes, till by its Number of Fibres, it receives a greater expanſive Force, by the warm Vapour it receives from below, than what is ſupplied by the Lobes, which now burſt the incloſing Shell, and by this Force, from below, are impelled above Ground, when the *Lobes* ſeparate, and the *Plume* appears, which is now enlarged, and its Leaves ſpread abroad, and becomes a perfect Plant, and the Lobes or *Secondines* drop off as uſeleſs.

A Plant and a Tree are hydraulick Machines, and are ſupported and made to grow by the two Agents *Light* or *Heat*, and *Spirit* or *Cold.*—As either one of theſe act upon the Parts of the Plant or Tree, ſo does its Growth and Increaſe go on.—A Tree is compoſed of a
Root

Root which is in the Ground, a Trunk above the Ground, and Branches which are spread in the Air, anfwering to the Roots below.— Now it is found by Experience, that you may pull up a young Tree by its Roots, plant the Boughs or Branches in the Ground, and let its Roots fpread in the open Air, as its Boughs ufed to do, it will grow in this Form, pufh out Leaves, Bloffoms, Fruit, and Seed.— The Leaves are formed wide, thin, and full of Pores, and anfwer the fame Purpofe to Plants, that the Lungs do to Animals, to perfpire the fuperfluous Vapour fent up from the Roots.—Thus, in warm Weather, when the Sun fhines on the Leaves, the Light or Sun-Beams enters their Pores, expands their Juices, and as foon as they are fpecifically lighter than the Atmofphere, are forced off by it.—Hence a *Vacuum* is there formed, which is immediately filled up and fupplied by frefh Vapour afcending through the Tree or Plant, from the Roots.—In this Manner the Juices received by the Roots, are carried throughout the whole Plant or Tree; and, after it has collected

collected such a Portion of it as is fit for the Support of every Part, the superfluous Moisture is perspired by the Leaves:—This continues all the Day, till the Heat of the Sun-Beams begin to decline in the Evening, and the Cold increases.—Thus, as that comes on, the Cold condenses some of the Moisture in the Atmosphere, and presses it down towards the Earth, as the Heat goes off.—The cold, moist Air and Spirit enter the open Pores of the Leaves, and as they overpower the Heat, force the Juices through the whole Substance of the Plant, down to its smallest Roots, which they force out and elongate.—In this Manner the Plant grows and increases in Bulk, till the Cold is so very powerful, to contract or press the Juices into a *Concreate*, when all Vegetation ceases, and the Leaves drop off as useless.

Thus, as the Cold of Autumn comes on, the Juices of the Tree are inspissated, the Buds and outer Rind are covered with a gummy Substance, in the same Manner as is used to cover the Silk of a Balloon, to prevent

vent the common Air from having any access within.—As soon as this is done, the Trees which are used to shed their Leaves, drop them off as useless, and continue in a torpid State till the next Spring.—In April, the Sun-Beams have sufficient Power to enter the Bark of the Tree, which then expand its Juices, and make them fluid; and, by the continual Increase it receives every Day, it acquires a Force one third greater than the Pressure of the Atmosphere.—The Wood of the Tree being of a closer Nature, and resisting more than the Rind, the Juices are made to expand in the *Series* of Vessels between the Bark and the Wood, which communicates through every Part of the Tree, and particularly with the Buds, which have Openings made for that Purpose, through all the Integuments of the Bark, &c. where this expansive Force enters, develops the Buds, and forces out the Leaves; and when they are quite expanded, the Tree becomes a perfect hydraulick Machine, as was before described, and grows, and is supported as above.—Thus, as soon as the Leaves are pushed forth, the

expansive

expanſive Force of the Juices is gone, the Tree will no longer bleed, but inſpires or expires, and thereby keeps up a continual Motion of the Juices, till they are concreted by the coming on of the Winter cold.

Having explained the Operation of Vegetation, which Moſes tells us was performed on the third Day, by the natural Agents already found to be good, and capable to do the Office God aſſigned to them.—He now put them into Action, and by this Expreſſion, *let the Earth bring forth Graſs*, gave them Power to do it.—*Thus ended the third Day, or the third Revolution of the Earth.*

It gives me Satisfaction to find, that the Method and Agency of Vegetation above deſcribed, are repreſented to be the ſame in the Scriptures, and that in this Inſtance they ſpeak philoſophically true: For Moſes informs us, (w) that Vegetables could not grow, till the Earth was ſupplied with Water or Rain, and that they were made to grow by a
moiſt

(w) Gen. II. 5, 6.

moist ascending Vapour, which watered the whole Face or Surface of the Ground; and that *to those who hearkened to the Voice of the Lord, he will open his good Treasure, the Heavens, to give Rain to the Land, in his Season, and to bless all the Work of their Hands;* (x) and Job informs us, that Vegetables are nourished and supported by Earth and Water; and the Agents which perform this Operation, are the solar Light and Heat of the Day, and the Dew and Moon Shine; for, says he, *can the Rush grow without Mire or Mould? can the Flag grow without Water?* (y) Thus Moses, in his Blessings on the Tribes of Israel, tells the Tribe of Joseph, *that the Blessings shall be on their Land, for the precious Things of Heaven, for the Dew, for the precious Fruits brought forth by the solar Light, and for the precious Things put forth by the lunar Light;* (z) and in Samuel we are informed, that *the tender Grass springeth out of the Earth, by clear shining after Rain.* (1) And Job tells us, that *though the Root*

(x) Deut. XXVIII, 12.—(y) Job. VIII, 11.—(z) Deut. XXXIII. 12, 13. (1) 2 Samuel XXXIII, 4.

Root of a Tree wax old in the Earth, and the Stock thereof die in the Ground, yet there is Hope, if it be cut down, that it will sprout out again, and *by the Scent of Water or Vapour, issuing from the Earth, it will bud and bring forth Boughs like a Plant.* (2)

It may be remarked, that Animal Life is carried on and supported by the same Agents which carry on and Support the Vegetable, viz. *Light or Heat,* and *Spirit or Cold.*

Some Years ago I had the Honour of being acquainted with a Lady of Fortune, who lived in a large House, but did not keep a great deal of Company; she had a large Parlour which was made but little Use of.—In October I was shewn a Bat, who had taken up his Winter Lodgings on one of the Cornices.—I saw him many Times afterwards, between that and Christmas, when he appeared Motionless, as if dead.—At Christmas I persuaded the Lady to have a Fire in the Room, to see if it would procure Life to the Bat.

(2) Job. XIV. 7, 8, 9.

Bat.—She accordingly agreed that we should spend one Day in that Room, and have a large Fire therein.—Some Time after Dinner, when we did not think of it, we were entertained with the Flight of the Bat, who flew round the Room with great Life and Vigour.—But we found, the next Day, after a cold Night, that he was returned again to a torpid State.—The same Thing may be observed by bringing Flies into the Warmth any Time in the Winter; but what puts this beyond Doubt is, the hatching of Chickens in Stoves.—The Egg, like the Seed of Vegetables, is covered with a Shell, and these Eggs may be preserved in their present State, a long Time, if prevented from having only a proper Degree of Heat; but put them under a Hen, or in a Stove, of a proper Temperature, in three Weeks a Chicken will be produced, who will then break the Shell, live, breathe, and feed, and be so far a compleat Animal as to feed itself.

On the 4th Day we are informed, that God made two great Instruments of Light, and placed

placed them in the Firmament of Heaven, to regulate or rule the Day and the Night; that they were to divide between the Day and the Night—and that they were to be the *identical Instruments*, to point out and divide the Seasons, the Days, and the Years.— Thus it may be observed, that on this fourth Day, the Motion of the Heavenly Bodies began, and was carried on by the natural Agents; for God tells us, that he saw that they were good, and *capable to perform the Offices assigned to them.*—Here then, (as it is natural he should,) Moses begins his Chronology. (3)— The first four Days, till the Sun and Moon were formed, the Rotation of the terraqueous Globe was under the immediate Direction of God; but, now it was an *Automaton*, under his deputed material Agents, the Sun, (the Moon, the Stars, and the Heavens,) unless he thought proper, at any Time, by a Miracle, to stop or to alter their Agency, and so to convince skeptical and unbelieving Men.

I am, dear Sir, with the greatest Sincerity,
 Your obliged Friend,
F. PENROSE.
STONEHOUSE,
 Oct. 25, 1783.

(3) Introduction, P. 5.

To F. PENROSE, Esq.

Mr. Heaviside professes a great Inclination for the Study of natural Philosophy, though he had been prevented from attending to it so much as he wished.—He then puts the following Quere.—In that general Dissolution of Substances, which you suppose at the Deluge, why where not Shells, Bones, Shrubs, &c. *dissolved, as well as Rocks, Stones, &c.*

DEAR SIR,

I Cannot but take Shame to myself, at Sight of the Dates of the Letters you favoured me with, which I am sorry to say is above three Months ago; more especially as they were such as I felt, and still feel myself so much obliged to you for.

The only Apology I have to make, (and I wish I had not had it to make) is, that I was not well during the whole Autumn.—I was first seized with a Disorder in my Bowels,

(the

(the firſt I ever had) which continued three Weeks, and left a low Fever upon me, which continued as many Months.—I, however, kept on Foot all the Time, but very uncomfortably; till being quite weary of ſo long and diſagreeable a Viſitor, I determined to take a Ramble, and try to loſe him, which I put in Execution, and with Succeſs: For having rambled, for three Weeks, thro' the North of England, I returned Home very much better, and have been very well, thank God, for above a Month paſt; though, perhaps the conſtant Hurry I have lived in, during that Time, may have contributed not a little, to keep me well.

I employ this, my firſt Hour of Leiſure, to acknowledge and thank you for the Trouble you have been ſo good as to give yourſelf, to explain your Ideas of the Cauſes of thoſe Appearances we now ſee on this terraqueous Ball.—But pray do not imagine, that becauſe I have not made it ſo much my Study as you have, that therefore I take no Pleaſure in Natural Philoſophy, or that I am ſo eaſily tired

tired of the Subject, as not to wish for the Sentiments of so ingenious and well-informed a Searcher into Nature, as you are.—Far otherwise; for though I have been debarred of proper Opportunities of Information, and my Habits of Life have been such, as to prevent me from any close Application to Study, yet I have always felt a Propensity to know and account for the Phenomena of Nature, and the Causes of those various Appearances, which every Moment, and every where, strike the Eye of the least attentive Observer.

But as my Inlets to Knowledge have been few, very few indeed, compared to yours, it would be extreme Folly in me to contend *seriously* with you on this Subject; and therefore would wish you to look on what I object to your System, as rather designed to draw out *Information*, than to produce *Conviction*. In this Light, give me Leave to ask you, why, in that general Dissolution of Substances, which you suppose to have taken Place at the Deluge, those Shells, Bones, Shrubs, &c. that are undoubtedly found (as you

you say) in all Parts of the World, both on the Summits of Mountains, and in the Depths of the Earth; *why were not thoſe Subſtances diſſolved likewiſe?* And what Reaſon can be given, why the Cauſe, (whatever it was) that could diſſolve Rocks, and Marble, ſhould not diſſolve thoſe Subſtances which are of ſo much looſer a Contexture? This is a Queſtion which has juſt now occured to me, on looking into the Beginning of your Letters; and I muſt confeſs, it ſeems to me as rather favourable to my Hypotheſis than yours.—I ſhall therefore be much obliged to you for your Thoughts upon it; and as my preſent Leiſure will not allow me to enter further into your Theory, at this Time, I ſhall beg Leave to defer my further Conſideration of it, till my Hurry is a little over, when I ſhall, with your Permiſſion, trouble you with what further Remarks may occur to me upon it.

I am,
  Dear Sir,
   Your very obedient,
    And faithful Servant,

Prince's-Street,
     J. HEAVISIDE.

Sunday, Jan. 11, 1784.

LETTER IX.

To JOHN HEAVISIDE, Esq.

Prejudices of Education hard to be overcome, therefore many Things in Mr. Penrose's Theory may appear doubtful at first, as they differ from some which are generally taught: There may be Arcana *in Nature, which human Reason may not be able to explain.—Answer to Mr. Heaviside's last Query.—A Constitution and Custom observed by the Royal Society, concerning Disquisitions.—The Waters the Outside of this terraqueous Globe, not sufficient for the Flood.—Centre of Gravity altered at the Flood.—Causes assigned why Bones, Shells, &c. were not dissolved.*

DEAR SIR,

YOUR Mind being prepossessed with *Ideas* very different from many Things in my Theory, I doubt not but some will *stick* with you, *at first,* (whatever they may do afterwards) I am sure they did so with me; but as neither you or I are any further concerned

cerned than for the Amusement of ourselves, and the Investigation of Truth; so we shall be more likely to agree about them, than the generality of Disputants; whose Endeavours are often to explain the Truth away; and I trust, we shall be both ready to embrace it, let it be found by either of us.

In Order to get at *Truth*, we ought to suspect our own preconceived Opinions, to divest ourselves as much as may be from our Prejudices, and make use of the greatest Impartiality in Judgement; for we must observe, how greatly all People are *biassed* to the *Ideas* which have been ingrafted on their *Understanding, by Education and Custom*; notwithstanding some of them may be the greatest Absurdities.—Thus, for Instance, we find many of the Wives of the Indian Kings are brought to believe, that by Self Murder, *(a Crime which we think the greatest, and most contrary to Nature!)* they shall inherit the greatest Bliss.—Under this Persuasion, many throw themselves into the Funeral Pile with their dead Husbands; encouraged and animated

mated to it, by thofe who are believed to be the beft and wifeft of their People.— We may alfo obferve, that a Perfon educated in Italy, will be a Catholick; in England, a Proteftant; in Turkey, a Mahometan; in India, a Gentoo.— *Errors*, from the fame Caufe, reign in Philofophy as well as Divinity; our philofophical Opinions are generally formed in the fame Manner, *from Education, and the Company we keep*; and often under the Protection of fome great *Name*, whofe Notions few dare to oppofe, or even to inveftigate or examine. — Thus the Earth, Moon, and Planets were believed to circulate round the Sun, by the Ancients, down to *Pythagoras*.—After that the *Ptolemean* Syftem took Place, then the *Tychonic*, and now the ancient Syftem is again recovered by *Copernicus*, and his Followers, and demonftrated to be true by the *immortal Newton*, and believed by nearly All.

The above Obfervations fhew us how eafily we are made to believe falfe Opinions by Education, and with what Difficulty they are

are eradicated afterwards.—A great many of them are often believed to be innate, and implanted in our Mind by God.—Hence, in Matters of Confequence, we fhould not receive *implicitly* thofe Opinions we have been taught, or are generally believed as true, *without Examination*; wherever this is the Cafe, it muft be a great Obftacle to Improvements in Arts and Sciences.—For the above Reafons, though I may obferve fome Things which are contrary to your preconceived Ideas, or to general received Opinions, or what you may have been taught to be true; yet, I hope, from your known Impartiality, you will not difcard them without Examination.

You have chofen a Queftion, the Anfwer to which will affift to elucidate my Theory, and I hope my Explanation of it may prove fatisfactory to you; although, as you obferve, it has a contradictory Appearance.—" Why
" in that general Diffolution of Subftances,
" which you fuppofe to have taken Place at
" the Deluge, thofe Shells, Bones, Shrubs,
" &c. that are undoubtedly found (as you
" (fay

"say) in all Parts of the World, both on
"the Summits of Mountains, and in the
"Depths of the Earth; why were not these
"Substances dissolved, and what Reason can
"be given, why the Cause (whatever it was)
"that could dissolve Rocks and Marble,
"should not dissolve these Substances which
"are of a much looser Contexture?"

In the first Place, I shall beg Leave to observe, that though the whole Operations of Nature are ALL carried on in a *mechanical Manner*, yet there may be some *Arcana* which may be out of human Power to explain.—But it is the Duty of every Searcher after Truth, not to evade the Question.—But if he cannot explain it, to confess it.—I hope, from what follows, that you will think, that I do not make the above Observation with a Desire to get rid of your *Query*, but only to lay in my Claim, lest I should want it hereafter.—However, you shall find that I will answer quite to the Point in Question, without Evasion.

I shall

I shall now pursue the same Method I did in my former Letter, first giving the historical Account of the Event, and then prove it to be true from Facts or Observations.

It may be observed, that Moses, in giving us the Account of the Flood, (which in Fact is the only one we have, or can have) tells us, that God said "*I, even I*, do bring a "Flood of Waters upon the Earth."—According to this Account, it was a *Miracle*, performed by God himself, by altering the Operations of Nature; but yet performed by material Agents, in a *mechanical* Manner.— Had it not been performed by material Agents, it could not be Evidence to our Senses, neither could we understand it, whilst our whole Machine, by which we receive our Ideas, is material.

In Order to explain these seeming Contradictions, I shall observe the Method directed by the Royal Society.—" The Con-
" stitution and Custom of which are, that
" every Disquisition must either terminate in

"a mathematical Demonstration, or be form-
"ed upon some one or more Experiments,
"Observations, or Histories of Facts, for a
"Foundation of Reasoning, and the Con-
"clusions drawn, must necessarily appear to
"flow from the Premises; and the Danger
"of drawing general Conclusions in natural
"Philosophy, and Physical Disquisitions, lies
"not in Arguments, *a Posteriori*, from the
"Effect to the Cause; but in the *hypothetick*
"Way, that is, by Parity or Similitude; to
"Parity and Similitude of Effects, which
"must be often a fallacious Method, and the
"Source of many Errors; for this same
"Cause, acting by one and the same Power,
"according to the same Laws, is often made
"to produce not only different, but even
"contrary Effects, according to the specifick
"Differences of the Subjects acted upon.—
"Thus Heat makes Clay hard, but softens
"and melts Wax, Metals, &c."—The Case
before us is another Instance of the same
Kind.

Here we have two Facts open to our View,
(besides

(besides a Number of others of the same Original) viz. the hardest Rocks shew us, that they were in a State of Solution, when the Shells, Bones, &c. were mixed with their very Substance; on the contrary, that these Shells, Wood, and Parts of Vegetables, are almost in a perfect State, though of a much looser Contexture.

I believe all Philosophers, who have wrote on the Flood, have allowed, that there was not a sufficient Quantity of Water on the Outside of this Globe, to cover it a tenth Part so high above it, as we are told the Waters prevailed.—If this is so, and the Fact is true, we must search some other Place for it? none will be found but within the Bowels of this Earth; accordingly Moses tells us, that this Flood was brought on " by the breaking up the " Fountains of the great Deep, and opening " the Windows of Heaven."—(Or, as it is expressed in the Original) opening the Cracks and Chinks, whereby Air passes through the Earth.—That Steam or Vapour is continually passing through them, is at this Time observed by Miners. It

It appears, before this *Phenomenon* could succeed, that the Centre of GRAVITY (let it be a Power inherent in *Solids* or *ab extra*) and the Attraction of Cohesion must be altered.—Let us suppose (for suppose it we must, as we are not informed of it) that God by his own Act, (I even I, says Jehovah) altered the Place of the Centre of Gravity, from within the Earth, to such a Distance on the Outside; the Consequence would be as Moses has told us it was.—The Waters would flow outwards by all the Fountains, Openings, and Chinks of the Earth, Rocks, &c. (the Number of which will be more easily conceived by viewing our Cliffs of Marble, than can be described) which would make no Resistance (Gravity being altered) but would be dissoved and carried away by the Impetuosity of the Efflux, and with many other Bodies, make one common *Colluvies*.

It may be observed in this common Destruction, that Earth, Rocks, Stone, &c. (which were kept or bound together by *Gravity or Attraction of Cohesion,*) on the Alteration

ation of the Centre of Gravity, and the Efflux, caused thereby, of the Waters, must be reduced, if not quite, *nearly* to their smallest Parts.—— On the contrary, Shells, Bones, Shrubs, Leaves, &c. which are not held together by Gravity, or Attraction of Cohesion, but by Fibres, Sinews, Tubes, Membranes, &c. tied, twisted, and complicated together in a wonderful Manner, would not be affected by it; the Attraction of Gravity would not untwist their Fibres, therefore those Parts of Animals and Vegetables, notwithstanding their soft Texture, would remain as before.

After the Waters had prevailed God's appointed Time, Moses tells us that God remembered Noah, and would not suffer him to be destroyed, which he must have been, had the Waters not assuaged.—God, by his own immediate Act, by *his Spirit*, or what may be called Ether, (this is the same Word as translated Spirit, Gen. 12.) restored the Power of Gravity to the Place appointed to

it

it before the Flood; and the terraqueous Globe was again restored to its pristine Form. (4)

From what has been observed, the following Conclusion seems naturally to arise, that Gravity was the Agent which forced off the Waters.—If so, is Gravity a material Power? If it is, does it lie in Solids or Fluids?—No great Difficulty seems to be in giving an Answer to the above Questions!

Farewell, my dear Friend, till I write you again, which I will do soon.

F. PENROSE.

STONEHOUSE,
Feb. 2, 1785.

(4) See Let. I. III.

To JOHN HEAVISIDE, Esq.

As the first material Agents cannot come within the Knowledge of our Senses, so different Philosophers have formed different Opinions. But Astronomy may be proved by mathematical Demonstration.—History is no more than a Romance without Chronology; which is not certain, unless proved by Astronomy.—Where to begin our Astronomical Epoch.—Moses's Account of the Place *of the Sun and Moon at the Creation, proved by Mathematical Demonstration.—First Meridian proved by an Observation of Dr. Bradley's.—As Mr. Penrose is not fearful of being convicted of Error, Leave is given to Mr. Heaviside to shew this Letter to any Proficient in Astronomy, and get their Criticisms on it.*

'Dear Sir,

I Thank you for your Present of the Book, on the Deluge, which I have read already—It is coming down in Betsey's Box, on board the Rose; when it arrives, I shall give it another Reading, and doubt not but I shall receive Satisfaction from some Parts of it; and I shall, (which I assure you I always do) *endeavour* to divest myself of all preconceived Ideas.—As the first material Agents, have not, neither ever can they come under the Examination and Knowledge of our Senses; so different Sects of Philosophers have formed different Hypotheses about them, which has been the Cause of such a Variety of Opinions.—For some Years past, my principal Study has been Astronomy.—A most sublime Science! The *Phenomena* of which may be proved from *mathematical Demonstration*; but even this Proof will be of no Signification to those who have *preconceived* Principles of a different Nature, and are thereby *prevented from examining* whether they be true or not.—There is another Thing against my Notions in Astronomy; it requires some Attention to understand them; therefore few will be proper Judges of them; some of them are contrary to the general preconceived Opinions, and as popular Prejudices are difficult to be overcome,

come, fo thefe Notions of mine will be oppofed.—This Study is certainly of great Ufe; for Hiftory is no more than a Romance, without Chronology, and there can be no Certainty in Chronology, unlefs proved by Aftronomy: Indeed without fome fixed and aftronomical *Era*, to which hiftorical Narrations may be referred, however true in themfelves, they will be deemed very little preferable to Romance. — Tho' I have heretofore troubled you with fome of my Notions on Philofophical Subjects, which, perhaps, you may have thought both a Wafte of Time and Trouble to read over; yet, you fee I am fo fond of fcribbling, that I cannot help perplexing you with a brief Account of fome of my aftronomical Ideas.

In the firft Place, I muft agree with *Keil*, who fays, " As in the Heavens there are cer-
" tain Points, from which Aftronomers be-
" gin their Computations of the Planets
" Motions, fo alfo there muft be certain
" Points, or Inftants of Time, from which,
" as from Roots, all Calculations muft begin;
" and

" and all memorable Actions are difpofed and
' recorded, according to the Series of Years
" which follows from that Root. Thefe
" Roots are called *Epochs* or Eras, from
" which we generally count our Years or
Times." (5)

The Beginning of Time may be confidered as an *indivifible Inftant*; but Time is a *determinate fucceffive Duration*, meafured by Motion; fo that Motion and Time are cœtaneous. If we trace it back to the firft Moment, it muft be the Inftant before planetary Motions had any Exiftence, or were Nothing; and when planetary Motions fhall ceafe, then cometh the End of Time.

If we know any thing when planetary Motion or Time began, (as moft Hiftorians pretend to,) it muft be difcovered, either by Obfervation or Calculation, or be revealed from God. But as there was no human Witnefs to the Creation, it could not be difcovered by Obfervation, neither could it be difcovered by

(5) Introduction, Page 7.

by Calculation: But Mofes has revealed it; and I have certainly the Liberty to take Mofes's Account as true, if I hereafter prove, from Mathematical Demonftration, that it is fo.

Hence I begin my Epoch of Aftronomy, on the fourth Day of the Creation, when, Mofes tells us, the Sun and Moon were formed and placed in the Heavens, *to point out Times and Seafons, Days and Years.* — Here then we have one *Datum* or Root, viz. the fourth Day of the Week, twelve o'Clock, (which it muft be on the Place in which the Sun was in the Meridian.) *Jofephus* tells us, the Jews reckoned their Years by the Sun, and their Months and Days by the Moon. Mofes alfo orders the Ifraelites (leaft they fhould be at a Lofs when to begin their Days) to keep their Sabbaths from Evening to Evening.[6] Hence we find that the Chronology of Time began, on the fourth Day, *at Evening*, which was the Day after the Moon's Oppofition, or when fhe was full; when they
(viz.

---

(6) Levit. XXIII, 32.

(viz. the Sun and Moon) enlightened the whole Earth, as Mofes tells us. — That the Ifraelites, and their Pofterity, might not be at a Lofs to know the Time of the Year, and alfo the Diftance of the Moon from the Sun, Mofes inftituted the Feaft of Ingathering, *(after they had gleaned up their Olive and Vineyards)* to be kept in Remembrance of that great Event.—This Feaft was to be kept on the 15th Day of the Moon (as it is in the Hebrew) or Month, in the *End or Revolution* of the *(Solar)* Year.[7] As every Month was begun on the Evening of the Vifibility of the Moon, fo this 15th Day muft be juft after fhe was paft the full. The Jews keep their Feafts of Tabernacles and Ingathering in this Manner, to this Day; and, according to their Tradition, it is in Commemoration of the Creation of the World, which happened at this Seafon; viz. at the autumnal Equinox, the Sun in *Libra*, at the full of the Moon. To be fhort. [8]

I fhall now affume the following *Data*, and prove,

---

(7) Exodus, XXIII, 16—Deut. XV, 13. —— (8) Indroduction, Page 6.

prove, by Mathematical Demonſtration, that they are true. Viz. 1ſt, that the Sun was formed on the fourth Day of the Week, at the Creation, at twelve o'Clock, in the firſt Meridian, at the Autumnal Equinox, or the Sun in Libra, the Moon 15 Days paſt the Conjunction, the Day after the Oppoſition.

Secondly.—That according to the Moſaic Account, A. D. 1753, is in Connection with A. M. 5760, and Time is meaſured, poſitively and abſolutely, by the Rotation of the Earth round its Axis, or a natural Day; and its annual Revolution thro' the Ecliptic. If, therefore, I prove that A. D. 1753, is the ſame identical Year with A. M. 5760, it muſt be mathematical Demonſtration that the above Aſſumitions are true. Now, (9)

A. D. 1753, we know to be the ſame Year as 6466, according to the Julian Period. I ſubſtract Moſes's Account of the Age of the World, 5760, from 6466 of the Julian Period, there remains 706, in Coincidence with the

---

(9) Introduction, Page 25.

the Year of the Creation. — The Julian Year is 11 Minutes longer than the Solar tropical Year, by which Means the Equinox fell back 44 Days, and, according to the Julian Kalendar, from Oct. 25, to Sep. 22, N. S.

Multiply 5760 the Number of annual Revolutions, or Solar Years.
By 1461 the Number of Rotations of the Earth round its Axis, or natural Days in a Quadriennium.

    5760
  34560
  23040
   5760

Divide by the Years in a Quadriennium. } 4)8415360 (2103840 Days in 5760 Julian Years.
Days of Retroceffion in 5760 Julian Years, 44 to be fubftrct.

Sun in Libra, A.D. 1753, A.M 5760, 2103796 A.I.P. 6466, *true Solar Days.*

To know the Day of the Week, add the extra Days before the Sun and Moon meafured Time.   4

Divide by 7) 2103800 (300542 Weeks
fince the Creation, or in 5760   (6)(Saturday.
Solar Years.

TABLE.

A. I. P. 706. Sun in Libra. Firſt Meridian	Interval. 5760 Years. 2103796 Days.	A. I. P. 6466. Sun in Libra. Firſt Meridian.
D. H. M. Oct. 25. 00. 00.		D. H. M. Sep. 22. 00. 00.

By

By a very accurate Obfervation, Dr. Bradley obferved that the Sun entered Libra A.D. 1753, September 22, on *a Saturday*. This had not happened before, fince the Creation, neither can it happen again, on the fame Hour and Minute, and Day of the Week, for many Thoufand Years to come; therefore 1753 muft be in Connection with A. M. 5760; this proves it to be as mathematically certain, that the Year, Day, Hour, and Minute, and Day of the Week, happened at the the Time when Mofes tells us it did, as it is to meafure the Diftance from Hatfield to London, by a Wheel: For Here are two Points, viz Hatfield and London; by running a Wheel from Hatfield to London, you will know how many Rotations the Wheel makes, between Hatfield and London: So here you have two Points, viz. the Autumnal Equinox, A. I. P. 706, or the Year of the Creation, and the Autumnal Equinox, A. I. P. 6466, in which Time the Earth performed 5760 annual Revolutions, and 2103796 Rotations round its Axis, which meafured the Interval, and united the two

Points

Points together.—Hence we have mathematical Demonstration that Moses's Chronology is true; and also, we have an *Epoch* whereon to begin our astronomical Enquiries.—The above is trifling Evidence, to what may be brought by the Astronomy of the Sun and Moon, by all the *Eclipses, Equinoxes, Solstices, new, and full Moons*, which have happened since the Creation.

I am not very fearful to be convicted of Error, in what I have said above, therefore (as perhaps you may meet with *Adepts* in Astronomy) I shall have no Objection to your shewing them what I have said; and, as Truth is the Object sought, I should be glad to hear their Criticisms on it.

I am,
  Dear Sir,
   Your obliged Friend,
    And Servant,
     F. PENROSE.

STONEHOUSE,
Wednesday, Feb. 9, 1785.

To F. PENROSE, Esq.

Mr. Heaviside having shewed Mr. Penrose's Letter to some eminent Astronomers, Members of the Royal Society; they " all agreed " that his Calculations were perfectly right, " and proved what He intended they should; " and that they would *have desired Leave to* " *have read the Paper at the Meeting of the* " *Royal Society; but that it was deemed to* " *be connected with religious Subjects, which* " *they never meddle with there.*" Queries to Mr. Penrose, *occasioned by the aforesaid Letter.*

DEAR SIR,

I AM highly obliged to you for your kind Letter, and for being so good as to state to me the Proofs of the Truth of the Mosaical History of the Creation: They are certainly very learned and ingenious; I have read them with great Pleasure, and have only to lament my own Ignorance, in not being able (for want of more Science in Astronomical Matters) to fully comprehend their Force. As you have always been so good as to make Allowance for my Ignorance on any Philosophical Subjects, and hear, without Offence, my Objections to some of your Opinions; so, I hope, you will pardon me for asking you a few Questions, not in the Way of *Objections*, but merely for Explanations, that I may the better comprehend the Whole of your Theory; which, I presume, is this, viz. that according to Moses's Account of the Creation, and the Number of Years he makes it from thence to the Flood; added to the Years from the Flood to the coming of our Saviour; and from thence to the Year 1753 of our Æra, making up the Number 5760, the true and real Age of the World, is thereby fully ascertained, and Moses's History proved to be a true one of the Creation *at that Time*.

You have proved, from Dr. Bradley's Observation, that the Whole Planetary System was in the exact Position, in the Year of our Lord 1753, that they were, and must necessarily farily have been at the Creation; and that they had not, nor could have been in the like Situation for 5760 Years before; nor will, probably, be so again, for as many to come. I shall therefore call this 5760th Year, the Year of the great *Cycle* of the Universe: But whether I call it properly so, or not, I do not know; nor does it much signify, if you will give me Leave to use it as a Term, by which you may understand my Meaning. Now I would ask what Proofs can be adduced, that the same Cycle, or Number of Revolutions, may not have happened over and over again, before Moses's Date of the Creation.

I must also beg you to explain the Use of your Table, and why in the one is Oct. 25, and in the other Sept. 22. I subjoin the Table as I copy it from yours.

TABLE.

A. I. P. 706. Sun in Libra. First Meridian.	Interval.	A. I. P. 6466. Sun in Libra. First Meridian.
H. M. Oct. o oo.	5760 Years. 2103796 Days.	D. H. M. Sep. 22. oo. oo.

I know that I expose my Ignorance in asking this, but I am not ashamed of doing that to you, who already know it so well.

The above I wrote (as what occurred to me on the first attentive Perusal of your Scheme) as soon as I had read it; and, having your Permission, I afterwards copied it, and shewed it to two or three of my Friends, whom I thought better acquainted with Astronomy than myself.

One of these I knew to be intimate with an eminent Astronomer, of the Royal Society; and, as I wished, he asked my Leave to shew it to him, which I readily gave him. He called on me a few Days ago, and told me that that Gentleman was much pleased with it, and had kept it till now, that he might shew it to his Astronomical Friends of the Society; and that they *all* agreed that your Calculation was *perfectly right*, and *proved* what you intended it should do: But, at the same Time, they made the same Observation upon it that I had done, viz. that it did

not

not prove that there had not been previous Revolutions (or Cycles, as *I* call it) to that mentioned above. You will not wonder that I was both surprized and pleased, to find that *I*, who am *un-*learned in such Subjects, should thus have *blundered* upon what had struck all these *learned Men*.

I must add, that the Astronomical Gentleman would have desired Leave to read the Paper at the Meeting of the Royal Society; but that it was deemed to be connected with *religious* Subjects, which they never meddle with there.

I find you will, in Time, give me an Itch for Philosophizing likewise, which hitherto I have only amused myself with now and then, as it has fallen in my Way. As a Proof of this, I have lately often thought of our Conversation at Hatfield, wherein you explained Sir Isaac Newton's Assumption of the inexplicable Terms of Gravitation and Attraction, and in their Place, affirmed that Fire, or Heat, answered all the Purposes equally, and

was

was a Subftance, or Quality, known and allowed by all. As we had not then Leifure to develop the Whole of your Ideas on that Subject, I fhould efteem it a great Favour if you would be fo kind as to give me a general View of your Opinions upon it, whenever you have Leifure, and find Inclination to gratify me with it.

I am,

Dear Sir,

Your very obedient,

And obliged Servant,

J. HEAVISIDE.

Prince's-Street,
March 20, 1785.

To JOHN HEAVISIDE. Esq.

Moses's History of the Creation ought to be examined by Chronology and Astronomy, which is the true Test of all History. — The Cycle of Years explained; — Answer to Mr. Heaviside's last Queries; — Ether the Cause of Gravitation; — Gravity and Levity relative Terms. — The Agency of the Ethers explained; — they are the Cause of Winds, Hurricanes, Earthquakes, &c. — they alter or destroy Attraction, Gravitation, Cohesion, &c. Is the Cause of the different Motions of the Earth, and its spheroidal Shape; the Cause of Tides, &c.

DEAR SIR,

I Thank you for your last Letter, which (by informing me, that what I had written to you had received the Approbation of some eminent Astronomers, Members of the Royal Society) gave me great Pleasure, as their Approbation does me a greater Honour than

than ever I expected to receive.—So learned a Body of Men (by the Discouragement they have given to Guess, Speculation, and Hypothesis) have been the Means of those distinguished Improvements, which the Sciences have received: It being one of their Constitutions to admit Nothing *but what must terminate in Mathematical Demonstration, or what is founded on Facts, and Reasonings and Calculations which necessarily flow from them.* — I think we should pay the *same* Regard to Moses's Account of the Creation, as we would do to any other Historian. — For, as I observed in my last Letter, History, if not proved by Chronology, is no more than a Romance; and there can be no Certainty in Chronology, unless proved by Astronomy.— On the Contrary, History and Chronology, which is proved by the Situation of the Sun and Moon, at the Time these Events happened, and confirmed by Eclipses, when the Moon intersects the Earth's Orbit; together with her Oppositions and Conjunctions, &c. must be as true as that there is a Sun and Moon; for their Conjunctions and Oppositions

tions will occur, at their appointed Seasons, as long as Time shall last. — Thus we know, by Calculation, that *Ptolemy*'s Account of the most ancient Eclipse of the Moon to be true; as we find, by Calculation, it must have happened, at the Time He mentions, either at Alexandria or Babylon: — I would try Moses's Account of the Creation in the same Manner.

The Gentlemen you shewed my Scheme to, as well as you, very justly observe, that the Exactness of it depended upon a *Cycle* of Years, and tho' my Calculations were perfectly right, *yet they did not prove but that there might have been many Cycles before the Time mentioned by Moses.* — In Regard to the Time of the Creation; it must have been known, (if known at all,) either, 1st from Observation, or, 2ndly, it must be proved by Calculation; or, 3d'y, it must be revealed. — It could not be observed, as there was *then* no Human Person to observe it; neither could it be found out by Calculation: But Moses informs us it was revealed, and to confirm his Account,

Account, has given us the Situation of the Sun and Moon, and Day of the Week, at that Minute of Time.—*These are Facts!* and I think it cannot be imagined that Moses (who wrote at a Time when Astronomy was little known) should be able to calculate the exact Place of the Sun and Moon, at the particular Instant of Time of that Event, which he tells us happened more than Two Thousand Years before he was born.—I therefore, think that if, on Calculation, we find that his Astronomical Account be true, we ought to allow his Fidelity, as an Historian, to be confirmed.

In order to find the Cycle of Years,

      Multiply 525949 the Minutary Measure of a Solar tropical Year,
      Into   5760 the given Number of Solar tropical Years.

Divide the Product
By 2103796) 3029466240 (1440 equatareal Minutes sought.
The Number   4 Cycles.
of the Earth's Rotations
about its Axis.   A. M. 5760 in Connection with A. D. 1753, when Dr. Bradley made his Observation at Greenwich.

In Regard to your other Question, *Why I made*

made *Time* to begin Oct. 25, and the *Cycle of Years* to end Sept. 22?

To explain myfelf as well as I can, why thefe *Cycles* began Oct. 25, and ended Sept. 22. I obferve, that the *Julian* Year confifts of 365¼ Days, (or Rotations of the Earth,) but this Quadrant, or Quarter of a Day, or fix Hours, is not compleated on the fame Meridian where the Rotation began, but 11 Minutes more Eaftward on the Equator.— This Preceffion of 11 Minutes *of Rotation Eaftward*, makes 11 Minutes *in Time Weftward*, (as in the Calendar); fo that the precife Length of the Year is 365D. 5H. 49M. Thus, if the Solar Year began in any Meridian, exactly at Noon, the fecond Year it would begin 11 Minutes before fix in the Evening; the third 22 Minutes before Midnight; the fourth 33 Minutes before fix in the Evening, and end 44 Minutes before Noon.— Hence a Day is added to every four Years, and that Year is what we call *Biffextile or Leap Year*: And in a Cycle of 1440 Years, having paffed every Minute on the *Equator*, the

the Year and Day will begin again together, in the same Meridian, but not on the same Day of the Week. — Hence the Day of the Week, and not the Day of the Month, must be the *Characteristick* to distinguish the Cycle.

The Julian Year (as observed) being 11 Minutes longer than the solar tropical, the Day of the Month, (according to the Julian Calendar,) from the Year of the Creation, or the Year of the Julian Period 706, had receded 44 Days, which brought the Day of the autumnal Equinox from Oct 25, which it was in the Julian Year 706, to Sept. 11, O. S.; but 11 of these Days being thrown off, in the Year 1752, in Order to bring the Equinox *nearly* on the same Day of the *Julian Month* which it was at the Nicene Council, which was held 1439 Years before; it brought the Day of the Month, (when the Sun entered Libra,) from Oct. 25, at the Creation, to Sept. 22, N. S. 1753.

In Regard to what passed between you and me, about Sir Isaac Newton's Assumption of

Gra-

Gravitation and Attraction, I think you misunderstood me: I did not oppose them, as *Effects*; but I would not have it understood that we ought not to be satisfied in going thus far, and no farther; — I contended that we ought to have Liberty to enquire what Agent, or Agents, were the Cause of these Effects; and not to make Use of Words which seemed to point out some occult Quality, and that it was the *ne plus ultra*, and improper to enquire any farther. — No! We ought to use these Words, as *Sir Isaac Newton* has directed, only to express *Phenomena* in Nature, to which he was going to apply his mathematical Demonstrations: Thus in his *Opticks*, (which was one of his last Works,) says he, " I would have Gravitation and Attraction to be understood as an *Effect only*, *which might be occasioned by the Pressure of a most subtle Ether*, (with which the Space, from the Sun to the Extremity of the System *might be filled*,) *or to something which he did not know*."

Daily Experience shews us, that Gravitation

tion and Attraction are *relative* Terms only, as Gravity and Levity, and are always in Proportion to the *Specific Gravity* of the Body, and the Denfity of the Medium that furrounds it. As, for Inftance, drop a piece of Cork out of your Hand, in the Air, it will be forced to the Ground, by being of a greater fpecific Gravity than the Atmofphere; put this Piece of Cork at the Bottom of a Bafon, cover it with Water, and the Cork will be forced upwards, and lie in the *Medium* between Air and Water, higher or lower in Proportion to its fpecific Gravity. The Experiments on Balloons greatly confirm and explain the above Theory.

The following Axioms (I think) are allowed by all Phylofophers: 1ft, that Matter connot act but when acted upon; 2dly, that it occupies Space, and cannot act in two Places at once, but only in the identical Space it occupies; therefore it cannot act at a Diftance from itfelf, or in any Place it does not occupy. Hence it muft be the *furrounding Medium* which caufes the Gravitation of Bodies.

dies.—Thus, as was obferved by the Cork; — a Body, placed in any fluid Medium, will rife or fall, in that Medium, in Proportion to the fpecific Gravity of that Body, and the Denfity of the furrounding Medium.

My Affumption is, that the *firft Agent* in Nature muft be the moft *fubtile* (or *active*) and *univerfally expanded*, and capable of entering all Pores, and Interftices, of the moft denfe Subftances in Nature, even *Adamant!*— And I fuppofe that the *Ether*, which Sir Ifaac Newton imagined, [9] might, by its Pulfion, be the Caufe of Gravitation and Attraction, & be compofed of two Qualities; which, for the Purpofe of being underftood, (not being able to find more proper Names,) I will call Heat and Cold.—I fuppofe this *Ether* to occupy all Space, from the Sun, at the Centre, to the utmoft Extremity of the Syftem; which *two* Qualities are in continual Conflict, in the Manner we have obferved [10] the cold and hot Air, or Atmofphere to be.— Thefe Ethers, mixed with the Atmofphere,

being

[9] P. Def. V, VIII——Lib. I, Sec. II.
[10] See Letter IV, Page 161.

being the Cause of the Conflict, we always observe, between hot and cold Air; each endeavouring to possess the Place occupied by the other;—the Heat expanding, and the Cold compressing. If they are the first Agents, their Power will be indefinite, and capable of destroying all material Substances, as we have numberless Instances and Experiments every Day, which confirm it. Does not the Experiments in Electricity prove that it is universally expanded and enters all Substances, and that it is in all Matter, Ice not excepted?

Boerhaave, and a great many Philosophers, have thought that Motion and Fire were synonimous Terms, as has been observed.[11] Viz. where Fire abounds, there will be the greatest Motion, and Cold the opposite.—Hence we see the Cause of all Winds, Hurricanes, Earthquakes, &c. which destroy every Thing, and force all before it: *in those, the Phenomina* of Attraction, Gravitation, and Cohesion, are all lost.—Hence may be observed, that all Matter, by having Fire added to it,

is

---

(11) Letter V. 169.

is expanded, and occupies more Space. Thus the Sun Beams, ftriking againſt the Earth, a great Part of them are reflected, and of Confequence there muſt be a greater Quantity of thefe Sun Beams, or Heat, at the Surface, than at an Inch from it, and a greater there than at two Inches, and fo on.—When the Rarefaction is made on the Surface of the Earth, the Cold, or more denfe *Ether*, ruſhes towards the Earth, together with the Atmoſphere, and forces this *light*, Heat, or rarefied Air, upwards from the Earth; and with it every thing that is of lefs fpecific Gravity than the Atmofphere. — The Earth, being placed and furrounded with thefe Ethers, it has no more Refiftance than a Body, of the fame fpecific Gravity, placed in the middle Part of a Tub of Water;—it would neither rife to the Top, nor gravitate to the Bottom, but would remain in the Middle, and move as the Body of Water moved; unlefs by Means of Heat, or fome other Caufe, the watery Medium, on one Side, fhould be expanded, & made to occupy more Space, and to be of lefs fpecific Gravity than it was on the other:

K k

If

If this was the Cafe, then the Medium, or Water, on the other Side of the Body, having greater Gravity or Preffure, would force itfelf into that Place of leffer Gravity, and of lefs Refiftance; and, by that Preffure, would force the Body to turn round together with it. — Thus the Earth, being placed in and furrounded with Ethers, can have no Refiftance: The fide of the Earth next or oppofite the Sun, having the Atmofphere heated and rarefied, and the other Side covered with cold and denfe Ether;—this cold and denfe Air, by forcing itfelf into the Place occupied by the hot and rarefied, carries the terraqueous Globe round with it. Thus, the Heat from the Sun, and the Cold from the Extremities, continually acting, caufe the perpetual Motion of the Earth. Hence, whilft thefe two Motions remain a Ballance to each other, fo long would the Earth go round the Sun; going round its Axis alfo at the fame Time.— Does not all Experiments in Electricity, Gunpowder, and the late Experiments on Balloons confirm it?

Hence

Hence, the greatest Heat, or Rarefaction, being on the Earth, every Body of greater specific Gravity than the Atmosphere, is forced towards it; and contrary, all Bodies of less specific Gravity, are forced from it. hence the spheroidical Shape of the terraqueous Globe; for if the Water, or fluid Parts, are pressed by the cold at the Poles, more than they are at the Equator, they must form a Spheroid, as Experiments on the Shape of the Earth have proved it to be.—Hence also, we are informed of the Cause of the Tide, or Sea, always flowing from the Poles to the Equator; (as Cook, in his Voyage to the South Pole, found they always did); and this is also observed at Nova Scotia, Newfoundland, that the Tide always flows from the North Pole towards the Line; which is contrary to the Doctrine of Attraction; for the Earth being a Spheroid, longest at the Equator, the Tide flows uphill, or from the Centre of Attraction.— The fall of Bodies is also proved not to be in an exact Perpendicular to the Place they fall from, but more towards the Equator, or where the Rarefaction

is

is the greateſt, and Reſiſtance the leaſt.— Another Experiment, which alſo ſeems to prove the above is, that when they drop a Weight, or Lead, into the Sea, to try its Depth, the Preſſure, or Weight, on the Finger, cannot be felt at more than Two Hundred Fathoms, let the Weight be as great as may be; and the Preſſure of the Line, on your Finger, becomes leſs and leſs every Fathom it deſcends.—Was the Attraction the greater, the nearer it comes to the Centre of the Earth, the contrary of this would be the Caſe.—I ſhould imagine, that was a Barometer to be carried down Two Hundred Fathoms, into ſome of our deepeſt Coal Pits, the Quickſilver would ſink in Proportion as you deſcended, in the ſame Manner it does when you aſcend into the Atmoſphere: But this is a mere Hypotheſis, which I believe has never yet been tried; but I much wonder at it, as we are ſo curious in Experiments.—If you have any inquiſitive Acquaintance amongſt the Coal Miners, who may be willing to make this Experiment, I think it would be a uſeful one.

Thus,

Thus, you see, I do not oppose any of Sir Isaac Newton's mathematical Demonstrations, (who, perhaps, was the greatest Mathematician that ever lived,) nor his Calculations of the *Effects* the Sun, Earth, and Moon, &c. have on each other; — I only lay a Claim for Liberty to explain the *Causes* of these *Effects*. — The whole Difference lies in This; whether the first *Agents* in Nature be Solids or Fluids: — Most of Sir Isaac Newton's Followers believe that they are in *Solids*. I, on the contrary, think they are in Fluids; the most subtile, the most active; therefore, as from Experiments, Fire seems to be the most subtile and active; of Consequence the *first material Agent*. —— Indeed there was one Thing else, which was contended for a great While; but, I believe, is *now* given up: Viz. that the Space between the Sun, Moon, and Earth, was *void* of Matter, a *Vacuum*; otherwise, say they, if it contained Matter, it must have Resistance, which, on these Principles, would have overcame all Motion before now.—For, say they, a Body once put in Motion, will allways
continue

continue in Motion, if it meets with no Refiftance, but if it meets with Refiftance, it would be continually lofing Part of its Motion, every Minute, and in Time ftand ftill; which muft have been the Cafe with the Planets, before now, if they met with any Refiftance.

I am,

DEAR SIR,

Your obliged and

Faithful Friend,

F. PENROSE.

STONEHOUSE,
Monday, April 11, 1785.

To F. PENROSE, Esq.

Doubts proposed concerning some Parts of Mr. Penrose's Philosophy, in Order that Truth *may be ascertained. Queries concerning* cold Ether; *and the Pressure of that cold Ether into the* Hot, *or where it is more rare.— What is the Cause of the Motion of the Earth?— What is the Cause that the Earth does not fall into the Sun? — Do you impute it to a Current of Ether? — Answer to the last Queries conclusive, if it be allowed that Moses was so far ignorant of Astronomy, as to be incapable of calculating the Eclipses which preceded his Time. — He is said to have been learned in all the Learning of the Egyptians;— State of the Sciences in Chaldea and Egypt.*

DEAR SIR,

I SHOULD have thanked you for your obliging Letter sooner, but that I have been a good Deal out of Town; and I have

had

had a lurking Sort of rheumatic Fever hanging upon me for more than a Month paft, which broke my Reft and Spirits very much, and thereby made me reluctant either to write, or to fet about any Thing elfe. Thank God, I have almoft got rid of it within the laft Fortnight, fince the Weather has been warm. I am greatly obliged to you for the Trouble you have been fo good as to take, to inform me of your philofophical Principles, and fhall make no Apology for offering fome of my Doubts to your Confideration; becaufe without a fair and candid Difcuffion, of any Subject, *Truth* cannot be afcertained. In ftrict Propriety indeed, I ought rather to fay, I muft beg fome farther Illuftration, on fome Points which I do not underftand, nor fee the Confequences which you draw from the Premifes.

I have lived a Life of fuch Hurry lately, that the above has been wrote at *twice,* and each Time a Week from the other, tho' I have taken every probable Opportunity of having Half an Hour to myfelf; and 'tis odds whether

whether I shall not be interrupted now, in five Minutes.

To begin—Heat and Cold are certainly relative Terms, as up and down are; and some Philosophers deny them totally: But I do not mean to quibble about Terms; for no Doubt there are such Effects produced as we call by those Names.—Nor have I any Objection to your *Ether*; for I think there probably may be such a subtile Matter, which pervades every sensible Substance that we are acquainted with.—But when you talk of the *cold* Ether driving out the *hot*, do not you recur to that *Gravity* which you want to explode? For by saying that the *Density* of the former causes it to rush into the Place of the latter, because it is there more rarefied, &c. is allowing of a Principle, little if at all different from our Ideas of Gravity.—The Instances of a Cork, or Piece of Wood put into Water; the Air Balloons, &c. &c. all go to the same Principle; for they will all of them *rest* when they come into a Medium of equal *Density* with themselves; and *in this Case*,

Denfity and Gravity feem to me fynonimous Terms.

I will alfo readily grant you, that the Sun Beams acting ftrongly upon that Surface of the Earth, which is oppofite the Sun, will rarefy the Atmofphere there, and that the denfe cold Air on the oppofite Side the Earth, will then pufh it forward into that rarefied and lighter Atmofphere: Nay, I will grant you that it will caufe the Motion round the Axis of the Earth, (though I by no Means think that a *rotary* Motion muft *neceffarily* follow from it,) yet I would afk why the Earth did not proceed in a ftraight Line directly to the Sun? ——— We will fuppofe the Earth this Inftant formed, and at reft: The Sun Beams play upon it, and rarefy the Air on that Side which is oppofed to them; (I fhall take the Liberty of ufing the Word *Air*, as a fhorter Word, inftead of *Atmofphere)* the denfe Air on the other Side will pufh it forward into that lighter Air moft certainly; but I do not fee why it fhould caufe a rotary Motion round the Axis of the Earth; much

lefs

less can I see any Reason for its elliptick, annual Motion from *this* Cause; Recourse must therefore still be had to an original Impulse, or trajectile Force, for its annual Motion; and then what is the Power that brings it back from that immense Distance at which it is, in the Summer Solstice? or prevent its flying off in a Tangent? If the mere Rarefaction of the Air was sufficient for this, would it not cause the Earth to fall plump into the Sun, and not take that circuitous Course which we see it does? Would you impute it to some Current of the subtile Ether? We know and allow that there is such a Current from North to South, which is the Cause of Magnetism; but that will not serve to carry the Earth round its annual Orbit.— Or would you assign various Currents for that Purpose? If so, there must likewise be a Cause assigned for them, which I fear will be still more incomprehensible than Sir Isaac's Doctrine of Gravitation and Propulsion.— In short, this is the great *Desideratum* in your Theory, which puzzles me, and to which you have not spoke at all in your Letter.—I

readily

readily assent to the Idea that Motion and Fire are the same Thing; *I have always thought it so:* For Fire or Heat has no Existence till Motion is excited.—The Principles of Fire, I presume, lye in Steel and Flint; but it must be drawn out, and put into Action by Collision, and then there is evident Motion. I will not dispute the Cause you assign for the spheroidical Shape of the Earth; though I think that Shape is sufficiently well accounted for by the centrifugal Force, (which cannot be denied to exist) acting upon the Globe while yet moist, during its rotary Motion round its Axis.—I dare say that your Hypothesis, that Quicksilver would fall in Proportion to the Depth it was carried into a Coal-pit, would prove true; and I will endeavour to get a Trial made of it; for I think it would be curious to know whether it falls *in the same Ratio* beneath, as above the Surface of the Earth, and I have a Friend in the North of England, whom I can trust, and hope he will get the Experiment made for me.

I give you many Thanks for the Explanations you favoured me with, refpecting the Queries in my laſt; they are very concluſive, provided that it be allowed that Mofes was fo far ignorant of Aſtronomy as to be incapable of calculating the Eclipfes which had preceded his Time.—For though he is faid to have been learned in all the Learning of the Egyptians, who were at that Time the moſt learned People in the World: And though the Ifraelites were originally from Chaldea, (if I miſtake not) who were the firſt People who ſtudied Aſtronomy; yet I am willing to allow that neither of thofe Nations were capable of calculating a Series of Eclipfes for two thoufand Years backwards.—The Confequence is, that Mofes muſt have wrote from Infpiration, and that his Account is a true one.—Yet if I had Leifure, I ſhould like to ſtate fome Difficulties which arife from the State which the Arts were certainly in, fome hundred Years ago in China; the long Duration of that Empire, (I do not mean their fabulous one) and the numerous Strata of Lava which are found one under another, to great

Depths

Depths under the Earth, and which muſt have been vomited out many Ages before hiſtorical Times; (perhaps before the Invention of Letters) and which would ſeem to carry us back to Times long before Moſes's Account of the Deluge.—But this I muſt leave to ſome other Opportunity, having no *preſent* Proſpect of more Leiſure than I have now; and I have had ſo little lately, that 'tis above a Fortnight ſince I began this Letter, and have hardly been able to write five Lines at a Time; ſo that I fear you will find it a very confuſed and unconnected one; which I truſt you will excuſe, as it ariſes from a Wiſh to ſhew the Senſe of your Favour, the firſt Moment it has been in my Power, rather then defer it longer in order to write a more correct one.

  I am,

   Dear Sir,

    Your very obedient,

     And obliged Servant,

      J. HEAVISIDE.

Prince's-Street,
 May 16, 1785.

To JOHN HEAVISIDE. Esq.

*Mr. Heaviside's Quere answered.—Calculations of the Motions of the Heavenly Bodies demonstrably true; but the Principles of natural Philosophy cannot be demonstrated with that Clearness and Precision as those in Astronomy.—Three Principles of Matter.—Gravity explained.—*Cold *and* Hot Ether *described according to* Sir Isaac Newton.—Centre *of* Gravity *supposed formerly to be placed in the* Centre *of the Earth, but late Experiments prove that* Gravity *does not tend to the Centre of the Earth, but to the Superficies, and to the Place where there is the greatest expansive Heat.—*Gravity *proved to be increased or lessened in Proportion as* Heat *and* Cold *prevail.—The* Pressure *of the* Cold Ether *or* Gravity *acts exactly in the same Proportion on the Poles and the Equator, as the spheroidical Shape of the terraqueous Globe shews it does.—The* Centre *of* Gravity *proved to be near the Surface of the Earth, where every Thing tends.*

DEAR

DEAR SIR,

BY your laft Letter, we were forry to be informed that your Conftitution had been fo much difordered both in Health and Spirits; but as you found Benefit from the Change of the Weather from Cold to Warm, we hope that the late fine Weather has made a perfect Cure.—I am afraid my long and tedious Letters difturb you, and put you to great Inconveniencies, both by reading and writing Anfwers to them.—Notwithftanding I imagine this to be the Cafe, I will trouble you with *One* more; as, what I am going to obferve may, perhaps, appear fatisfactory *to fome*, that the World was created at the Time Mofes informs us it was.—There may be others who imagine, or *pretend to imagine*, that the World is *eternal*; fuch Perfons, I apprehend, neither mathematical Demonftration, nor any Thing elfe will convince.

In your former Letter you fay, that notwithftanding the Sun and Moon were in the Places Mofes records them to have been at the

the Time he mentions the Creation to have happened; yet, fay you, "may there not have been many Cycles before that Time?" And you obferve, that the Chinefe Hiftory makes that Empire to have been in Being fome hundreds of Years before.—In Anfwer to this I fhall again remark, that Hiftory, without Chronology, is little better than a Romance; and there can be no Certainty that Chronology is true, unlefs proved by Aftronomy; but when the Sun and Moon give their Teftimony to it, there cannot remain a Doubt, they are two faithful Witneffes.

Now, Sir, as to this Queftion, I obferve, that I never undertook to prove, by Mathematical Demonftration, that there might not have been a Series of Years before the Time in which Mofes places the Creation.

To prove a Negative is always attended with great Difficulty, and often impoffible! What I attempted was to try Mofes's Hiftory and Chronology, by the Evidence of Aftro-
mony,

nomy, and to examine whether the Sun and Moon were in the fame Places in the Heavens, as Mofes tells us they were, at the Time when the Creation happened; which your aftronomical Friends allow I have done.—This appears to me to be Evidence fufficient to eftablifh any other Hiftory: If fo, why fhould it not Mofes's Hiftory?—And it is not credible that he would have calculated thofe Places of the Sun and Moon, two thoufand Years before he was born.—If he could not, and we find it in his Hiftory, it muft be revealed from God, as he tells us it was!

As I obferved to you before, I affume, (from Mofes's Hiftory, and Dr. Bradley's Obfervations) that the Moon was Full, and in her Node, A. I. P. 706, Oct. 24th Day, 10th Hour, 24th Minute, at Night, in the Meridian of Greenwich Obfervatory; between that Time, and the Year 6490, which is in Connection with A. D. 1783, when, on a Wednefday Night, the third Year after Biffextile, there happened an Eclipfe of the Moon,

Moon, Sept. 10th Day, 12th Hour, 40th Minute.—Between thefe two Points of Time the Earth made 5789 Revolutions through the Ecliptick, and was interfected in her 5790 Revolution, by the Moon, 12th Day, 16th Hour, 14th Minute, before fhe entered Libra; during this Time fhe made 2114741 Rotations round her Axis.—While the Earth was performing thefe Rotations, the Moon performed 71,612 fynodical Revolutions, and interfected the Earth as above.— Here we have two Points of Solar Time, Oct, 25th, 706, Julian Period, the Sun in Libra, and Sept. 22d Day, 16th Hour, 54th Minute, 6490, I. P. the Sun in Libra, meafured by the Number of Rotations the Earth made between them.—We have alfo Oct. 24th Day, 10th Hour, 24th Minute—706, when the Moon was in Oppofition to the Sun; and Sept. 10th Day, 16th Hour, 40th Minute, 6490, when the Moon was obferved to be in her Node, and exactly oppofite to the Sun, (by the Eclipfe which then happened.)— Between thefe two Points, the Time is meafured by the Number of Rotations the Earth has

has made, *with as much Eafe, and as great an Exactnefs,* as the Diftance between any two Places are by a Surveyor's Wheel.

Hence alfo by knowing the Quantity of the Motion of 71,612 Lunations, we fhall have the precife Length of Time of one Lunation.—Here you have *mathematical Precifion!* As the Interval which lyes evenly between thofe two Points, is meafured by the Number of Rotations the Earth has performed during that Time; and alfo the Point of Interfection where the Moon ends her 71612th fynodical Revolution, meafured with the fame Exactnefs, and alfo the Diftance between that Point of Interfection, and that other, when the Sun entered Libra.—Hence I remark, that the Revolutions of the Moon, when compared to thofe of the Earth, are fo complicated, fo curious, various, and exact, that it requires 7,948,800 fynodical Revolutions, which are more than 600,000 Years for Her to go through all her Variations, and to caufe the Moment of her mean Oppofition to fall again on the fame Point of the Equator,

tor, in the same Meridian, on the same Day of the Week, and the same Year of Bissextile. (a) —This appears to me to be sufficient Evidence, that the World was created at the Time when Moses informs us it was, and that the History of the Duration of the Empire of China is fabulous.

I have teased you thus far on a Subject that must appear *dry* to any one who does not take a particular Pleasure therein; with a Desire, (if it is not too troublesome,) that you would shew it to those Gentlemen who joined with you in Quering whether there might not have been *Solar* Cycles before the Time when Moses places the Creation to have happened.

In Order to give you some Satisfaction for this Trouble, I will promise that I will ask no more such Favours; for I am satisfied, the Trouble of perusing and making Remarks thereon, must be very vexatious to one who has so little Time to spare.—If you should

(a) Kennedy's Chron. P. 196.

should have an Opportunity of shewing the above to the Gentlemen who saw the other, be pleased to inform them, that the above Calculations were made without *Tables, Equations,* or *Anamolies,* after a most easy and simple Manner; by the first four Rules of Arithmetic only. [b]

I observed to you in one of my Letters some Time ago, that as the first Principles of natural Philosophy could not be demonstrated with that Clearness and Precision as those of Astronomy, I deferred entering upon them.—In Astronomy we only calculate and demonstrate the Phenomena of the Motions, which the Heavenly Bodies are known, and *observed,* to have.—Sir Isaac Newton, in his Philosophical Calculations, went no farther than this, and therefore they are *certainly true:* But if we Philosophize, or draw Inferences from them, we must always take Care that they flow easily from, and are not in the least contradictory to the known Principles of Matter.—Now, Sir, the following are

[b] Introduction, P. 8o.

are Principles of Matter, which I believe are allowed by all Philosophers.—1st, that Matter occupies Space, and has Resistance.—2d, that no two Particles of Matter can occupy the same identical Space, at one and the same Time.—3d, that it can only act where it is present, *not the least Distance from the Place it occupies.*

Now, I believe, you and I, and all Philosophers, have seen and observed the EFFECTS which the Heavenly Bodies have on each other, known by the Name of *Gravity.* I endeavour to account for these Effects by the Ethers, *or the Matter* which fills the Heavenly Space, in the same Manner as Sir Isaac Newton supposed, and consequently is in *Contact* with them. [c] This is my Theory and my Ideas of it.—Without this *Ether* occupying the Space between them, I shall be glad to be informed how they act on each other, in a *Mechanical Way,* and not by saying *that Gravity is the Cause of it*; which is no more than saying that a Ship sailed from London

[c] See Let. IV. P. 162.

London to Plymouth, without telling us that the Air was a continued Medium between the two Places, and that a Current of that Air or Wind carried her there.— Do you suppose that Gravity is (as it is often explained) *something superadded* to Matter? If so, is it spiritual or material? If material, it must act according to the known Laws of Matter.—If you say it is spiritual, there must be an End of the Controversy, for it is what I don't understand, and must not pretend to explain.—I should also be glad to be informed, that if the Motions of the Earth or Planets are occasioned from an *original Impulse or trajectile Force, how this Force is continued and supported?* For if you allow Matter to reach from the Planets to the Sun, and to the End of this System, it must *resist*, and if it resists, it must have taken off such a Quantity of the trajectile Force, that they must have stood still Ages ago; when, in Fact, we know their Motions are the same they were some thousand Years ago.—These are Difficulties which I think will not be surmounted, till we allow the *first Agency in Matter to be*

in

in Fluids, and not in Solids, and the more *Subtile* the Fluid, the *greater* the Agency.

In my last Letter, when I mentioned the different Modifications of Ether, I told you that I used *Heat* and *Cold*, (if possible,) to explain my Ideas of them, though I did not think them proper ones, but I could find no better; but then I did not join the Ideas of the Sensations which Heat and Cold have on our Bodies, but pure elementary Heat and Cold, such as may be observed from the Effects of Lightning, and electrical Experiments.

These Ethers I endeavoured to explain by a Quotation from Sir Isaac Newton, who calls them *Spirit* and *Light*; I there desired to be understood in the same Manner whenever I make use of them.[d]

In this Year's Philosophical Transactions, there is the History of Experiments made on the Influence of Cold on the Earth, and, at the

---

[d] Letter IV. P. 163.

the same Time, at different Heights from it; which are curious and worthy to be read: The Gentleman that made them, (whose Name, if I remember right, is Cavendish,) observes, that Cold is reflected, rises or flies off from the Earth, as well as Heat.—According to my Theory, both *Heat* and *Cold* must be intercepted by the Earth, and be reflected from it, by interrupting their Passage, whereby they are made to rebound from it.

As you seemed to be puzzled by the Use I made of *Heat* and *Cold*, and that you understood thereby, that I wanted to explode *Gravity*; I shall therefore endeavour to explain my Ideas of that *Phenomenon* of Nature, which is certainly a just and true one, and not to be disputed; therefore, I hope, you will not imagine I wanted to explode it.— My Design is to clear it from some Difficulties attributed to it, and to elucidate its Power.—In Order to do this, I shall take the immortal *Newton* for my Guide, who tells us,

us, [e] "That the *Ether* which fills the heavenly Spaces, is a *Medium* which pervades all Bodies, and that there is *no* Vacuum but what it fills; that it readily pervades all *Bodies*, and by its elastic Force, is expanded through the whole Heavens, and that it may suffice *to impel* Bodies from the denser Parts of the Medium to the Rarer, with all that Force or *Impulse* which we call GRAVITY." [f] He also describes this Medium to act with a *two-fold Quality*, which he calls *Light* and *Spirit*.—The one expanding itself from the Sun, and the other condensing and pressing this expanded *Ether* towards the Sun.—That these opposite Forces are carried on in a *vibrating* Manner, being alternately in Fits of easy Reflection, and easy Transmission.—In Order to shew the Place where the Centre of Gravity is supposed to be, and how it acts, I shall give you the Description of it by Mr. Ferguson. "Bodies, says he, are heavier near the Poles, than those towards the Equator, *because they are nearer the Earth's Centre, where*
"the

(e) Optick, P. 323, 325.— (f) Letter IV. P. 135.

" *the* whole Force *of the Earth's Attraction*
" *is accumulated.*—Bodies carried from the
" Poles towards the Equator, gradually lose
" their Weight.—Experiments prove that a
" Pendulum, which vibrates Seconds near
" the Poles, vibrates flower near the Equa-
" tor, which shews us that it is lighter or
" less attracted there.—To make it oscillate
" in the same Time, it is found necessary to
" diminish its Length.—By comparing the
" different Lengths of Pendulums swinging
" Seconds at the Equator, and at *London*,
" it is found that a Pendulum must be $2\frac{160}{1000}$
" Lines shorter at the Equator than at the
" Poles." (g) It is also observed that the *cold
Ether* at the Poles, gives a *gravitating* Power
to Bodies removed there from the Equator,
nearly as $\frac{1}{222}$ —— Does not this Fact shew us
that the *cold Ether*, or, as Sir *Isaac Newton*
calls it, *Spirit*, makes Bodies to gravitate,
and is the Cause of Gravity as he supposed it
did? Thus we find that the *cold Ether* presses
at each Pole, just in the same Proportion,

more

(g) Ferguson. P. 50, S. 117.

more than the *hot Ether* at the Equator. As the equatorial Diameter of the Earth exceeds the polar Diameter in Meafure.—By the Experiments of *Meſſrs. Maupertuis*, &c. in the Years 1736 and 1737, the equatorial Diameter of the Earth was found to be $36\tfrac{3}{100}$ Miles more than the Polar, which is $\tfrac{1}{200}$ nearly.

Hence it may be obferved, that the fpheroidal Shape of the Earth is exactly according to *Gravity* or the *ethereal Preſſure*.—For the cold Ether is found to prefs or make *all* Bodies to increafe in Gravity there, juſt by the fame Proportion as the Equatorial Diameter of the Earth is longer than the Polar.

Now, Sir, if the cold Ether gravitates in that Proportion, more at the Poles than it does at the Equator, the terraqueous Globe muſt be in the Shape it is found to be.—For it is the Property of Fluids to *move eaſily* in every Direction, and *to acquire* a uniform Surface in Proportion to the Preſſure on it.

Thus

Thus the Air is a fine elaſtick Fluid, ſurrounding this terraqueous Globe, and is found by Experience, to be compreſſed or condenſed by *Cold*, and expanded or rarefied by *Heat*. The Seas are a watery Fluid, giving Way to Preſſure, and ſurround this Globe; therefore if they are preſſed more at each Pole, occaſioned by the *Cold*, than at the Equator, where they are expanded by *Heat*, they muſt be in the ſpheroidal Shape as $\frac{1}{222}$ nearly.

Having ſhewn that the *cold Ether, preſſing more* at the Poles than at the Equator, is the Cauſe of the ſpheroidal Form of the Earth, I ſhall endeavour to find, from Experiments and the *Phenomena* of Nature, where the Centre of Gravity is, or the Place where it tends.

It was obſerved in my laſt Letter, that Dr. *Halley*, many Years ago, found that a Weight dropped from above, does not deſcend according to the Perpendicular of that Place, but a little to the Eaſtward of the South, tending to the Place on the Globe where the Rarefaction

faction is the greateſt, and the Heat the ſtrongeſt.—The Tides at Newfoundland are found to tend in the ſame Manner a little towards the Eaſtward of the South.—In like Manner later Experiments have proved, that a Plumb Line placed on each Side of a Mountain, will not deſcend Perpendicular to the Centre of the Earth, but, *on both Sides*, tends towards the Mountain; the Place where the greateſt Number of the Sun Beams are reflected, and where the Heat is the greateſt.

It has long been an Obſervation amongſt Sailors, that Gravity was loſt about Two Hundred Fathoms under the Surface of the Sea: That when they ſounded with a Line longer than that, they could feel no Effect from the Weight, let it be ever ſo great; and by a late Experiment it has been found, that if you ſuſpend a Pound Weight at one End of the Scale Beam, and at the other End hang another Pound Weight, by a fine String, over a Shaft or Mine, and let it deſcend gently below the Surface of the Earth; it loſes Part of its Gravity as it deſcends, till

till it comes to Nothing; and the Weight muſt be leſſened in that Scale above Ground continualy, to make an *Fquipoize*.— From the ſame Cauſe it is found by Experience, that Candles will not burn but about Two Hundred Fathoms under the Earth's Surface.

The above Experiments ſhew us, that the Force of Gravity does not tend to the Centre of the Earth, as has been imagined, but to the Place where the *expanſive Force and Rarefaction from Heat, are the greateſt* —Thus, where the Sun Beams are moſt reflected, and their expanſive Force the greateſt, there the Preſſure of the *cold Ether* or Gravity will tend.—They alſo ſhew us the Reaſon of the ſpheroidal Form of this terraqueous Globe, and why the Waters or Tides are always flowing from each Pole, towards the Equator.— Hence it may be obſerved, that *Heat* and *Cold* are the Cauſes of *Gravity* and *Levity*; Heat enters, projects, and expands the Parts of Bodies, and makes them ſpecifically lighter. On the contrary, *Cold* preſſes them cloſer together, and increaſes their *Attraction of Coheſion*,

hesion, and adds to them *Gravity*.—Do not the above Experiments shew us the Cause of *Gravity*, and how it acts?—Thus, Sir, you may observe it is not my Design to deprive Gravity of any of its Powers, I only mean to endeavour to point out the Cause of that *Phenomenon*.

From what has been observed, it appears, that as *Heat* is the Cause of Projection and Expansion, so *Cold* is the Cause of Compression and Gravity: That these two Ethers are in a continual Conflict or Vibration; each endeavouring to jostle the other out of its Place.

You also imagine that *Density* and *Gravity* were synonimous Terms. The Ideas I used them for is quite opposite: I suppose Gravity an *Agency*, forcing every Thing towards the Body or Place to which it gravitates: On the contrary, I suppose the *Density of the Medium between* two Bodies, the Resisting Quality.—I never did or ever will make Objections to Author's Terms, so he does but explain what he means by them.—The Earth cannot fly off in a Tangent, no more than a Balloon can fly into the Sun. The Earth is placed in a *Medium*, (furrounding the Sun,) of *the fame Specifick Gravity* with it, therefore it cannot depart from, or approach nearer to the Sun, than that Medium reaches, in the fame Manner as a Balloon or a Cloud; it muft continue at the fame Diftance from the Earth, unlefs its fpecific Gravity is altered, by throwing out Ballaft, or letting out fome of the light inflammable Air. — By thefe Actions the Balloon will either rife or fall, as its fpecific Gravity is leffened (in Proportion to the Atmofphere) by throwing out Ballaft; or its gravitating Quality is increafed, by letting out inflammable Air. — Hence, as you juftly obferve, *Heat and Cold* are relative Terms, as all Parts of Matter are to each other.

I return you many Thanks for the Trouble you have taken, in Order to get the Experiments on the Barometer tried, in fome of our deep Coal Pits; I wifh you had joined

the

the Thermometer with it.—I am much surprised they have never yet been tried, as we live in an experimental Age.

I am,

Dear Sir,

With great Respect,

Your obliged humble Servant,

F. PENROSE.

STONEHOUSE,
June 18, 1785.

To

To F. PENROSE, Esq.

State of the Sciences about two thousand Years ago.—The former Query repeated: " *If the Earth, &c. were first put in Motion by the Heat of the Sun, rarefying the Atmosphere between these Bodies, why did not the Earth immediately gravitate into the Sun?—Must not a trajectile Force have been at first necessary to cause its annual Orbit?*"

Dear Sir,

'TIS now above ten Weeks since I was favoured with your last; a shameful Time I confess! And yet I wish that I had not so good Reasons to give for my seeming Negligence.— The Illness of a particular Friend confined me here in Town, during all the hot Weather, till near the Middle of August; by which I was reduced to such Weakness and Langour, that I could neither write, or do any Thing else; and if my Confinement here had continued much longer, I could not have supported it; for never having

got

got rid of the Illnefs I had laft Autumn, the clofe warm Air of this Town, for fo long a Time, quite overfet me; fo that when I was at Liberty to get out of Town for a few Days, I was not able to ride on Horfe-back more than fix or eight Miles at a Time; nor have yet been able to ride from hence to Potterels, without taking a Poft-Chaife at Barnet. About three Weeks ago I fet out, (but in a fingle Horfe Chaife,) on a little Ramble thro' Norfolk and Suffolk, which has done me a great deal of good, and enabled me to venture on a little Sea-Bathing, fo that I fhall fet out for Margate to-morrow Morning, where I hope to recover fome Part, at leaft, of the Strength I have loft.—However, my own Illnefs has not been the fole Caufe of my having fo long deferred to thank you for your laft obliging Letter.

Since I was favoured with your laft, I have had no Opportunity to fee any of my Mathematical Friends, they having left Town long ago; I muft therefore wait for their Opinion till Winter brings them back again; confequently

quently I can only give you a few of my own trivial Remarks upon it.

First then, I entirely assent to what you say, as to the Time of our Saviour's Birth. 2dly, I think there is *very great Probability* that you have also fixed the Creation of the World rightly, and proved that the Mosaic History is true.—I say, *very great Probability*, because it is still *possible*, that the World *may* have existed 600,000 Years, which you say it would require to compleat all those various Revolutions among the Heavenly Bodies, which are necessary to bring them again into the identical Situation they must have been in at the Time of the Creation.—What strongly induces me to believe the World cannot have existed so long, is, the very low State that all the Arts and Sciences, (particularly the former) are well known to have been in 2000 Years ago: Astronomy being almost the only Science that seems to have been cultivated prior to that Period.—Indeed, about that Time the Mathematicks and Mechanicks seem to have made a prodigious Progress grefs under Archimedes; but I think it appears that they were not generally underſtood, for tis plain the Romans were totally ignorant of them.

Another Proof, I think, is the total Want of Civilization among Mankind, at that Period; a very few Nations (if any) perhaps excepted.—So that you ſee I am far from objecting to your Opinions, though I am forced to draw my Reaſons for approving them, from other Fountains than you do, and by no Means ſo good ones.—I am not ſo *perfectly* well ſatisfied with your Natural Philoſophy, though I acknowledge that you Support your Ideas well; but being now upon the Wing, I have not Time to ſtate and explain my Objections ſo thoroughly as I wiſh to do.

In the firſt Place give me Leave to obſerve, that you have given me no Anſwer to the Query I put in my laſt, viz. That if the Earth, &c. were firſt put in Motion by the Heat of the Sun rarefying the Atmoſphere
between

between these Bodies, why did the Earth not immediately gravitate and fall into the Sun, as the Medium between them must have been much more rarefied then it could be any where else, or in the Course they took? And if so, must not a trajectile Force have been at first necessary to cause its annual Orbit? For I will allow that the Sun's Heat might cause the diurnal Motion, as you explain it in your former Letter, provided *that* Heat did not cause the Earth to fall directly into the Sun, as I said above.

You did not rightly apprehend my Meaning, I see, when I said that Gravity and Density were synonimous Terms; I only meant that Bodies gravitated through any Medium, in Proportion to the Density or Closeness of the Matter of which they are composed; as that a Pound of Lead will gravitate sooner than a Pound of Feathers, and so forth; but did not apply it to the Medium through which they were to fall, for *that* will certainly obstruct the fall of both, in Proportion to its Density, and the *Bulk* of the falling Bodies. After

After all, I fancy that I do not fully comprehend your Ideas of Heat and Cold, as to the Degrees and Situations of them.—I know that you suppose that the greatest Degree of the former is on the Surface of the Earth; in which you, no Doubt, are perfectly right: And it just now occurs to me that you dropped a Hint one Day at Hatfield, (which you did not pursue, or farther explain;) that you did not know but all the superior Regions of the Air were perfect Ice.—If I am right in this, perhaps some Conclusions may be drawn from this Coldness in the Upper Regions, in Answer to my Query; but I have not now Time to consider them properly, as the Time of sending to the Post is now at Hand, for Letters must, by the last Regulations, be sent to the receiving Houses by *Five* o'Clock, which is very inconvenient.— However, I cannot at present see how this Coldness above can prevent the Descent of the Earth to the Sun; because the Air being rarefied near its Surface, would move that Way; and as it advanced further and further, would carry the same Degree of Heat before it, till

it arrived at the Source of Heat, the Sun.—
I write this, (especially the latter Part,) in
great Hurry, and therefore hope you will allow for the Imperfections of all Kinds; but
I would not go again from Town without
telling you how much I think myself obliged
to you for the Trouble you take in answering
my idle Queries; and assuring you, that your
Letters give me infinite Pleasure; I therefore hope you will never entertain an Idea
that they can be too long.

I am,

Dear Sir,

Your much obliged,

And very humble Servant,

J. HEAVISIDE.

Prince's-Street,

Sept. 12, 1785.

To JOHN HEAVISIDE, Esq.

Heat and Cold Ether first Agents, according to Sir Isaac Newton, Boerhaave, *&c.— Internal Make of this terraqueous Globe described. — The Thickness of the Shell of Earth.—The confused Appearances on this terraqueous* Globe, *prove that it has undergone some tremendous Convulsions from within, and that the earthly Shell has been burst into Millions of Pieces.—Earthquakes examined, and their Effects described.— These Effects occasioned by Fire.—The Causes of Earthquakes explained,—which prove that there is an immense Quantity of Fire within the Earth.—The above Account agreeable with what is given in the Scriptures.*

Dear Sir,

I WAS sorry to be informed by your last Letter, that you had been so ill, but was glad to find you had nearly got the better of it; I hope the Sea Bathing will perfectly restore you to your former State of Health.

As

As you obferve, I did not perfectly explain myfelf, with Regard to all the Motions of the Earth. —It will require a long Letter or two to do it; but as you defire it, you muft thank yourfelf for the Trouble they will give you.—You want in particular to be informed, " why, according to my Explanation, the Earth does not proceed in a " ftrait Line to the Sun, &c."—And you fay that *Heat* and *Cold* are relative Terms.—They certainly are, with Regard to that Effect on our Senfes; but when we mean by them Sir Ifaac Newton's Ethereal Medium, *Light and Spirit*. [h] We mean firft Agents, which, according to his Definition of them, " fill all the Space between the Sun and Sa-
" turn, and beyond; that it is rarer at the
" Sun, than in the celeftial Spaces, and
" rarer there than at Saturn, and beyond;
" and may *impel* Bodies from the denfer
" Parts of the Medium, towards the rarer,
" with that Force we call *Gravity*."—This compreffing Agent he calls " *Spirit* or *Weight*;
" which, fays he, may condenfe thofe Va-
" pours

---

[h] See Letter IV. P. 163.

"pours and Exhalations afcending from the
"Sun, and make them fall back into him
"again, and by that Action increafe his
"Heat, after the fame Manner as it increafes
"a culinary Fire."—Hence it may be obferved, that Sir Ifaac Newton fuppofes a Circulation from the Sun, to the Extremities of the Syftem, by *two* vibrating Agents.—*The Ethers*;—the one, going out, iffuing from the Sun, in Form of *Light*, and the other returning in Form of *Spirit*.—And, as was before obferved, *Boerhaave* has proved by the heating and cooling of an Iron Bar, &c. that Heat is the firft *Agent* or *Mover*, and *Cold* the Compreffor, Contractor, or *Gravitator*.—But before I explain myfelf any farther, it will be neceffary to get the beft Information we can, concerning the internal Make and Contents of this terraqueous Globe: This appears to be a difficult Tafk! and if you remember, when we firft entered on thefe Difquifitions, I entered the following *Caveat*, "viz. [i] " That there may be fome *Arcana* in the Mechanifm of Nature, that may be beyond

[i] Letter IX. P. 224.

yond our Power to explain;" for it cannot be thought that we can give a mechanical Solution of all its Operations.—However, I shall not *now* take any Advantage from it, but endeavour to anfwer your Queftions in the cleareft Manner I can.

It is related in the Hiftory of the Deluge, that the Waters were fifteen Cubits above the higheft Hills; and that there was an Expanfion in the *Midft* of the terraqueous Globe; and that the Flood was occafioned by the Waters proceeding through the Fountains and Openings from the great Deep.— After the Waters had prevailed the Time God appointed them, he caufed a *Wind* or *Spirit* to force them back again from whence they proceeded, whereby the Earth became Dry. And Job tells us, [k] that God had made the Spirit the Inftrument of Gravity.

Now in Order to conjecture the Thicknefs of the earthy Shell, we will allow, three Miles above the Earth (which, is generally reckoned)

[k] Job XXVIII. 25.

reckoned) to be the Measure of the highest Mountains; four Miles for the Thickness of the earthy Shell, and other three Miles for the Waters within the Shell; all this will be but ten Miles.—But what will ten Miles be to nearly 4000, the supposed Number of Miles from the Surface to the Centre.—This is but as one to 400, which will be as thin a Shell or Covering, in Proportion, as what is made use of to cover a Balloon.

It seems reasonable to conjecture, (as an ingenious Author has observed,) from the natural Appearances of this terraqueous Globe, that it has been burst to Pieces by an expansive Steam from within; for we observe on it Mountains, broken Clifts, craggy Rocks, angular and impending Shores, subterraneous Caverns; together with a vast Variety of Fissures, Cracks, &c.—All these are particularly to be observed in the Marble or Lime Stone about Plymouth!—And, says this Author, that "without farther Inquiry, "these romantic Appearances are not the "Effect of a regular, uniform Law, but of
"some

"some tremendous Convulsions, which have
"burst its *Strata*, and thrown their Fragments into all this Confusion and Disorder:
"Nay, says he, the very Representation of
"Sea and Land, upon a Geographical Chart,
"seems alone sufficient to establish the Truth
"of such a Conjecture.—The Mountains in
"Derbyshire, and the Moorlands in Staffordshire, appear to be so many Heaps of
"Ruins:— The *Strata* lye in the utmost
"Confusion and Disorder; broken, dislocated, and thrown into all Directions;
"and their interior Parts are no less rude
"and romantic, *full of subterraneous Caverns*,
"with every possible Mark of universal Violence.—Also Blocks of Stone scattered over
"the Surface of mountaneous Countries,
"and blended with Soils to very considerable
"Depths, as if they had been originally
"ejected from their native Beds, by *subterraneous Blasts*, as Stones from Vesuvious
"and Ætna. [1]

"The Fragments near the native Beds are
"too

[1] Whithurst, P. 21.

" too numerous and maſſy for the Hand of
" Man to have placed them there, and are in
" as much Diſorder as Stones caſually thrown
" together.—The Banks on the Eaſt Side of
" the River Derwent, from Crick Clift, for
" twenty Miles up the River, are thus co-
" vered; and the ſame may be ſaid of many
" other Mountains in Derbyſhire and Staf-
" fordſhire.

" Theſe Stones lying ſo near their original
" *Stratum*, we may eaſily ſatisfy ourſelves
" that they are detached Parts thereof; and
" by Analogy, the more diſtant Fragments
" may be aſcertained with equal Certainty,
" though at the Diſtance of ten or twelve
" Miles.

" In the Neighbourhood of Utoxeter, in
" Staffordſhire, Blocks of Lime Stone are
" frequently dug up, of four or five Hundred
" Weight each; and yet there are no Quar-
" ries of the ſame Kind nearer than four or
" five Miles.

" Fragments

"Fragments of Stone, perfectly analogous to the former, were dug up at *Etwall*, in Derbyshire.—A Well being sunk to the Depth of eleven Yards, many of these Stones were found, intermixed *with other adventitious Bodies*, from the Surface of the Earth, to that Depth; some of them were six or eight Pounds Weight, and some smaller.—Now although *Etwall* cannot be less than fifteen or twenty Miles from any known Quarry of the same Kind; we cannot help concluding, that they were originally ejected to that Distance; since such Effects are frequently produced on subterraneous Explosions." (m)

The above accurate Description of the natural *Phenomena* of this terraqueous Globe, (as the Author observes,) appears to be Evidence, that the Shell of the Earth was burst and broken into Millions of Pieces, by an expansive Explosion from within; and these Pieces could not possibly fall together again into their primitive Order and Regularity, but must leave an infinite Number of Caverns,

(m) Whitehurst, P. 53.

verns, many Miles, probably many Hundreds of Miles in Length, below the Surface; and I think we may juftly conclude, that this happened at the Reformation after Noah's Flood.—Now in Order to fhew that there ftill remains a violent expanfive Force, occafioned from the internal Fire, I fhall give an Account of the moft remarkable Phenomena of late Earthquakes, from the above Author.

At the Earthquake at Lifbon, which happened Nov. 1, 1755, " The Mountains of " Arrabida, Eftretta, Julio, Marvan, and " Cintra, being fome of the largeft in Por- " tugal, were impetuoufly fhaken to their " very Foundations, and fome of them open- " ed their Summits, fplit and rent in a wond- " erful Manner, and huge Maffes of them " were thrown down into the adjacent Val- " lies. (m) This Earthquake was more dread- " ful in Barbary than at Portugal; at Me- " quinez, that Part of the City where the " Jews refided, was entirely fwallowed up.—
" The

(n) Hift. and Phil. Earth. P, 317.

" The Mountains were so strangely torn,
" that they seemed to be different Shapes
" now from what they were.—A large Moun-
" tain near Portmorant, near a Day's Jour-
" ney over, is said to be quite swallowed up;
" and in the Place where it stood, there is
" now a great Lake, of four or five Leagues
" over. (n) In this memorable Earthquake at
" Lisbon, not only the Sea, but Lakes and
" Ponds were violently agitated all over
" Europe.—Now as Mr. *Whitehurst* observes,
" as one of the Properties of the Steam is
" Condensation by a small Degree of *Cold*,
" the same Degree of expansive Force, can
" only exist during the same Degree of Heat,
" therefore the incumbent Weight cannot
" become elevated to any greater Distance
" than the subterranean Fire is continued.—
" But on Nov. 1, 1755, the Waters were
" agitated through an extensive Country, not
" less than 3000 Miles; so that the Steam
" must be in one continued Body thus far."(p)

Mr. Hook, in his Posthumous Works, P. 302,

(n) Philos. Transact. Low. Abrid. Vol. II. P. 417. (p) Whitehurst, P. 94.

302, informs us, "That from Sept. 24, to Oct. 9, 1650, the Island of Santitirum was dreadfully shaken with Earthquakes, but the People were more amazed to see a horrid Eruption of Fire break out at the Bottom of the Sea;—previous to the Appearance of Fire, the Water was considerably elevated in that Place, and the Wave spread itself round every Way; overturning every Thing it met, destroying Ships and Gallies, in the Harbour of Candia, which was eight Miles distant. [n]

"The Earthquake filled the Air with Ashes, and horrible sulphurous Vapours, and dreadful Lightnings and Thunder succeeded.—All Things in the Island were covered with a yellow, sulphurous Crust; Multitudes of Pumice and other Stones, were thrown up, and carried as far as Constantinople, and to Places at a great Distance.

"Nov. 20, 1720, a subterraneous Fire burst out of the Sea, near Tarcara, one of the

[n] Whitehurst, P. 64.

" the Azores, which threw up such a vast
" Quantity of Stones in the Space of thirty
" Days, as formed an Island about two
" Leagues Diameter, and nearly round.

" In the Year 1767, a solid Stone, measur-
" ing *twelve Feet* in Height, and *forty-five*
" in *Circumference*, was thrown a Quarter of
" a Mile from Vesuvius."

Now, Sir, in Order to confirm my Theory, I have extracted some Observations from Mr. *Whitehurst*'s State and Formation of the Earth, (the Book which you were so kind as to send me lately, as a Present,) he appears to me to be a diligent Inquirer into the component Parts of this terraqueous Globe, and a faithful Relater of the Observations he made himself, or received from others.—I shall therefore take his Advice, and follow his Example, viz. " *Not to find Faults with other Systems; but to avail myself of such Parts of them as are applicable to my own Design,*" but must beg Leave to differ from him *in Design;* for he tells us, " That his *Inquiry* was after
" the

Let. XVI.   *On natural* PHILOSOPHY.   311

" the *Laws* by which the *Creator chose* to
" form the World, and that the *only* natural
" *Datum* required, was the oblate, spheroidal
" Form of the Earth."—My Design is to enquire after, and point out, the physical *Causes*, how one Part of Matter, acts by *mechanical Laws*, on another.

From the above Observations we may naturally conclude, that all the apparent Confusion and Disorder of the *Strata*, are undoubtedly Convulsions and Effects occasioned by FIRE, and fiery Vapours continued within this terraqueous Globe.—But when we compare these tremendous Operations of Earthquakes, with those which the Earth underwent at the Deluge, when the Alps, the Andes, &c. were formed, it will hardly bear a Comparison.

Hence, as Mr. *Whitehurst* observes, [o] " their
" Effects leave no Room to doubt the *Existence, Force,* and *Immensity* of *subterraneous*
" *Fires*; not only under the Bottom of the
"   Ocean,

[r] P. 84.

"Ocean, but likewife *under Mountains, Con-*
"*tinents, &c. in all Parts of the World.*"

Thus, if the expanfive Power, (within this terraqueous Globe, which is occafioned by Fire acting in the fame Manner as has been obferved,) is continually increafing, it will gradually become equal to the incumbent Weight or Bond which furrounds it; thefe fame Caufes ftill continuing, they will become fuperior to the Preffure of Gravity from without:—It will then, by Degrees, expand and diftend the incumbent *Strata*, and caufe an Earthquake, and find a Vent to mix itfelf with the furrounding Airs without. After this, the Fire and Steam from within the Globe, having expanded themfelves, and being mixed with the Atmofphere, (which they will foon do;) the Gravity and Preffure from without, will again take Place, and *comprefs* and force the Parts of the terraqueous Globe towards the Centre, with the *fame Power* it did before this *Phenomenon* happened. But fince the aftonifhing Cataftrophe at the Deluge, which made fuch Alterations in the terreftrial terrestrial Globe, it cannot now be affected to so great a Degree as it was then:—For by the confused Manner the Fragments were forced back again into the great Deep, Mountains were formed, which we may conjecture to be nearly equal in Height to the whole Thickness of the earthy Shell; and, it is probable, that some of these huge Fragments may reach as much below the Deep, or Waters within the earthy Shell, as the Hills and Mountains do on the Outside; and as is observed, have left innumerable and large Caverns and Fissures, which reach from the fiery Expansion within, to the Tops of our highest Mountains without; where many of them, in different Parts of the World, have Volcanos on their Tops, and therefrom discharge their *superfluous Fire*, as Occasion may require.—By these Vents, whenever the internal Expansion is arrived to a Strength sufficient to overcome the outward Pressure, it forces itself up through these Vents, and expands itself into the common Atmosphere without; but if it happens to make its Way into any of those Caverns, that have not the aforesaid

aforesaid Vent, it there distends the incumbent *Strata*, and forms Earthquakes; and after it has found a Passage into the Atmosphere without, these Fragments are again forced together as before, but in a confused Order.—Hence it may be observed, that as soon as it arrives at a certain Force, it then spreads itself, and the *Equilibrium* is again restored.

Thus, as has been remarked, there will be left an internal *Void* of Space nearly 8000 Miles Diameter; which, from the above Observations, may be supposed to contain Fire and inflammable Air, and Steam.—Hence, this terraqueous Globe will be of no greater *Specifick Gravity* than the *Ethers* wherein it is placed; and that this is so, is confirmed by the Alterations made on the Flux and Reflux of the Sea into the Abyss; and this *only* by the Moon's intercepting the Pressure from the Extremities; so that this terraqueous Globe will be carried round the Sun, (and not fall into it) in the same Manner as Clouds, or in particular a Balloon, which is kept

kept fuspended at such a particular Distance from the Earth, viz. till its *Specifick Gravity* is altered, either by throwing out Ballast, to lessen that Gravity, and make it ascend higher, or by letting out some of the inflammable Air, and thereby increasing its Gravity.—If neither of these are done, or happens, by Accident or otherwise, the Balloon will continue at the same Height from the Earth, and be carried by the Current of Air wherein it swims, either North, South, East, or West; as that Current goes.—Heat and Cold are now allowed by all to be the Cause of the Current of Air we call Wind!—And what is very remarkable, the Person therein, let him be carried ever so fast, feels very little Effect from it.

Now it may be asked how is this Fire supported? If it does not receive some *Pabulum*, it must lose its Strength!—Certainly!—But it receives this Support by *Circulation* from without; as the Sun does by the *cold Ether* pressing into it from the Extremities of the System. — For the expansive Power from within

within the Shell of the Earth, may be observed to be in an exact *Equilibrium* with the compressive Power without.—For it has been often observed by Navigators, that at particular Places in the Ocean, there are certain *Gulfs* by which the Sea communicates with the *great Deep* below the Earth, particularly that Whirpool called *Maelstroom*, or *Navel of the Sea*, upon the Coast of Norway, where, says *Gordon*, in his *Geographical Grammar*, " The Sea, for upwards of two Leagues round, " makes such a terrible *Vortix*, that the Force " and Indraught of the Water, together *with* " *the Noise* and Tumbling of the Waves upon " one another, is rather to be admired than " expressed.—But, as in the Time of Flood, " the Water is drawn in with a mighty " Force, so during the Time of Ebb, does " it throw out the Sea with such Violence, " that the heaviest Bodies then cast into it, " cannot sink, but are tossed back again by " the impetuous Stream which rusheth out " with incredible Force."—Hence may be observed, that there is a continual Circulation, or alternate *Flux* and *Reflux*, between the

Seas,

Seas, without the earthy Shell, and the *Abyss* within; and that the *expansive* Force within is in so exact an *Equilibrium* with the *Compression* without, that no greater Force is required to cause this Flux and Reflux, than the Difference the Moon makes by her intercepting some of the Pressure from the Extremities, when she is either over, or at a great Distance from the Part.—Now the Waters, in running into the Abyss, carry with them Air enough for the *Pabulum*, or Support of the internal Fire.—On the Return of the Waters to the Expansion within the earthy Shell, they are again, by the Fire there, expanded into Vapour, which Vapour is forced up through the Caverns and Fissures from below, to the Tops of the highest Mountains, where by the Cold it there meets with, is again condensed into Water, falls into the different Cavities of the Earth, and is forced out in Springs, from thence into Rivers, and thence into the Sea.—Thus, as the Preacher tells us, "*All the Rivers run into the Sea,* "*yet the Sea is not full: Unto the Place from whence*

whence the Rivers come, thither they return again." (f)

It gives me Satisfaction to find that the Scriptures confirm the above natural Obfervations, and that they fpeak phyfically true concerning them.—Thus Job tells us (t), *" That the Earth is fufpended on the conftrict-" ing Mixture of Ethers;* the Place in the Heavens where thefe two ethereal Agents are in a juft Proportion to each other, and of the fame fpecifick Gravity with the Body of the Earth;

(f) Ecclef. I. 6.—(t) Job, XXVI. 7.

(t) What I have tranflated the *conftricting Mixture* of the Ethers, in the Englifh Bible is tranflated *Nothing*, but that cannot be the Signification of this Word: It is BaLIMaH, from BaLaM, which according to all Lexicons, fignifies *to conftrict, to bind, to reftrain*, as the Violence of an Horfe or Afs is by a Bridle; and is to be found but once more in the Bible, which is Pfalm XXXII. 9, where it is made ufe of as a participle paffive, for the reftraining an Horfe or Afs with a Bridle;—without the final *Mem*, it is often made ufe of as a *Mixture* of different Things, as dry and wet, &c.—It is probable that the Englifh Tranflators were led into this Error, by following the Latin Tranflation too clofely; which at that Time, was by many of the Church of Rome believed to be more infallibly true than the original Hebrew.

Earth; in which the terraqueous Globe is carried on in them, with as much Ease as a Cork is on the Water, or as if the whole Body was composed of Ethers; having neither *Projection* nor *Gravity*.—Hence, notwithstanding the terraqueous Globe is carried on by these Ethers, at the incredible Rate of more than one thousand Miles every Hour; yet the Inhabitants on it meet neither with Resistance or Pressure from these Ethers, and therefore find Nothing of this almost *inconceivable* quick Motion. — Much the same Thing has been observed by those who have been carried with the greatest Celerity in a Balloon; not finding any Thing of the Quickness of the Motion, or how it went.—*These* Ethers *compose the Swadling Band that surround it :* (u) *These are the* Pillars *which support it ;* (v) *when he gave his Decree that the Sea should not pass his Command.* (w)

Having now been forced to write a long Letter, in order to explain my Conjectures about the internal Make of this terraqueous Globe,

(u) Job, XXXVIII, 9.—(v) Job, IX. 6.—(w) Prov. VIII. 27, 28, 29.

Globe, I shall defer pointing out the Agents Nature makes Use of, and the Method they act by, in order to carry on the diurnal Rotation, and the annual Revolution, to my next Letter, which you will receive soon.

Adieu,

F. PENROSE.

STONEHOUSE,
Oct. 18, 178$\frac{5}{2}$.

To JOHN HEAVISIDE, Esq.

Mr. *Heaviside's Question,* " *Why does not the Earth gravitate into the Sun, &c.*" *answered.*—*All Space filled with* ETHERS, *which reach from the Sun, to the Extremities of this System, and are in continual Conflict, and cause a* vibrating Motion, *by their Endeavour of getting the better of each other. These* Ethers *the Cause of* Projection *and* Gravity.—*The Earth and Planets of different specifick Gravities, according to their Distance from the Sun.*—*The diurnal and annual* Motion of the Earth *accounted for. The Phenomena of Nature, and the Scriptures, confirm the Testimony of each other.*

Dear Sir,

IN the last Letter, I sent you my Conjectures on the Make and Form of this terraqueous Globe; by which you may observe, that I suppose the Thickness of the earthy Shell to be but small, in Comparison with the inter-

S s   nal

nal *Void* or *Hollow* in the *Midst* of it.—By the *Phenomena* of Earthquakes, &c. it appears that this Hollow is filled with Fire, inflammab'e Air, and Steam. — Thus the whole Body of the terraqueous Globe will be of no greater fpecifick Gravity, than the Ethers which furround it.—If this was not the Cafe, and it was folid to the Centre, it feems probable that it would be forced into the Sun: But, as it is of the fame fpecifick Gravity with the furrounding Ethers, they keep it at the fame Diftance from the Sun, and it fwims therein with as much Eafe as a Balloon does in the Air, above the Earth.

Having mentioned thus much, I fhall now endeavour to anfwer the two Queftions you were fo anxious about, which you propofed in your Letter dated May 16; and again repeated in your laft.—Firft, " If the Earth, " &c. were put in Motion by the Heat of " the Sun, rarefying the Atmofphere between " thefe Bodies, why did the Earth not im- " mediately gravitate into the Sun, as the " Medium muft be there more rarefied than
" any

"any where else?"—Secondly, "What is
"the Impulse or trajectile Force for its an-
"nual Motion; and then, what is the Power
"that brings it back again from the immense
"Distance at which it is at the Summer
"Solstice; or prevent it from flying off in a
"Tangent?"

In some of my former Letters [x] I observed it was the Opinion of the ancient Philosophers, that the Heavens were filled with Fire or Light and Air, and that these were the Agents which governed all other Things: Sir Isaac Newton seems to think so too, [y] for he supposed " that Light and Ether lay hid
" in *all* Bodies; that the *Light proceeded from*
" *the Sun*, and the *Spirit from the Extremities!*
" That if their elastic Force were expanded
" through the whole Heavens; and that if
" this Medium be rarer at the Body of the
" Sun, than at its Surface, and rarer at the
" Surface, than at the hundredth Part of an
" Inch from the Body of the Sun; and rarer
" there than at the fiftieth Part of an Inch
" from

(x) Letter IV. Introduction, P. 60.—(y) Opt. P.

"from its Body; and rarer at this Place,
"than at the Orb of Saturn; I see no Rea-
"son, (says he) why the Increase of its Den-
"sity should stop any where, and not rather
"be continued through all the Distances, from
"the Sun to Saturn, and beyond.—Then, if
"we suppose two vibrating Mediums, the
"one rarer at the dense Bodies of the Sun,
"Stars, Planets, and Comets, than in the
"celestial Spaces between them; so that if
"the elastic Force of this Medium may be
"exceeding great, it may suffice to *impel*
"Bodies *from the denser Parts of the Medium,*
"*towards the rarer, with all that Force or*
"*Impulse which we call Gravity.*

Hence we find, that it was the Opinion of Sir Isaac Newton, and the ancient Philosophers, that there was an ethereal Fluid, which filled *all Space*, from the Sun to the Extremities of this System.—That what issued from the Sun, in Form of Light, was more rare than that which was returned from the Extremities to the Sun, which he calls Spirit.— By these Agents, (the ETHERS)
all

all Motion was performed, and by the Spirit, every Thing was forced to the Sun, with that Power we call *Gravity*.—That the *Mixture* of thefe two Ethers was of a different fpecifick Gravity, in Proportion as one or other abounded.—Hence, that the Bodies of the Earth, Planets, &c. circulating round the Sun, muft be of different fpecifick Gravities, agreeing exactly with the fpecifick Gravity of the Medium *(Mixture,)* wherein they were placed.

Thus the Earth muft be of lefs fpecifick Gravity than *Venus*; *Venus* than *Jupiter*, &c. This may be explained fo far, as to underftand my Meaning, by placing a Glafs or Metal Bubble, of the exact fpecifick Gravity, between Water and Spirit of Wine —If we place this Bubble at the Bottom of a Glafs Tube, and pour on it an Inch of Spirit of Wine, it will be forced and kept at Bottom by its own Gravity; if we add an Inch of Water, it will then remain at Reft, in any Part of the Fluid:—If we again add another Inch of Water by Degrees, we fhall
perceive,

perceive, that the Fluid, by this Means, will acquire a greater fpecifick Gravity than the Bubble, and will then, (according to the Laws of Hydroftaticks,) be forced, *by Gravity*, down to the Bottom, and will then force the Bubble of lefs fpecifick Gravity, to afcend to the Top.—This Motion of the Bubble in the Fluid, may be made to move or change its Place, in the fame Manner by Heat and Cold. Thus by applying Heat to the Top, or any Side of the Fluid, it will expand its Parts, and thereby make it to occupy more Space: Hence its Pores being filled with Heat or Fire, it will refift lefs, and the cold and denfe Parts of the Fluid will prefs it towards, and into that Part which is more rare, and of lefs fpecifick Gravity, and refifts lefs.—Hence we may obferve, that Gravity and Levity are relative Effects.

Thus, the Earth being of the fame fpecifick Gravity, with the *Mixture* of the furrounding Ethers; thefe Ethers keep it at the fame Diftance it is from the Sun, and prevent it being projected farther from the Sun, or forced nearer to it. Having

Having obſerved thus much, that the Aſcent from the Sun, and the Deſcent to it, are occaſioned by the Rarity and Denſity of the different Mediums, as the different Mixtures of the Ethers, between the Sun and the Extremities, according as the Quantity of either one prevails; I ſhall now endeavour to point out the Cauſes of the *diurnal* and *annual* Motions of the Earth; but before I do this, let it be remembered, that Bodies of different Denſities, are a longer or a ſhorter Time heating, and alſo that they retain their Heat a longer or a ſhorter Time, according to their Denſities. (z) —Thus, Water will acquire a greater Heat than Air, and Earth than Water, &c.—This is obſerved to be the Cauſe of different Winds; for it is a known and invariable Quality of the Air, for the Cold to endeavour to force out the Hot, and the Hot to open and expand the Cold.— Thus the Earth being denſer than Water, it will acquire a greater Heat than the Sea.—
" It is obſerved, that the Sea Breezes blow
" towards the Land, in the Middle Part of
" the

(z) See Let. V. P. 181, 183.

"the Day, in *every Direction*; and in the
"Middle or coldest Part of the Night, the
"Land Breezes blow towards the Sea, and
"thus alternately they succeed each other.—
"Hence the Equilibrium of the Pressure of
"the two Atmospheres being destroyed, and
"the Land Atmosphere, by the Heat being
"rendered specifically lighter than the Air at
"Sea, the former ascends by the superior
"Pressure or Weight of the latter; therefore
"the Sea Breezes *blow towards the Land, in*
"*every possible Direction.*—When Night comes
"on, the Sun's Heat abates, until the Land
"Atmosphere becomes equally dense with
"that at Sea.—The Equilibrium of Pressure
"being thus restored, the Sea Breezes totally
"cease.—Thus, Cold increasing by the Ab-
"sence of the Sun, and its sudden Departure
"below the Horizon, accumulates on the
"Surface of the Islands, and condenses their
"incumbent Atmosphere more than that at
"Sea."

I shall now apply Deductions from the Phenomena observed, and by them I shall endeavour

deavour to explain the Motions of this terraqueous Globe.—First then, I suppose, there is a *hot Ether* or Light continually issuing from the Sun at the Centre, which is the Cause of *Projection*, Rarefaction, Expansion, and what we call a *centrifugal Force*, &c. and a *cold Ether* or Spirit continually descending from the Extremities of this System, to the Sun at the Centre, which is the Cause of Attraction, Cohesion, Pressure, *Gravity*, and what is called a *centripetal Force*.

Thus, Light or one Moiety of the celestial Ethers, (which is the rarer or finer Part,) is in continual Motion, from the Sun to the Circumference; and the other Moiety or *Spirit*, (which is the grosser Part,) is in continual Motion from the Circumference or Extremities of this System, to the Sun in the Centre;—that these two Forces, by Mixture, exactly balance each other at the Morning and Evening Edge of the Earth, and parallel with the Ecliptic.—The Motion of these adverse Forces causes an Expansion, and lays a Stress or Pressure on every Body, and every

Particle of the ethereal Fluid, (and is the Cauſe of Coheſion,) and forces the Bodies contained therein, either nearer or farther from the Sun, according as the different Mixture of theſe two Particles prevail, and the ſpecific Gravity of the Body.—Thus, when an Equilibrium is formed round that Body, it remains at Reſt, and continues ſo, till by Light or Heat an Expanſion is made on one Side, or Part of it; when Motion enſues, and continues ſo long as the Preſſure behind is of greater Force than the Projection or Expanſion before.

The Mixture of theſe two Qualities of Ethers, being rarer or denſer in Proportion to the Diſtance between the Sun, and the Extremities of the Syſtem.—Thus the Bodies of the Earth, and all the Planets, are formed of different ſpecifick Gravities, according as they are placed either nearer or farther off from the Sun, and are placed in a *Mixture* of Ethers, of the ſame ſpecifick Gravity with the Planets placed therein; and are thereby prevented from approaching nearer, or receding

ceding farther from him.—Thus the Light projecting on one Side of the terraqueous Globe, and Spirit pressing in at the opposite, causes the Earth's Motion round its Axis, in the same Manner as a Cork or Piece of Wood may be observed to circulate round, when a River is obstructed by a Bank, and the Water made to circulate round.

We will now suppose the Sun to be placed in the Firmament or Expansion, and the Earth in the same Place it now occupies; I will then suppose, (as Moses informs us) that it was first made to turn on its Axis by the immediate Power of God; after that, having finished his Work, it was an *Automaton*, and he saw that it was good, and every Part of it capable to perform the Office he designed it for.—Thus he left *Nature*, or the *material* Agents, to perform their own Work; *unless, by a Miracle,* he stopped or altered them, to shew his Power over them.— Thus, as has been observed, the *projectile Force* of the Light from the Sun, on that Side of the Earth opposite to it, was exactly counterbalanced

counterbalanced by the *gravitating Force* of the Spirit on the Backside of the Earth, opposite to the Extremities.—Now, it is well known, and has already been observed, that Bodies receive and retain their Heat, in Proportion to their Densities, and that this has been proved to be the Cause of Winds, Hurricanes, &c.—Thus, that Side of the terraqueous Globe, opposite the Sun, having its Parts greatly heated, and being more than one thousand Times more dense than the Atmosphere, it retains it a great While longer;— Thus, the Atmosphere at the Evening Edge of the Earth, is more rarefied and expanded by this Heat, and the dense Air or Spirit pressing in from behind, (and also from that Side opposite the Extremities) to form an Equilibrium, forces it round its Centre, towards the Morning Edge, or from West to East.— Hence the diurnal Motion;—the lateral Rarefaction being greater on this Quarter from Noon to Evening, or between South and West, than on its opposite, receives a different Impulse, in *a Diagonal* of these two Forces, viz. that of the projectile, on that Side the Earth

Earth next the Sun, and the gravitating, on that Side oppofite the Extremities.—Hence, the annual Impulfe through the Ecliptick, which makes an Angle of 23 D. 30 M. with the diurnal; and as thefe Forces are continually acting, fo the Earth will continue her Motion round her Axis, from Weft to Eaft, together with that through the Ecliptick;— As thefe Ethers are of different Qualities, both nearer or farther from the Sun; and as the terraqueous Globe is exactly of the fame fpecifick Gravity with this Mixture of the Ethers, wherein fhe is placed, (which is in a continual Current or Circulation round the Sun,) fo muft the Earth be carried round the Sun with it.

We may form fome Conception how thefe two oppofite Forces act by the Motions of a Pendulum, or a Weight fufpended by an inflexible Rod on a Pin, as its Centre of Motion.—" Its Weight or Gravity will hinder
" its approaching any nearer to the Centre,
" and the Rod or Projection will prevent its
" Weight or Gravity from carrying it farther
" from the Centre; but, neverthelefs, it is
" capable

" capable of being put in Motion by a *small*
" *lateral* Impulse, and will describe not a
" strait Line, but *Arcs* of a Circle, whose
" Centre is the Pin from whence it is sus-
" pended.—And as the two Forces are sup-
" posed equal, the Case of the Earth will be
" exactly analogous to that of the Pendulum!"

Thus the progressive or lateral Impulse being always exerted in the Direction of the Plane of the Earth's enlightened Hemisphere, where the mixt Force of these conflicting Ethers is equal, and Resistence nothing.—Which Plane is always perpendicular to the Rays drawn from the Sun to that Place.—If in any Part of the Earth's Orbit, the *Pressure or Gravity* be greater than ordinary, or *the Projection of the Light* less; the Earth, in either Case, will be made to approach in that Part of its Orbit, nearer to the Sun: Or, if the *lateral* Impulse be stronger or weaker than ordinary, the Earth will be forced farther off, or nearer to the Sun: And as the Moon and Planets are sometimes so situated, that if, by the Intervention of their Bodies, they

they interrupt the Action of *Spirit* or *Light*; this Interruption may leſſen or increaſe their Force, either to bring the Earth nearer to, or farther from the Sun. — Witneſs the Moon's Influence on the Tides!

The foregoing Account of the Phenomena of Nature, ſeems to confirm and explain to us the ſhort Hints thereof given in the Scriptures.

I ſhall therefore ſubmit to your Judgement and Candour, whether what I have ſaid may not illuſtrate the Moſaic Account of the Formation of the Earth, and Reformation of it, at the Deluge; and then conclude, that as the Phenomena of Nature, Reaſon, and Revelation ſo perfectly agree, whether that Coincidence may not be conſidered as a Teſtimony of the Truth of each.

Thus we are informed, that the all-wiſe Creator has obſerved the moſt exact Proportions, and has made ALL Things in *Number, Weight,* and *Meaſure:*—Who made *Weight*

for

for the *Winds* or, (which is more literal) *who made the Spirit the gravitating Inftrument, and weighed the Waters by Meafure.* (a) Who hath meafured the Waters in the Hollow of his Hand; and meted (or fpread) out the Heavens with a Span, and comprehended the Duft of the Earth in a *Meafure*;—who *weighed* the Mountains in Scales, and the Hills in a Balance. (b) " Who hath *bound the Waters* in a *Garment*; who hath eftablifhed all the Ends of the Earth: (c) Who fhut up the Sea with Doors, and made the Cloud the Garment thereof, and thick Darknefs a Swadling-Band for it; and faid hitherto fhalt thou come, but no farther; and here fhall thy proud Waves be ftayed. (d) The North declines, (or *gravitates)* to the empty Place, (or South) and hangeth the Earth upon Nothing, (in Hebrew) (the *Mixture of Ethers,)* (e) Thefe, as we are informed, (f) are the *Pillars* of the Earth, and the Lord has fet the *World* upon them.

Adieu,

F. PENROSE.

STONEHOUSE,
Oct. 20, 1785.

(a) Job. XXVIII. 25.—(b) Ifaih, XL. 12.—(c) Proverbs. XXX. 4.—(d) Job, XXXVIII. 8, 9, 10, 11.—(e) Job, XXVI. 7.—(f) I. Sam. II. 8.

Let. XVIII. *On* ASTRONOMY.

To JOHN HEAVISIDE, Esq.

Dear Sir,

IN your laſt Letter, you were ſo complaiſant as to aſſure me, that my long Letters gave you infinite Pleaſure, and that I had not anſwered your former Queſtions.—In my two laſt, I endeavoured to do it in as clear a Manner as I could; I hope they will find your Health quite reſtored, by your Journey into Norfolk and Suffolk, together with your Sea Bathing.

I herewith ſend you a New Year's Gift, for A. D. 1786, in Hopes to profit by the Remarks of yourſelf and Friends.

It is two Diagrams, (an original Deſign of my own) conſtructed to ſhew the Places of the Sun and Moon, for every Day next Year, according to the Julian Calendar.—You will find ſome Part of it to differ from what is generally taught in Aſtronomical Lectures, and received as true, viz. the Diviſion of the Ecliptick

Ecliptick, and the Preceffion of the Equinoxes, but thefe appear to me contrary to the Operations or Laws of Nature; I therefore wifh to have them examined by Perfons well verfed in thefe Sciences; and as the Improvement of Knowledge is the fole End of my Defign, fo if you will fend me the critical Remarks of your Mathematical Friends thereon, I doubt not but all thefe Difficulties will be cleared up.

I am,

DEAR SIR,

Your faithful

And obliged Friend,

F. PENROSE.

STONEHOUSE,
Dec. 26, 1788.

Let XIX.   *On* ASTRONOMY.

To F. PENROSE, Esq.

The Observations of Mr. Heaviside's astronomical Friend, on Mr. Penrose's Diagrams, not conclusive.

DEAR SIR,

YOUR laſt Favour found me very early in the new Year at Potterels, where I had been for two Months, ſo far from well, as not to have ſtired out of Doors hardly in all that Time. My little Excurſion into Norfolk and Suffolk, was of ſome Service to me for a While, but I ſoon grew worſe again, and was unable to ſtir; indeed I have not been able to ride ten Miles on Horſeback, in any one Day, for near a Year and Half paſt; however, I have been recovering full as faſt as I can expect, for the laſt five or ſix Weeks, and have got up my Fleſh and Strength again amazingly, if I can but keep free from Colds, to oppreſs my Lungs, which are ſtill in a Situation too ſuſceptible of Injury.—This State of Health has detered me from

from staying in London more than a Day or two at a Time, when Business obliged me to it, till very lately; when, upon Trial, I found myself, thank God, equal to staving here without Prejudice.—For these Reasons I had no Opportunity till very lately of shewing your Diagrams, (with which you favoured me, and for which I think myself very highly obliged to you) to any of my learned Friends; but I do assure you, that I did not neglect the very first I had; and this very Day the Gentleman called, when I was out, and left it for me, with a Note, of which you will find a Copy in the Margin; I would have sent the Note itself, but that it would have made it a double Letter.

As I do not think he has entered so deeply into this Business as he should have done, I am by no Means satisfied with the little he has said, and therefore shall endeavour to find out some other Astronomer, who will give it more Consideration than I fear he has done; I should therefore have defered writing till then, but that as I think it probable you may

wish

wish to have the Plate engraved soon; I trouble you now, to beg you will give me your immediate Directions for having it done, if you wish to have it done *now*, and I will use my best Endeavours to find out a good Engraver.— Pray what think you of this Gentleman's Idea on that Subject?

On the other Side you will likewise find what my Friend Dr. Alexander, (to whom I wrote some Time ago, to get some Experiments made relative to the Weight of Bodies at different Depths in Mines,) says on that Head: His Account seems in some Measure to contradict your Opinion as well as my own.—If you are not satisfied with this Answer, and would put any more particular Questions to him, pray send them to me, and I will endeavour to procure an Answer to them; for it will give me great Pleasure to procure you any Information or Satisfaction in your laudable Pursuits after Knowledge and Philosophy.— Nor would I have you think, that because I am too idle a Fellow myself, to apply closely to the Study of Philosophy

losophy as you do, that therefore I take no Pleasure in such Enquiries; far otherwise; I really have great Pleasure in it, and should follow the Pursuit closely had I Leisure, and any Friend near me to assist or join me in it.

The astronomical Gentleman who had the Examination of your Diagrams, presents his Compliments, and has returned it, and observes, that " He fears some of the Positions " it contains will not be found to have been " corrected up to the latest Discoveries, or " rather *newest Opinions.*"

I am,

Dear Sir,

Your very obedient,

And obliged Servant,

J. HEAVISIDE.

Prince's-Street,
Feb. 22, 1786.

To JOHN HEAVISIDE, Esq.

Dear Sir,

YOUR last very kind and obliging Letter came to Stonehouse when I was in Cornwall, where I had been a great Part of the Months of February and March:—For this last Month I have been confined with the Gout:—I thank God, I am now able to walk again.—It gave us very sincere Pleasure to be informed, that you were recovered from your late Indisposition.

I am greatly obliged to you for the Trouble you have taken, in consulting your Astronomical Friends, about my Diagrams.—As I differ therein from what is generally taught by Astronomers, about the Division of the Ecliptick, the Precession of the Equinoxes, which appear to me to be Things of great Importance, I did hope that they would have thought it a Matter worthy their Examination, and that I should be confirmed either that I was right, or that my Errors, if any,

would

would be pointed out and corrected.—I therefore join entirely in your Opinion concerning it, viz. that they have not entered so deeply into the Business as I could have wished they had done.—For, as they observe, " *the Positions therein differ from the latest* " *Discoveries, or rather the newest Opinions*." For that Reason I wished to have them thoroughly examined, as Truth is my Object.

If you have not yet met with an Astronomer, whose Opinion may be depended on, I hope, from your great Acquaintance, you soon will have an Opportunity of doing it.—I have sent one of these Diagrams to Oxford, with a Desire that it might be examined by the Geometricians and Astronomers there, but I have not yet received any Intelligence concerning it.—I am afraid that many Teachers of Science go on by Rote, with the same String of Experiments and Arguments that they have been taught, without giving themselves Freedom and Trouble to examine the Truth of them.

I

I give you and Dr. Alexander many Thanks for the Intelligence he sent you, concerning the Rise and Fall of the Mercury in the Barometer, when under the Earth.—I am afraid that Dr. Alexander, by consulting Miners, who *had the Rudiments of Philosophy*, has answered the Inquiry from Theory and not from Experiment.—All Experience tell us, that the deeper we dig under the Surface of the Earth, the Heat is the greater, and of Consequence the Air is the rarer;—therefore, for that Reason, I am fearful that those Persons, whom Dr. Alexander applied to, have imposed on him, and answered his Queries from the Ideas they had of the Matter, and *not* from Experiment.—If they had made Use of a Thermometer, instead of a Barometer, I believe their Theory would prove true.—I could only wish for an Experiment without Theory.—Let a Barometer be carried down into a Mine, mark the Height of the Quicksilver on the Surface of the Ground, and also every thirty or forty Fathom you descend.— If they had also a Quicksilver Thermometer, and likewise mark the different Heights of the Mercury, it would be more satisfactory. I am sorry that you and Dr. Alexander should have had so much Trouble, and that he should have met with so many Difficulties about it.—All this I can most readily believe, as I have met with the same.—It might be imagined that I could get a Thing of this Kind easily done in Cornwall.—I have applied to many of my Acquaintance for that Purpose, and told them that I should be glad to pay a Man for his Trouble in doing it.—I have been often promised it, but have never yet been able to get it performed.—If I could go down in a Mine myself, I could easily get it done! A Gentleman, when I was last in Cornwall, promised me to get it done, but I am fearful it will be some Time before it will be brought about.

I am,

 Dear Sir,

  Your obliged and faithful Servant,

    F. PENROSE.

STONEHOUSE,
April 10, 1786.

Let. XXI.   *On* ASTRONOMY.

To F. PENROSE, Esq.

DEAR SIR,

I AM ashamed to see that it is now six Weeks since I was favoured with your very kind Letter, and that I cannot even now answer it satisfactorily, either to myself or to you; for having been so much out of Town, (in which I dare not stay long at a Time, on Account of my Cough,) and having had so very much to do when I am here, and now finding that *real* deep Philosophers and Astronomers are much more thinly sown than I apprehended, I have not been able to get at any one who has ventured to give me any *decided* Opinion upon your Diagrams. — I want much to get them shewn to Dr. Maskelyne, but have not yet been so luckly as to meet with one Acquaintance of mine that knows him enough to do it; however, I do not yet despair of finding such a one, if your Friends at Oxford fail you.

I have wrote again to my Friend, Dr. Alexander,

exander, to try if he can procure a more exact Experiment to be made with a Barometer, in a Coal-Pit; which I dare say he will do if he can; but I need not tell you how difficult it is to put those Miners, (or indeed any Body else) out of the Way in which they have been used to tread, unless it were possible to impress them with a Desire of real Knowledge, unadulterated with Prejudice, *or make it* their Interest.

I am,

DEAR SIR,

Very truly,

Your Friend, and obedient Servant,

J. HEAVISIDE.

PRINCE'S-STREET,
June 29, 1786.

Let. XXII. ASTRONOMY.

On the MOON and LUNAR MOTIONS.

To JOHN HEAVISIDE, Esq.

The Moon not a Planet, but a Satellite attending the Earth.—The recorded Observations of Astronomers, concerning Her, collected.—Her Make and Motions described.—The Chaldean Cycle, with the Methods they made use of for calculating their Eclipses.—The physical Causes of these Motions explained, and confirmed by the Observations of Mr. Herschel, and the French Astronomers.

DEAR SIR,

I GIVE you many Thanks for the Trouble you have taken to get a decided Opinion on my Diagrams, &c.— As you express a Hope, in your last Letter, to get Dr. Maskelyne's Opinion on them, I have herewith sent you my Theory on the Moon, and the lunar Motions, in Hopes that you may, at the same Time, get his Sentiments on the

lunar

On the MOON and LUNAR MOTIONS.

lunar Motions alfo, and perhaps he will let you know what Objections he has to any of them.

The lunar Motions are called irregular; but, on Examination, we fhall find no Irregularity belonging to the Moon or her Motions, but all of them performed according to the moft exact and perfect Harmony and Mechanifm; and that their apparent Intricacy proceeds from our Incapacity to comprehend their almoft innumerable Variety of Motions. If we ftudy them with a proper Attention, we fhall find, that, inftead of being irregular, they are performed with the greateft Harmony and Regularity, according to the moft ftrict Laws of Geometry, Number, Weight, and Meafure; and though their Number and Variety exceed the Power of comprehending them, or even of believing their Regularity, unlefs by thofe who make them their particular Study; for though the Moon requires 7,948,800 fynodical Revolutions, (which are more than 600,000 Years) for to go through all

On the MOON and LUNAR MOTIONS.

all her Variations, and finish her Period or Cycle; (g) yet all these various Motions are carried on in the most curious, exact, and mechanical Manner, according to Number, Weight, and Measure, and cannot be calculated or understood by no other Method; therefore if any Theory concerning them will not bear the Test of Geometry and Numbers, it must be discarded.—Having premised thus much, I shall, in the first Place, collect the recorded Facts and Observations of Astronomers concerning them; from which I shall endeavour to draw the most natural Inferences, to explain these various Motions, and to point out their physical Causes.

The Moon is not a Planet but a Satellite, attending the Earth; which, together with the Sun, are allowed to be the principal Cause of her Motions.—These Motions are generally divided in a three-fold Manner; which are not only connected with each other, but are also connected with those of the Earth's,

in

(g) Kennedy, P. 196, 210.

On the MOON and LUNAR MOTIONS.

in a moſt wonderful Manner.—In the firſt Place, ſhe has a Motion round the Earth from Change to Change; or, from Sun to Sun, which ſhe performs in 29 D. 12 H. 44 M. 1 S. 45 T. which is called a *Lunation*.—2dly, She has a forward Motion, compounded with this Lunation, from Weſt to Eaſt, attending the Earth through the Ecliptick, round the Sun;—this ſhe performs in twelve Lunations, 10 Days, 21 Hours, and 39 Seconds.— Theſe twelve Lunations are called a *lunar Year*, and the 10 Days, 21 Hours, and 39 Seconds, are the Time required for her to get up with the Sun again. Theſe 10 Days, 21 Hours, and 39 Seconds, are not dropt or loſt, but go on as Part of the next Lunation, and is called *the Epact*, and is the Difference between the lunar and ſolar Year.—She does not keep the Earth's Path round the Sun, through the Ecliptick, but goes round the Earth in a progreſſive Circle, like a Screw, and forward, through the Ecliptick, at the ſame Time, together with the

On the MOON and LUNAR MOTIONS.

the Earth; always, (throughout her whole Orbit,) keeping nearly at the same Distance from Her;—that is, Half the Diameter of her Orbit; which is supposed to be about 240,000 Miles. — These Motions of the Moon in her Orbit, round the Earth, and through the Ecliptick, is so well described by Mr. *Ferguson*, in his Astronomy, [h] that I shall take the Liberty to send it you, in his own Words.—" The Moon's absolute Mo-
" tion *(says he)* from her Change, to her first
" Quarter, is so much *slower* than the Earth's,
" that she falls 240 thousand Miles, (equal
" to the Semidiameter of her Orbit) behind
" the Earth, at her first Quarter; that is,
" she *falls back* a Space equal to her Distance
" from the Earth:—From that Time, her
" Motion is *gradually accelerated* to her Op-
" position or Full, and then she is come up
" as far as the Earth; having *regained* what
" she *lost* in her first Quarter.—From the
" Full to the last Quarter, her Motion *con-*
" *tinues*

[h] Ferguson, P. 194. S. 267.

ASTRONOMY.   Let. XXII.

On the MOON and LUNAR MOTIONS.

"*tinues accelerated*, so as to be just as far *be-
"fore the Earth*, (at her third Quarter) as
"she was *behind* it at her *first*; but from
"thence to her Change, her Motion is *re-
"tarded*, so that she loses as much, with
"Respect to the Earth, as is equal to her
"Distance from it, or to the Semidiameter
"of her Orbit; and by that Means she comes
"in Conjunction (at the Change) as seen
"from the Earth."

These Motions of the Moon, both round the Earth and round the Sun, are performed from West to East, and from Left to Right, in the same Manner as the Earth goes round the Sun:—But, besides these two *joint* Motions of the Moon, there is a Motion or an *ecliptick* Current of Ethers, *absolutely* belonging to the Moon.—This *Current of Ethers* goes also from West to East, as do the Earth and Moon, but with this Difference, that as the Earth and Moon proceed Eastward, from Left to Right; so this proceeds just in the opposite

On the MOON and LUNAR MOTIONS.

oppofite Manner, from Right to Left, and may moft properly be denominated *the Path of the Nodes or Eclipses.*—This alfo creeps round the Ecliptick in a progreffive Circle, in 18 Years, 10 Days, 19 Hours, 46 Minutes, and 15 Seconds; when it again meets the Sun in the fame Point of the Ecliptick, and then begins a new Cycle.—This was in Ufe in *Chaldea,* and is called the *Chaldean Cycle of Eclipfes:*—For, in this Period, there will be a regular Return of the *fame Eclipfe* for many Ages; only the Eclipfe get 28$'$ 12$''$ forward at every Return; and, by thefe flow Degrees, comes in at one Pole of the Earth, and after having paffed quite over it, goes out at the other:—Thus thofe which come in at the North Pole, go out at the South; and thofe which come in at the South, go out at the North; after which they are again loft in the Expanfe, but require more than one thoufand Years to do it.—Hence it may be remarked, that the *Chaldeans,* (from amongft whom Abraham was called) had a

Method

On the MOON and LUNAR MOTIONS.

Method of calculating Eclipses; for they had only to keep an Account of Number of Days and Years; the Method the Patriarchs and Israelites were taught to calculate the Returns of the Weeks, Months, and Years, and to keep their Chronology. (i) Thus by *only numbering* and keeping an Account of the Days and Years of this *Chaldean Cycle*, which was finished every eighteen Years, and the same Eclipse was sure to make its Appearance again; for at the End of every eighteen Years, the Sun, Moon, and Nodes meet the Earth on the same Point of the Ecliptick, and they then begin a new Cycle.—To illustrate this, I shall here add the Calculations of the fourth and fifth Return of that remarkable Eclipse which happened at London, May 3, N. S. 1715—at 9 H. 51 M. or 2 H 9 M. before twelve o'Clock, when the astronomical Day is compleated, so that it was May 2 D. 21 H.

(i) Introduction, P. 27, 28.

On the MOON and LUNAR MOTIONS.

H. 51 M. fubftract this from the three Days of May, and it leaves D.H.M.
                                    28   2   9—1715
    To which add June 15 4 56—1787 the Eclipfe
    ─────────────
It makes in the Whole   43   7   5——72 Years, 43 D.
    ─────────────   7 H. 5 M.
                        Years D. H. M.   D. H. M.
4th—4 Cycles———   72 43 7   5— June 15 4 56 P. M — 1787
5th—1 Cycle ———   18 10 19 46 15 June 26 0 42 15 P.M   18
    ─────────────   ─────────────
It makes in the Whole   90 54 2 51 15   1805

From the above Example we may obferve with what Eafe and Certainty the Chaldeans might calculate the Return of the Eclipfes, viz. by knowing exactly the Length or Quantity of Time which the Sun, Moon, and Nodes require to perform their Circle, or to meet again in the fame Point of the Ecliptick at which they parted; for though they do not meet precifely at the fame Point, yet it wants only 28′ 12″. ——— Thefe Calculations make it appear, that the Nodes move forward to the Eaftward as well as the Earth and Moon, and alfo that they move a contrary

Way

On the MOON and LUNAR MOTIONS.

Way from them, and by that Means the Moon crosses them twice every Lunation.

In this Cycle there are 223 Lunations
      229 Nodes
And   18 Julian Years, 10 Days, 19 Hours, 46 Minutes, 15 T.

Hence the Regularity and the Harmony of the Sun, Moon, and Earth, may be remarked, and the Method of the Ancients in calculating their Eclipses, which they did in so *mechanical* a Manner, that they had no Occasion to know which of them moved, or whether any one of them did; yet were able to calculate, to prognosticate, or foretel these supposed portentous Events.

Thus, as has been observed, the ecliptick Path of the Eclipses, goes forward from West to East, but a contrary Way to the Earth and Moon, and makes an Angle of 5 Degrees 20 Minutes, with the ecliptick Path of the Earth.

The

Let. XXII. ASTRONOMY.

On the MOON and LUNAR MOTIONS.

The Moon makes her Orbit round the Earth, by an Angle of 45 Degrees, with the Ecliptick;—but as this Angle is not the fame throughout her whole Orbit, as the Moon, in one Part of her Orbit, is Half the Diameter of it *before* the Earth, and in another Part, fo much behind her, fo fhe does not make the fame Angle with the Ecliptick quite through her Revolution. — Thus, at the Entrance into her *third* Quarter, fhe cuts the Ecliptick *diagonally*, and *flackens* her Motion two-thirds, (when fhe enters the South, or Summer Part of her Lunation,) and, (as was obferved by Mr. Ferguson,) *falls back*, and proceeds to the Weftward, by an Angle of 45 Degrees.—Thus fhe keeps on with this Angle, till fhe comes to the Change; when it is altered to the Complement of that Angle, which is alfo 45 Degrees; which Angle is continued from the Change to her *firft Quarter*;— at which Point fhe croffes the Ecliptick, and enters the North or Winter Part of her Orbit.—Here this Angle

On the *MOON* and *LUNAR MOTIONS*.

is altered from 45 Degrees, to 19 Degrees, 50 Minutes, and her Motion is *increased* two-thirds, and she now recovers the Motion *she lost at her third* Quarter; and, by this Means, she gets so forward to the Eastward, in the Ecliptick, as to be exactly in a Line with the Earth and Sun at her Opposition.— From this Place she returns round the Earth, and continues her *accelerated* Motion, till she arrives again at her third Quarter, where she is again a Semi-diameter of her Orbit, *before the Earth*; and from this Place she goes on as above described.

The Moon's Orbit, round the Earth, is marked by Astronomers with four Divisions: The first is from Star to Star; which she performs in 27 Days, 7 Hours, 43 Minutes, 4 Seconds.—This would compleat her Orbit, did she not go forward in the Ecliptick at the same Time.—The second is from Apogee to Apogee, which requires 5 Hours, 35 Minutes, 39 Seconds more.—These 5 H. 35 M. 39 S.

On the MOON and LUNAR MOTIONS.

39 S. shew us how much her progressive Motion, forward, in the Ecliptick is, during the Time of her going from Apogee to Apogee.—The Earth's progressive Motion forward, through the Ecliptick, during one Rotation round her Axis, or twenty-four Hours, is four Minutes; hence, 1 H. 50 M. 12 S. belong to the Earth, and the remaining 3 H. 45 M. 27 S. is the Quantity of the Ecliptick *forward* Motion which belongs *absolutely* to the Moon during that Time.—Thus we may observe, that the Moon's absolute Motion *forward, through the Ecliptick,* is more than double to that of the Earth's.—This causes her to compleat her Orbit round the Sun, in less Time than the Earth does. This is also confirmed by the Motion of the Moon's Shadow over the Earth, during the Time of an Eclipse, which Mr. Ferguson tells us, [k] moves at the mean Rate of $30\frac{1}{2}$ Minutes of a Degree every Hour.—The third Division is from Node to Node.—This is not generally distinguished

---

[k] Ferguson, P. .-6. S. 338.

On the MOON and LUNAR MOTIONS.

diſtinguiſhed in this Manner by Aſtronomers, as they have ſuppoſed that the Motion of the Nodes receded from Eaſt to Weſt, and did not proceed forward, (as I do) from Weſt to Eaſt, which requires 1 D. 4 H. 51 M. 8 S. 44 T. Time to compleat it, than from Apogee to Apogee.—The fourth Diviſion wants 18 H. 34 M. 10 S. 1 T. to be added to the laſt, to bring the Moon to the Sun, or compleat the Lunation; which, as was before obſerved, is 29 D. 12 H. 44 M. 1 S. 45 T.

When the Moon comes to her Apogee, ſhe has compleated her Orbit round the Earth, in the Ecliptick; but as the *ecliptick Current of Ethers*, (as they move forward in a progreſſive Circle) has got 1 D. 3 H. 51 M. 8 S. 44 T. before the Moon, during that Time, ſo it requires for the Moon to go juſt ſo much beyond her Orbit, to meet and croſs it,—At the very Point, where the Moon, in her Orbit round the Earth, *croſſes the ecliptick Current of Ethers*, is her Node, and a
Line

On the MOON and LUNAR MOTIONS.

Line from Node to Node, crossing the Centre of the Ecliptick, is called the *Line of Nodes.*—Thus the Line of Nodes cross the Ecliptick every sixth Lunation, when the Node that was last in Conjunction with the Moon, *now* crosses the Ecliptick 4 D. 15 H. 25 M. before the Moon meets the Sun; and as the Nodes are diametrically opposite to each other, so this other Node wants the same Time to meet the Sun; but as the ecliptick Current of Ethers goes forward every Half a Node but 9 H. 17 M. 5 S. so the Moon comes in Conjunction only 9 H. 14 M. 5 S. after the Node.

The Nodes then cross each other, and change Places; the ascending one to the descending, and the descending to the ascending: Hence, whenever either Node at the End of the sixth Lunation, is 4 D. 15 H. 25 M. before the Moon, the other Node (being the same,) will meet the Moon in the Ecliptick, and cause a total and central

Eclipse

On the MOON and LUNAR MOTIONS.

Eclipse.—But, as all these Points are of such different Lengths, and vary so much, it is not to be wondered at, that we have so few Eclipses; more especially, as the Orbit of the Moon is divided into 360 Degrees, and the Moon must pass the Node within 17 Degrees of it, at the Change, and within 12° at the Opposition, to cause an Eclipse; otherwise the Moon's Shadow will not touch the Earth, nor the Earth's Shadow the Moon.—In Order to make more clear what has been observed, I shall describe the Nodes and Eclipses for this Year, A. D. 1786.

The Nodes move forward so much faster, through the Ecliptick, than the Moon, that at the End of every twelfth Lunation, that Node, which was in Conjunction with her, when she began her first, is got 9 D. 6 H. 50 M. 0 S. 12 T. before her; and just Half that Quantity, or 4 D. 15 H. 25 M. 0 S. 6 T. at the End of every sixth Lunation.—The Nodes change Places every sixth Lunation,

On the MOON and LUNAR MOTIONS.

tion, when the ascending Node becomes the descending, and the descending the ascending one.

Now to explain their Motion this Year.—We will suppose the two Nodes to be marked A and B—The Nodes crossed the Ecliptick Jan. 14 D. 12 H. 0 M. when A became the descending Node, and B the ascending one.—The Moon comes in Opposition to the Sun, 44 Minutes after, and causes a total Eclipse.—14 Days, 9 H. 5 M. after that, the other Node was in Conjunction with the Sun, and caused an Eclipse of that Luminary; after this, the Moon in her Orbit round the Earth, never crossed the ecliptick Path of the Nodes, *near enough* the Sun, to cause an Eclipse, till July 6, at 16 Minutes past twelve at Night, when the Node A will cross the Ecliptick 3 D. 15 H. 9 M. before the Moon was in Opposition; and, the other Node B will also want just as much to be in the Ecliptick, by that Means the Node B will

On the MOON *and* LUNAR MOTIONS.

will be in the Ecliptick, 54 Minutes only after the Moon is in Conjunction, and cause a total Eclipse of the Moon, July 11.—On the next Change, fourteen Days after, viz. July 25, the other Node A will meet the Moon in the Ecliptick, and cause an Eclipse of the Sun, and then will become the descending Node again.

The above are the collected Observations of Astronomers on the Moon, and the lunar Motions, from whence we may infer, that they are all caused and governed (as immortal Sir Isaac *Newton* has supposed) by the subtile *Ethers* with which the heavenly Space is filled, and by which they are surrounded.— For, according to him, " these ETHERS " are expanded through the whole Heavens, " and *impel* Bodies from the denser Parts of " of the Medium, towards the rarer, *with all* " *that Force* and *Impulse* which we call " GRAVITY. [1] That these *Ethers* act in a " double Capacity, the one as *Light*, pro-
" ceeding

[1] Lec. IV. P. 169.

On the MOON and LUNAR MOTIONS.

"ceeding from the Sun, and the other as *Spirit*, descending towards the Sun;—and thus a *Circulation* is carried on between these two vibrating Mediums."—Thus *they act by a continual Conflict, in a vibrating Manner, with a Force in Proportion as the one or the other prevail:—When the Light prevails*, it opens, expands, and projects *every Thing:*—On the contrary, *when the Spirit prevails*, every Thing is *compressed*, and their Parts *are forced in closer Contact.*—Thus all Bodies, by being compressed into less Space, are increased in their specifick Gravity, and they are also made to adhere with all that Power or Force called *Gravity, Attraction* of *Cohesion*, &c.

I think it must add to the Veneration we have for the Scriptures, to find that they speak justly in physical Matters, about the Mechanism of Nature.—Thus *Job* tells us [m] that God *made a Weight for the Winds*; this

[m] Job. XXVIII, 25.

On the MOON and LUNAR MOTIONS.

this is according to our English Translation, but the Hebrew is more clear and expressive, it is there said that God made the *Wind* or *Spirit*, the *Instrument* of Gravity.

In the first Place, the Earth is carried through the Ecliptick, round the Sun, by *a Current of Ethers*, and the Moon, as a Satellite of the Earth, is carried round the Sun, throught the Ecliptick with it.—The Moon has also a circular Motion of her own, round the Earth, which Motion intersects the ecliptick Motion by an Angle of 45 Degrees.

In Order to explain myself the better on these two Motions of the Moon, I shall instance the Sailing of a Ship, which is also affected, *(at the same Time,)* by two Forces, the Wind and the Tide, and her going forward is occasioned as either one or other prevail.—Thus, as the Sailors always observe the Ship is accelerated or retarded in her Sailing, according as she goes either with or against

On the MOON and LUNAR MOTIONS.

gainſt the Tide, and that which ever of the two prevails, either the Wind or the Tide, ſo is the Ship carried on, either North or South; or, if both meet in an Angle, her Courſe is in a Diagonal between them; but if they meet exactly oppoſite to each other, both Forces are deſtroyed, and the Ship ſtands ſtill in the ſame Place.—Hence, if a Ship receives a Force from the Wind, to ſail two Miles an Hour, and the Current or Tide runs one Mile an Hour; this one Mile an Hour of the Current, ballances one Mile an Hour of the Force ſhe receives from the Wind; ſo the Ship will looſe the Force of one Mile an Hour in her ſailing, and in Fact, will be found to proceed forward one Mile only.—On the contrary, let her turn back with the ſame Wind and Current, ſhe will then go forward with the joint Forces of both; and will then proceed forward three Miles an Hour.—Much in the ſame Manner the Moon is carried round the Sun, through the Ecliptick, as a Satellite of the Earth to-

On the MOON and LUNAR MOTIONS.

gether with her; but as her *absolute* Force round the Earth is double to what carries the Earth round the Sun, and this Force or Current of Ethers which belongs to the Moon *only*, makes an Angle of forty-five Degrees, in crossing the Ecliptick: By this Means she is in one Part of her Orbit, round the Earth, Half of a Diameter of that Orbit, before the Earth, in the Ecliptick; and at another Part of her Orbit as much behind the Earth, and at her Conjunction and Opposition, exactly in a Line with it; always keeping nearly the same Distance from the Earth.—Thus being acted on *jointly* by both these Forces, when she comes to her third Quarter, she is then carried with an Angle of 45 Degrees, against the Current of Ethers which forces the Earth round the Sun, through the Ecliptick, and carries on the Earth four Minutes every twenty-four Hours, or a natural Day; which, as has been observed, is but Half the Force with which the Moon is carried round the Earth, so this ecliptick Current of Ethers

resists

On the MOON and LUNAR MOTIONS.

refifts one Minute of that Force, and the Moon's abfolute Motion forward, being refifted by one Minute out of two, fo fhe proceeds but one Minute every fix Hours, or ninety Degrees.—Hence it may be obferved fhe lofes a Moiety of her Force, and goes forward one only.—As foon as fhe comes in Conjunction with the Sun, fhe is then forced towards her firft Quarter, by the Complement of the Angle fhe makes from her third Quarter to her Change.—This is alfo 45 Degrees; and, as fhe ftill continues to go *againft* the ecliptick Current, fhe keeps that flow Pace, till fhe comes to the End of her firft Quarter; at which Point fhe changes, and inftead of going againft, and being obftructed by the ecliptick Current, fhe receives its additional Force to carry her on.—Thus, as has been obferved, her own Force carries her forward *two*, and the ecliptick Current *one*;—and inftead of going with that flow Motion of one, which fhe did from her third Quarter to her firft, fhe now goes three;

and

On the MOON and LUNAR MOTIONS.

and being a Semi-diameter of her Orbit, behind the Earth, occasioned by her *flow* Motion from her Change to this Place; so now, by her accelerated Motion, she recovers this second Quarter what she had lost in the first, and by that Means comes opposite to the Sun at her Full.—She, now by the same Means, continues the like *accelerated Motion*, till she arrives at her third Quarter, at the Entrance of which she goes on with her flow Motion as before.

The above Description of the Phenomena of the Moon's Motions, and the Conjectures how they are caused, seem to make it appear, that the Body of the Moon, and probably the Bodies of all the Planets, are formed much in the same Manner as this terraqueous Globe is described to be, [n] viz. of a thin Shell on the Outside, with a large Hollow or Void in the Midst, filled with Fire, Steam, or inflammable Air; and consequently of the same

---
[n] Let. XVI. XVII.

On the MOON and LUNAR MOTIONS.

same specifick Gravity with the Ethers that surround them.—Thus the Moon is carried round the Earth by these Ethers, in the same Manner as the Earth is round the Sun; and by being exactly of the same specifick Gravity with these Ethers, *at the same Distance* she is placed from the Earth; she meets with no Resistance from them, but is carried on by and with them, with as much Ease as we see a Glass Bubble, of the same specifick Gravity with Water, will be carried on by it, never altering its Place, but goes with it in the same easy Manner as if it was a Part only of the Water; neither can she be moved nearer to the Earth:—As the expansive or projectile Power or Force of the Light, reflected from the Earth, prevents it; nor can she be carried farther from the Earth, as the compressing Power of the Spirit, from the Extremities, prevents it : — Which two Powers, by a joint Mixture, being of the same specifick Gravity with the Moon, she constantly moves in the same Direction that

these

On the MOON and LUNAR MOTIONS.

these do, and with as much Ease as a Balloon does.

Since this Letter was written, Mr. *Herschel*'s Discoveries of the *Volcanos* in the Moon, confirm the above Conjectures to be true, and that the Body of the Moon is formed much in the same Manner as we have described the Earth to be; indeed it seems difficult to conceive how any large Body of Matter can be supported and constrained in the heavenly Spaces, by the surrounding Ethers, unless it is of the same specifick Gravity with them; and the only Method found or observed to do it, has been by filling their internal Void with Fire; by this Means a Body of Gold, or the heaviest Metal, may be made to be of so small specifick Gravity as to be forced to the greatest Distance from the Earth, by the surrounding Air.—Thus we find that all Nature is formed in a *mechanical* Manner, and relative to each other *in Number, Weight, and Measure*.—Hence, as has been already observed,

On the MOON and LUNAR MOTIONS.

observed, these Volcanos, both in the Earth and Moon, appear to be the most proper Method to regulate the Gravity of these Bodies, to the specifick Gravity of the surrounding Ethers.—These Vents being a Means, whenever the internal Expansion, *from the internal Fire,* becomes too great to throw off and discharge the superfluous Fire, and the remaining is condensed, much in the same Manner as may be observed in the Fire Engine; so that it never can arrive to such an Height as to destroy the Body, unless these Vents were effectually stopped. (o)

Mr *Baudy*, a Citizen of Geneva, a great and able Astronomer, has published a Letter against Mr. *Herschel*'s Discoveries, wherein he has treated them as imaginary Visions, for says he, " If within the Compass of his Te-
" lescope alone, he can count from 60 to 110
" Stars, (Mr. *Pictet*'s Assertion) that may
" prove the Perfection of his Instrument, but
" in

(o) P. 312.

On the MOON and LUNAR MOTIONS.

" in a Zone of 15 Degrees in Length, and 2
" in Breadth, could he have seen passing in
" an Hour, 50,000 ? *so prodigious a Number*
" *could not be so easily nor so readily told!*"
He then criticises these Discoveries in the
following Manner.—" Mr. *Herschel*, (says
" he,) a learned Astronomer, gives Scope to
" his Imagination, but pays no Regard to the
" Reality of his Experiments; for, (conti-
" nues he,) by the exact Observations I have
" taken the Pains to make and repeat, in dif-
" ferent Climates of Europe, with excellent
" Telescopes, I am sure that the most crowded
" Parts of the *Heavens* cannot contain so
" great a Number of Stars, united in the
" Focus of the best Instrument whatever.—
" Whenever the Sky is clear of all Kind of
" Vapours, Stars are, or seem to be in Mo-
" tion; so that their *continual Vibration* oc-
" cupies the Eye in such a Manner, that the
" Objects *multiply* in Proportion as you
" count them.—*This is what generally de-*
" *ceives those who trust too much to Appear-*
                                      " *ances!*

Let. XXII.　ASTRONOMY.

On the *MOON* and *LUNAR MOTIONS*.

" *ances!*—From thofe Illufions fprung the
" Idea of Volcanos in the Moon, *which would*
" *deftroy the very Idea* of the Planet being in-
" habited as ours."—Hence I obferve, that notwithftanding the above judicious Remarks of
fo able an Aftronomer as Mr. *Baudy* appears
to be, yet, I think, with Regard to the *Volcanos* in the Moon, he fhould have tried his
pre-conceived Idea *of the Moon being inhabited
by the Matter of Fact only*;—whether thefe
were Volcanos or not?

Since the above Publication of Mr. Baudy,
the French Aftronomers appear to have afcertained the Certainty of the Fact; for in a
Letter *M. De la Laude* has written in the
Paris Journal, dated March 8, 1788, he obferves, that " on the 13th Inftant, from Se-
" ven to Nine in the Evening, *Dom. Novet*,
" one of the Aftronomers of the Royal Ob-
" fervatory, perceived in the unlighted Part
" of the Moon, what Mr. *Herfchel* has called
" a Volcano, like a Star of the fixth Magni-
" tude,

ASTRONOMY. Let. XXII.

On the MOON *and* LUNAR MOTIONS.

" tude, or one of the cloudy ones, the Bright-
" nefs of which increafed, from Time to
" Time, as by Flafhes.—Other Aftronomers
" have perceived it, and Mr. *de Villeneuve*
" had feen it before, on the 22d of May,
" 1787.— We *cannot*, (fays he) *therefore*
" *doubt* of the Exiftance of this Volcano in
" the Moon, Mr. *Herfchel* faw it the 4th of
" May, 1783, and particularly the 19th of
" April, 1787.—In the Eclipfe of the 24th
" of June, 1778, *M. d'Ulloa*, a well-known
" Spanifh Aftronomer, had feen on the dark
" Difk of the Moon, a bright Point; and in
" the total Eclipfe of 1715, certain curious
" Obfervers faw fome Flafhes of Lightning.
" There is no fenfible Atmofphere. in the
" Moon, it is true, and Chymifts may dif-
" pute about the Name of Volcanos being
" given to *fuch apparent Eruption*; but the
" Name after all is of no Confequence, and
" we muft certainly fubfcribe to Mr. *Herfchel*'s
" Opinion.—This Volcano is fituated in the
" North-eft Part of the Moon, about three
                                    " Minutes

On the MOON and LUNAR MOTIONS.

"Minutes from the Moon's Border, towards the Spot called Helicon, marked N°. 12, in the Figure of the Moon, in my Aftronomy."

As I was defirous of fending you my Theory of the lunar Motions, it has occafioned my Letter to be of a greater Length than I propofed.—I had alfo a Defign of fending you my Calculation of the Eclipfe which is to happen on the 25th of this Month; but fhall now fend it you in a feparate Letter next Week.

I am,

DEAR SIR,

Your Friend and Servant,

F. PENROSE.

STONEHOUSE,
July 5, 1786.

To JOHN HEAVISIDE, Esq.

To confirm what Mr. Penrose has observed in his last and former Letters.—He has sent Mr. Heaviside a Calculation of the Eclipse which is to happen July the 25th.—It is calculated by the Method made use of by the Ancients, to measure and record Time:—But to shew how certain their Method was, it is also calculated according to the present, *by Equations and Anomilies.—It may be remarked, that both these Methods differ from each other only 8 M. 11 S.—That the Patriarchs and Chaldeans had more Knowledge in Astronomy than is generally allowed them. This is proved by the* 18 *Years Cycle of Eclipses, and also the* 19 *Years Cycle of the Moon, both which, it is certain, we received from them, and without these Cycles, Astronomers would be at a great Loss.—* Data *on which the Calculations are made, and Conclusions infered from them.*

DEAR SIR,

ACCORDING to Promise, I herewith send you a Calculation of the Eclipse which

which will happen July 25; with a Recapitulation of some former Observations, to confirm what has been observed in my last and former Letters.—The ancient Patriarchs and the Chaldeans, measured their Time, and recorded Events, by the simple, easy, and natural Method of keeping an Account of the Days and Years.—That this Account might be remembered with the greatest Exactness, Moses tells us, God ordered the Sabbath Day, (or Cycle of seven Days) to be kept as a Festival, in Commemoration of the Creation, and to transmit to Posterity, an Account, that the Powers and Operations of the heavenly Bodies, were not eternal, nor inherent in them, but was given to them by Him.—And in Order to commemorate their Months, they were ordered to keep the *new*, or *first* Appearance of the Moon, as a Festival also; that, by this Means, it might not be forgot.—And that they should not mistake or forget when one Year or annual Revolution ended and another began, they were to keep the Feast of Ingathering, at the *End or Revolution* of the Year, *after* the Fruits of the

the Earth were ripe and gathered in. (p) —— That this was the Method in Use about six hundred Years after the Flood, is most certain; for when Jacob was brought before Pharoah, Pharoah said unto him, "*how old art thou.*"—In the Margin of the Bible, there is a literal Translation of the Hebrew, "How many are *the Days of the Years* of thy Life. (q) Jacob answered in the same Style, "An hundred and thirty Years; few and evil have *the Days of the Years* of my Life been."—This shews us that it was the Method of Computation *then* in Use, both by the Patriarchs, and also by the Egyptians, who were supposed to be possessed of the greatest Learning.—After this, by some Means or other, Astronomers either dropt or lost this Method of measuring and keeping an Account by *Days and Years*; and since that Time, have made their Calculations, by dividing the annual Orbit of the Earth into 360 Degrees, and measured it accordingly; and not by the Number of Days as *Nature* performs it, and as the ancient Patriarchs did

did it.—By this Means, in Order to make the 365½ Rotations of the Earth, in her annual Orbit, to tally and agree with the 360 Degrees of the Equator, they were obliged to contrive and use artificial Numbers.—In my Calculations, I have adopted the ancient Method, as the most easy and certain, and the Method Nature directs.

It appears to me that the Patriarchs and Chaldeans had more Knowledge in Astronomy than is generally attributed to them.—Nay, it appears by what I observed in my last Letter, on the lunar Motions, that they knew very well how to calculate the Return of an Eclipse.—It is allowed by all, that we received the Cycle of 18 Years, for the Calculation of the Return of Eclipses, from them; which is called the *Chaldean Cycle* to this Time.—We also received the lunar Cycle of 19 Years from them; for we are certain, that *Meto*, the *Athenian* Astronomer, made use of it more than 430 Years before Christ. (r)— Now, Sir, take away these two Cycles from Astronomers,

Aſtronomers, and they will find themſelves at a great Loſs, notwithſtanding the aſtoniſhing Improvements in Arts and Sciences, particularly in Opticks.— For my Part, I do freely acknowledge, (notwithſtanding it is ſo unpopular to do it, in an Age when all Speculations which aggrandize the Dignity of Reaſon, are ſo eagerly received,) that I cannot conceive how Adam, juſt after he was created, could have Knowledge and Underſtanding ſufficient to give *ideal* Names to *all* Animals, &c. unleſs that Power was given from God.—If God gave him a Power to ſpeak and underſtand Language; is it unreaſonable to ſuppoſe that he had Inſtructions from the ſame Original, how to calculate and know when the appointed Seaſons were, which God commanded him to keep holy? It belongs *only* to a Tyrant to make Laws which cannot be obſerved!—Moſes taught the Iſraelites when to *begin* their Days, their Weeks, Months, and Years.—This has much the Appearance of Chronology and Aſtronomy!

It

It is allowed by *All*, that Astronomers calculate Eclipses, (which are not of long standing) with great Precision; therefore, in Order to confirm what has been observed, I herewith send you Calculations of the succeeding Eclipse, (which will happen on July 25,) by both Methods, viz. the ancient one, by Days, Years, and Lunations, and the present one by Equations and Anomalies, from which you may observe, that the Difference of Time is 8 Minutes and 11 Seconds only: But the Calculations of all Eclipses, by both Methods, will not always agree with the same Exactness; for the Motions of the Moon with the Earth, are so various and complicated and eccentrick, that the Angle of her visible Appearance often deceives us, so that equal, true, calculated Time will not agree with that of Observation, occasioned by the Eccentricity of the Moon's Motions, and the Angle of Vision.—This Difference is occasioned much in the same Manner as the variable Angle the Shadow of the Sun makes on a Dial, and the equable and true Division of it by a well regulated Clock.—

Hence,

Hence, when we truſt too much to Appearances and Obſervations alone, (as Mr. Baudy obſerves) they often deceive us, as all Aſtronomers allow.—But, as theſe Calculations of Time, and the Places of the Sun, Moon, and Earth, by Days, Years, and Lunations, cannot deceive us, they are therefore the moſt proper and certain to try Chronology by, and to meaſure the Diſtance between any two Points of Time.

In my former Letters, I have endeavoured to prove, that the Year of the Creation, according to the Moſaic Chronology, happened at the autumnal Equinox, in the Year anſwering to 706, of the Julian Period; and that at this very Point or Inſtant of Time, the Duration of this terraqueous Globe is to be dated from. (f) — In that Point, I have made all Calculation to *begin*, and to *end* at ſome certain Inſtant of Time, in which we cannot be miſtaken or deceived; as at an Equinox or Eclipſe.

Now,

(f) Introduction, P. 7, Let. X.

Now, if we know the Number of the Rotations the Equator has made between thefe two Points, we muft be mathematically certain of its Length and Duration. (t) And to fhew you that it will do fo, I have collected the following Data, and prove, by Calculation, that thefe Data are true.

1ft That at the Creation, the Sun was placed in Libra, at Noon, in the firft Meridian, on a Thurfday, the fourth Day of the Week; when, according to the Mofaic Hiftory, Chronology began.

2dly, That the Mofaic Chronology places the Year of the Creation, in the Year 706, according to the Julian Period.

3d, That if the Moon had been in Being, fhe would have been Full the Day before, at Noon.

4th, That there were four Days, or four Rotations of the Earth, before the Sun was placed in the Haevens.

5th.

(t) Introduction, P. 16, 78 1:3.

5th, That Moses begins his Chronology on the fourth Day of the Week, at six o' Clock in the Evening, at the going off of the Sun, when the Moon made her Appearance, and they *then jointly* began to perform the Office God designed them for; to *point out Times, Seasons, Days, and Years;*— and that they then enlightened the *whole Earth* from Pole to Pole. [u]

This Year, (1786) is the 6499th of the Julian Period; therefore in Order to know the Number of annual Revolutions, since the Creation, I substract 706 from 6499, which leave 5793; the Number of annual Revolutions since that Time; the last of which will be compleated at this next autumnal Equinox, at the next Full Moon after the Sun enters Libra.— Hence we can measure the Distance between these two Points with a *mathematical Exactness, superior* to a Surveyor measuring a Garden Walk with his Wheel; and that as Nature performs it, by Days, Months, and Years.

(u) Let. X, XIV.

Let. XXIII. *On* ASTRONOMY.

The CALCULATION.

```
                                    A. D. 1786
Multiply by the Number of  ⎫    Julian Years
Minutes a Julian Year is   ⎬       5793
longer than a Solar Trop.  ⎭         11
                                   ─────
                                    5793
                                    5793
                                   ─────
Divide by Numb. of Years   ⎫  1440)63723(44 Days
which compleat the Sun's   ⎬      )5760(
Cycle                      ⎭      ─────
                                   6123
                                   5760
                                   ─────
  Hours in a Day    ─────           363
                                     24
                                   ─────
                                   1452
                                    726
                                   ─────
              Divide 1440)8712(6 Hours
                        )8640(
                        ─────
                           72
 Minutes in an Hour        60 Minutes
                      1440)4320(3
                          )4320(
                          ─────
                           0000
```

Julian

```
                    Julian Years.
            A. M. 5793              A. I. P. 6499
                          1461 Num. of Quadrants in
                          ——   a Quadriennium.
                    5793
                    34758
                    23172
                    5793
                   ───────       Days.    H.  M. (J. Y.
Years in Quadriennium 4)8463573(2115893  6   0 in 5793
                                 1      44   6  3 Retroc.
                                      ─────────
             Sun in Libra        2115848 23  57  1ft M.
  add to bring Meridian of Greenwich      10  24
                                      ─────────
             Sun in Libra        2115849 10  21 Lond.
  Days from Kalends of Jan. to Oct. 25   298
                                      ─────────
                                 2116147 10  21
  Julian Biffext. 11 D. deduct for N.S. 2115882
                                      ─────────
   Days from January 1ft inclufive   265 10  21
        Sun in Libra, Sept.           22 10  21
```

According to thofe Calculations, the Sun will enter Libra this Year, at Greenwich Obfervatory, Sept. 22d Day, 10th Hour, 21ft Minute, and that it was placed in Libra, at the Creation, (or in the 706 of the Julian Period,) at Noon, in the firft Meridian, Oct. 25.—But as Mofes begins his Chronology at Six o'Clock in the Evening, when the Moon

was

was placed nearly in Oppofition to the Sun, being a little paft its Full, the two Luminaries together enlightened the whole Earth. Thefe fix Hours being added, brings it to fix in the Evening, Oct. 25th Day, 6th Hour, 0 Minute, P. M.

Another Method.

	D.	H.	M.
Retroceffion	44	6	3
Deduct for N. S.	11		
	33	6	3
Deduct for Meridian of Greenwich		10	24
	32	19	39

	D.	H.	M.	
Oct.	25	6	0	
Sept.	30			added to make a Subtraction
	55	6	0	
	32	19	39	true Retroceffion
Sept.	22	10	21	

Mofes informs us that his Chronology began at Six o'Clock in the Evening, which was fix Hours after the Sun was placed in *Libra*; hence it may be obferved, that it was the firft Year of the *Quadriennium*; therefore if we add One to the Year of the World,

World, it will always give us the Year of the *Quadriennium*, by dividing that Sum by four, the Remainder the Year fought.

$$\text{Thus } \underset{\quad 1}{5793}$$

$$\text{Divide } 4\overline{)5794}\underset{2\,(\text{Second}}{(1448}$$

This History also lets us know, that the Sun was placed in the Heavens, and the Earth began her annual Orbit on a Thursday, the fourth Day of the Week; therefore if we add those four *extra. Days*, to the Number of Rotations the Earth has since made, and divide the whole Number by Seven, it will give us the Number of Weeks since the Creation, and the Remainder will be the Day of the Week.

Thus we find, that from the Sun's entering *Libra*, in the Year 706, A. I. P. to Sept, 22, this Year, when the Sun enters *Libra*, the Earth will have performed 5793 annual Revolutions, and

Let. XXIII. *On* ASTRONOMY.

```
           2115849 Rotations round its Axis
                 4 extra. Days
   Divide 7)2115853(302264 Weeks
              5 Friday
```
——According to this Calculation, we find that Sept. 22, 1786, being the second Year of the Quadriennium, will be on a Friday, the fifth Day of the Week.

Having now proved, by Calculation, that the Sun will enter *Libra* this Year, Sept. 22d Day, 10th Hour, 21ſt Minute, on a Friday, as it will be found to do from Obſervation :—I ſhall now try if the lunar Motions, meaſured by the Rotations of the Equator, as they are performed by Nature, will alſo confirm the ſame.

A. M. 5793 ending at the autumnal Equinox.

Julian Years.

```
Years in a Cycle, divide by 19)5793(304
                               57
                               ──
                                93
                                76
                                ──
                                17
   Lunations in a Year         12
                               ───
                               204
   Intercalatory Lunations       5
                               ───
                               209
```

3 D

On ASTRONOMY. Lct. XXIII.

```
                    304
                    235 Lunations
                    ―――
                   1520
                    912
                    608
                   ――――
                   71440
Lunations          209 Lunar Years
                12) 71649 (5970
                    60
                    ――
                    116
                    108
                    ――
                     84
                     84
                    ――
                     09 Lunations


                        Lunar Years.
Years in a Period   30) 5970 (199 Periods
                        30
                        ――
                        297
                        270
                        ――
                        270
                        270
                        ――
                        000
```

The Moon's Lunations being a small Fraction lefs than 29 D. 12 H. 44 M. 1 S. 45 T. caufe one Day, (as may be obferved) to be thrown off in 138 Periods, or 49,680 Lunations.

Rotations

Let. XXIII. *On* ASTRONOMY. 395

	Rotations or Days	H.	M.	S.
In 138 Periods are	1467078 (24)	9	00	
In 60 Ditto	637860	10	30	00
In 1 Ditto	10631	0	10	30
In 9 Lunations	265	18	36	15

Full Moon, 1st Meridian	2115835	5	25	45
add to bring to Greenwich Observatory		10	24	
Full Moon, London	2115835	15	49	45
add Days from Kalends of Jan. to Oct.	24	297		
	2116132	15	49	45
Julian Bissex. 11 D. deduct for N. S.	2115882			
Days from Jan. 1 inclusive	250	15	49	45
Full Moon, Sept.	7	15	49	45
to bring to New Moon add Half Lunation	14	18	22	
New Moon, Sept.	22	10	11	45

This is Sept. 22d D. 10th H. 11th M. 45 S. Morning, according to the Julian Reckoning.

```
Full Moon  2115835
           4 extra. Days
       ─────────────
    7) 2115839 (302262
           5 \ Friday.
```

According to the preceding Calculations, the Sun will enter Libra, at the Greenwich Observatory, Friday, Sept. 22d Day, 10th Hour, 21st Minute, (1786,) being the second Year after the Quadriennium, or after Leap

Leap Year.—The Earth will then have performed, since she entered Libra, A. I. P.

         Rotations or Days   H. M.
706 ———— 2115849 10 21

In which Time the Moon will have made 71,649 Revolutions round the Earth, from Sun to Sun, which she has performed in

           Days.   H. M.
         2115835 15 49

Full Moon	14	18	32 EPACT
Half Lunation	14	18	22
New Moon		10	EPACT

                D. H. M
New Moon, Sept. 22 10 11
Half Lunation   14 18 22

        Full Moon   7 15 49
according the Julian Reck. 8   3 49 Morning.

The aforesaid Motions of the two Luminaries, or more properly, of the Earth and the Moon, as they are performed by Nature, and measured by the equable Rotation of the Equator, (the just and true Root of all Measure,) prove that the Sun and Moon are now in the same Place, in the Heavens, which they were 5793 Years ago.

                                  As

Let. XXIII. *On* ASTRONOMY. 397

As there will be an Eclipse of the Sun, July 25, this Year, (1786) though invisible to us; I shall first calculate this Eclipse, according to the foregoing Method, and then make a Calculation of it from *Ferguson's Tables,* in Order to try whether it will confirm or disprove it.

$$
\begin{array}{r}
\text{A. M.} \\
19)\overline{5793}(304 \\
57 \\
\hline
93 \\
76 \\
\hline
17 \\
12 \\
\hline
\end{array}
$$

Intercalary Lunations
$$
\begin{array}{r}
204 \\
3 \\
\hline
207
\end{array}
$$

$$
\begin{array}{r}
304 \\
235 \\
\hline
1520 \\
912 \\
608 \\
\hline
71440 \\
207 \\
\hline
\end{array}
$$

$$
12)\overline{71647}(5970 \\
60 \\
\overline{116} \\
108 \\
\overline{84} \\
84 \\
\overline{07}
$$

On ASTRONOMY. Let. XXIII.

```
30)5970(199
   30
   ---
   297
   270
   ---
    270
    270
    ---
    000
```

	Rotations or Days.	M.	S.	
In 138 Periods are	1467078 (24)	9	00	
In 60 Ditto————	637860	10	30	00
In 1 Ditto————	10631	0	10	30
In 7 Lunations	206	17	8	12

```
          2115776  3 57  4
                  10 24
          ---
          2115776 14 21 42
                  10 24
          ---
          2115776 14 21 42
             297
          ---
          2116073 14 21 42
          2115882
```

Full Moon   191 14 21 42
Half Lunation   14 18 22
               ---
               206 8 43 42
New Moon, July 25 8 4 24

Days since the Creation.
2115790
      4 Extra. Days
---
7)2115794(302256 Weeks
         2 Tuesday

According to these Calculations, this Eclipse
of

Let. XXIII. *On* ASTRONOMY.

of the Sun will happen on a Tuesday, July 25th D. 8th H. 43d M. 42d S. We will now try what is the Time according to *Ferguson's Tables*.

1786	New Moon. D. H. M. S.	Sun's Anomaly. S. D. M. S.	Moon's Anomaly. S. D. M. S.	Sun from Node S. D. M. S.
March	18 5 21 30	3 28 6 7	5 11 34 19	2 7 53 12
4 Lunations	118 2 56 12	3 26 25 17	3 13 16 02	4 2 40 56
New Moon, July	14 8 17 42	0 24 31 24	8 24 50 21	6 10 39 8
1st Equation	1 42 6		8 24 11 33	38 48
Once Equated 2d Equation	14 6 35 36 9 40 3	4 0 19 51	8 24 11 33	
Twice Equated 3d. Equation	13 20 55 33 4 12			
Thrice Equated 4th Equation	13 20 51 21 32			
Old Stile, July add for N. S.	13 20 51 53 11			

New Moon and Eclipse of the Sun,

	D. H. M. S.	
July 25	8 51 53	according to Ferguson's Tables.
July 25	8 43 42	Tuesday—according to Mosaic History of the Creation.
	8 11	Difference.

	H. M. S.	
July	20 51 53	after Twelve at Noon, July 24
	D. H. M. S.	
that is, July	25 8 51 53	

By comparing both these Calculations together, viz. that from the Time and Place of the Sun and Moon at the Creation, according to Moses's History of them, measured by the Rotations of the Equator, as Nature performs them; the other from *Ferguson's Tables*, which being some of the newest, we take it for granted that they are most correct. By comparing both those Calculations together, we find a Difference of 8 Minutes and 11 Seconds only.—Supposing *Ferguson's Tables* to be precisely true, this small Quantity of Difference in Time, can be of no Consequence in 5793 Years or annual Revolutions.

Let it be observed, that there were here two Points given, viz. the autumnal Equinox, 706, of the Julian Period, and the autumnal Equinox, 6499, of the same Period.—Between these two Points the Earth has performed 5793 Revolutions round the Sun, and 2,115,790 Rotations round its Axis. During this Time the Moon has made 71,647 Revolutions round the Earth, and Half of another, when she intersected the Earth's Orbit,

Orbit, and caufed an Eclipfe of the Sun.—
Both thefe are meafured by the equable Rotations of the Equator.

From the Facts and Obfervations in my former Letters, confirmed by the above Calculations, I fhall infer the following Conclufions.

1ft. That the equable Rotation of the Equator, round its Axis, is the Root or Standard by which Diftance, Duration, and Progreffion of Time are meafured.—By dividing the Equator into twenty-four Parts or Hours, the Duration and Progreffion of Time is known; by its being divided into 360 Degrees, that of Meafure or Diftance.—Thus a Revolution of 15 Degrees in Meafure, anfwers exactly to an Hour, or the twenty-fourth Part of the Revolution of the Equator.—In a Minute of Time there will be a Revolution of 15 Minutes of the Equator.—In a Second, a Revolution of 15 Seconds.—Hence, by knowing the Diftance or Number of Rotations and Degrees moved forward, or the Length of Time paſt, the other may be as eaſily known, by converting Rotations and Degrees into Time, or ♀ *contra*. Time into Meaſure.

Thus the Diſtance between any two Points of Time, *(it being a Strait Line)* may be meaſured with the greateſt Exactneſs and Preciſion; for the Number of Rotations the Equator makes, is a ſtrait Line, the exact Length between theſe two Points;—and it is the Property of a ſtrait Line to meaſure the Diſtance between two Points, with a Mathematical Exactneſs.—By the equable Rotation of the Equater, the annual Orbit is meaſured. By the ſame Means, the Moon's Lunations, and her other Motions are meaſured; and by this Method the foregoing Eclipſe, and all the others, have been meaſured and calculated; which Method will always prove mathematically true, if we know the Number of Rotations, and the Remainder, between any two Points, let their Diſtance be ever ſo great, as may be obſerved in the foregoing Calculations.—The mathematical Exactneſs

of

Let. XXIII. On ASTRONOMY.

of this Meafure may be obferved, as you may begin at either Point, or at any intervening Eclipfe, and they will all come out the fame, which no Tables already formed have been able to do.—This Calculation begins at the Point when the Moon came firft in Oppofition to the Sun, after the Sun entered Libra, 706, of the Julian Period; and ends at the Point of Interfection, when the Moon will be in Conjunction with the Sun, the 25th of this Month.—In this you have not only the Meafure between thefe two Points, by the Earth's Orbit, but you have alfo the Point where the Moon, in her Orbit round the Earth, interfects the Earth in her annual Revolution round the Sun.—The Moon does not meafure her own Orbit or Motions! but by her Interfections of the Earth's Orbit, with the Affiftance of the twelve Signs or Stars, Chronology is afcertained, and Times and Seafons pointed out with a mathematical Precifion.

2dly, That as Calculations may be made equally true between any one, two, ten, or ten thoufand Years, (each beginning and ending

ing when the Sun enters Libra, making thefe Calculations according to 365 Days, 5 Hours, 49 Minutes, being the exact Length of the folar tropical Year;) fo it muft prove that the Length of the folar Year is 365 Days, 5 Hours, 45 Minutes exactly.—And alfo that the Length of the Year is precifely the fame it was 5793 Years ago.

3dly. That as all or any one of the Moon's Interfection of the Earth, in her annual Orbit, may be calculated with equal Exactnefs; fo I conclude, that the Length of her Lunation is properly afcertained; and that in 706, (the Year of the Julian Period, when the Creation happened, according to the Mofaic Chronology,) fhe was precifely in the Place in the Heavens affigned to her;—that her Orbit is exactly of the fame Length it was 5793 Years ago; and that fhe is now no nearer the Earth than fhe was then.

4thly. I conclude, (as thefe Calculations prove) that the Moon was Full, or in exact Oppofition to the Sun, Oct. 24, at Noon, in in the 706th Year of the Julian Period.— That the Sun entered Libra that Year, Oct. 25, at Noon, one whole Rotation of the Earth, after the Moon was in Oppofition to the Sun.—That this happened on a Thurfday, the fourth Day of the Week.—That the Moon rofe and began to enlighten the Earth at fix o'Clock in the Evening, fix Hours after the Sun was placed in the Heavens, when the Chronology of Time began. That the Moon was then thirty Hours paft her Oppofition, but that her Declination was fo fmall, as not to prevent the Sun and Moon to enlighten the WHOLE Earth.—That the Moon, by being departed one Quadrant, or fix Hours, from the Sun, fhews us that 706, A. I. P. muft be the Beginning of the fecond Year of the Quadriennium.

5thly, That thefe Places of the Sun and Moon, in the Heavens, the Year of the Quadriennium, the Day of the Week, and the Minute of the Day, have not happened again fince that Time, viz. in 5793 Years; nor can it happen again for many Thoufand Years to come.

I

I now conclude with assuring you, that I am, with great Truth,

DEAR SIR,

Your real and affectionate Friend,

F. PENROSE.

STONEHOUSE,
July 12, 1786.

F I N I S.

ERRATA.

Page	Line	Correction
4	4,	*for* Equatereal, *read* Equatoreal.
Bottom 8		*for* LET. XVII. *read* LET. XXIII.
Bottom 10		*for* LET. VII. *read* LET. XI.
12	14,	*for* Elipse, *read* Ellipse.
	18,	*dele* That
13	16,	*for* is, *read* are.
	Last Line,	*for* Anomilies, *read* Anomalies.
15	4,	*dele* by.
16	15,	*for* Elipse, *read* Ellipse.
20	19,	
Note at Bottom		*for* Horns, *read* Focus, *and is for* arc.
25	2,	*for* 3420, *read* 4320.
	10,	*for* 1783, *read* 1753.
Bottom 26		*for* LET. VIII. *read* LET. X.
33	3,	*for* this, *read* their.
	4,	*for* their, *read* this.
37	17,	*for* rectify, *read* rectifies.
51	11,	*for* Equinox, *read* Equinoxes.
52	24,	*for* Strauchas, *read* Strauchius.
61	13,	*for* Portes, *read* Partes.
74	10,	*for* Sceptic, *read* Skeptick.
78	4,	*for* 2116214, *read* 2116219.
	6,	*for* 30216, *read* 302317.
	7,	*for* two Days, *read* Nothing.
	11,	*for* sixth, *read* four.
	12,	*for* Saturday, *read* Thursday.
96		*for* 11 H. *read* 1 Hour.
102	21,	*for* 5th Hour, *read* 10th Hour.
139	1,	*for* America, *read* Africa.
175	18,	*for* eliptical, *read* elliptical.
207	2,	*for* Placentia, *read* Placentæ.
237	17,	*for* Assumitions, *read* Assumtions.
274	9,	*for* would, *read* could.
277	13,	*for* Quering, *read* Querying.
279	7,	*after* not, *insert* at.
316	12,	*for* Vortix, *read* Vortex.
362	6,	*after* 44 F. *read* more.
363	9,	*for* this, *read* the.
380	0,	*for* Anomilies, *read* Anomalies.

www.ingramcontent.com/pod-product-compliance
Lightning Source LLC
Chambersburg PA
CBHW022138300426
44115CB00006B/236